2/88 - 9/88

Horseback Honeymoon

They left their hearts in the West, and after returning to New York, Quincy and Ella found themselves hoping that some day, in one of the far mountain valleys, a house would be waiting for them beyond an open gate.

HORSEBACK HONEYMOON

The Vanishing Old West of 1907 Through the Eyes of Two Young Artists in Love

DOROTHY BALLARD
With drawings and photographs
by Ella and Quincy Scott

Two Continents Publishing Group, Ltd.
and
Morgan Press

Library of Congress Cataloging in Publication Data

Ballard, Dorothy.
    Horseback honeymoon.

    Includes index.
    1.   Northwestern   States—Description   and   travel.   2.   Overland
    journeys to the Pacific.   3.   Scott, Ella, 1882–1971.   4.   Scott,
    Quincy, 1882–1965.   I.   Title.
    F597.B35   917.7′04′30924   75–15042
    ISBN 0–8467–0105–7

Production by Planned Production
Text design by Carol Basen
Printed in USA

Two Continents Publishing Group, Ltd.
30 East 42 Street
New York City   10017
and
Morgan Press

Contents

For my brothers, Hugh and Allen Scott

FOREWORD

> Most of the Wests have been touched
> by the magic figure of the horseman.
> Wallace Stegner*

Every family needs a saga, some tale of peril, achievement or humor that can withstand many tellings. The events don't have to be grandly heroic. If the story gives the oncoming generation a sense of family identity and uniqueness, it will do.

Hugh and Allen and I were fortunate. About two years before the eldest of us was born, our parents started on a wedding journey that combined achievement and comedy with a seasoning of danger. By the time we children were old enough to listen, the account of that summer of 1907 had developed into a saga of sorts. We soon discovered that we possessed something unusual. Whatever distinctions our playmates might lay claim to, none of their parents had set out to ride horseback from St. Paul to Seattle.

The romance of America's frontier determined their means and direction of travel. And they weren't a moment too soon. The West was changing fast, shrinking under the assault of the twentieth century as a body of water shrinks under the sun, drawing back from one lowering margin after another until it stands in isolated pools. Although covered wagons had creaked over the Oregon Trail as recently as 1895, by 1907 automobiles were daring the miserable cross-continent roads, and in four years more the first airplane would fly from coast to coast. A New West that saw its future in trains, planes and autos didn't know what to make of anyone who preferred to adventure on horseback.

It certainly wasn't the best way to cross the country in 1907. Feed was scarce, accommodations for both riders and horses were falling into disuse. Except in its arid heartland, the open-handed, unquestioning hospitality of the Old West was being replaced by suspicion and calculation. Yet the "magic figure of the horseman" continued working its spell. Children were not the only ones to ask the travelers wistfully, "Are you *really* cowboys?" And even when the door had been slammed shut, the curtains might be slyly drawn aside so that a cautious farmer could watch the two strangers turn out of his lane and ride westward in the dusk.

The flavor of the times and the character of the people were caught in the day-by-day journal kept by Quincy and Ella Scott, and elaborated in the light-hearted letters they wrote to anxious families on either side of the continent. They took snapshots and made pencil sketches—they were both professional artists—and the following winter Quincy wove the notes and memories into a book. Over two dozen black-and-white drawings were completed, some by Ella in her detailed illustrative style, some by Quincy in his free-swinging cartoonist's exuberance. One of the major New York publishers accepted the results, but the book was not printed because of the firm's closing.

Journal, letters, photographs, manuscript and drawings followed the Scotts around the country for the next sixty years. Periodically Quincy or Ella would talk about rewriting the book. But there were too many other interesting things to claim their attention—children, careers, church and civic responsibilities, stints in two World Wars for Quincy, and eventually golf, grandchildren and great-grandchildren. So it finally came to me, with the encouragement of my husband and brothers, to tell the story of the horseback honeymoon, from the records kept by my father and mother during their summer ride, from my memory of many re-tellings, and from information supplied by my mother during the few years between my father's death and her own. However, I wanted to make it a *story*, not just a string of notes. So the account has been supplemented with descriptions, action and dialogue that seemed to fit. There are one or two slight shifts in sequence. Names have been changed for most of the individuals and families met along the way, but towns and geographical features bear their real names, and significant details of the journey were not tampered with. I have used some material, both verbatim and rewritten, from Quincy's manuscript, particularly in the conversations at Medora and Fourth of July canyon, for I could not better my father's ear for dialect.

Throughout the writing I have tried to be faithful to the sources, but also to see those two young lovers in the clarifying light of time.

NOVATO, CALIFORNIA   *Dorothy Ballard*

---

* *The Sound of Mountain Water* by Wallace Stegner © 1969 by Wallace Stegner. Quoted by permission of Doubleday and Co., Inc.

An abandoned sod house, a memorial to the prairie settlers.

MAY: *The farmer's prairie*

As my eyes
search
the prairie
I feel the summer in the spring.

—*Chippewa Music*, Frances Densmore
BUREAU OF AMERICAN ETHNOLOGY

I It had no business to be snowing. Not in May, on the Mississippi. Summer snow-squalls might be waiting out there in the high passes of the Rockies, but St. Paul was supposed to be sunny and warm. That was the way Quincy and Ella had pictured it during all the months of planning. A lark would be singing as they rode out of town, and a soft prairie breeze beckoning from the west.

Instead, here was snow, mouthfuls of it spit out of a churlish sky. From the doorway of the livery sale barn, Ella looked accusingly at the fly-specked calendar nailed to the wall inside. May 3, 1907. She and Quincy had arrived by train from New York yesterday, a day proclaimed by the St. Paul newspapers as the coldest May 2 on record. Well, St. Paul could boast of May 3, too. It was just as nasty. Ella pushed her fingers farther up into the sleeves of her blue serge jacket and revised her picture of departure. It would still be snowing tomorrow when she and Quincy headed out for Seattle, equipped only with what they could wear on their backs and strap to the saddles of their two riding horses. No larks would sing, and the breeze would be a biting wind.

It never occurred to Ella to ask, *Will* we leave tomorrow? Quincy was in the livery yard now, bargaining for sound horses at a manageable price. Of course he would succeed, and of course they would leave tomorrow. A well-advertised honeymoon can't be postponed because of a little snow.

"From St. Paul to Seattle in the saddle." The clipping from the New York *Herald* was in her handbag. It showed, above the opening phrase of the story, the photographs of a dainty young woman with a wreath of daisies in her hair, and a grave young man in wing collar and white tie. "It will be about a two thousand mile horseback journey, and Mr. and Mrs. Scott expect to cover it in one hundred days, or at the rate of twenty miles a day," the story continued. "Quincy Scott is a well known young newspaper illustrator and cartoonist, whose work is familiar to readers of the Evening *Telegram* and other publications. His wife was Miss Ella Allen, of Seattle, Wash. She came to New York about a year ago to study art, and she and Mr. Scott met in the Art Students' League, of which both had become members. They were married last fall, but both were too busy then to indulge in any protracted honeymoon trip, so they postponed that luxury until now."

Luxury! Ella wished that enthusiastic reporter were shivering here beside her, lips blue, nose stinging with the ammoniac reek of the barn.

Describing two thousand miles on horseback as a luxury wasn't the only way the *Herald* reporter had dressed up his story, either. The next sentence: "Both Mr. and Mrs. Scott are excellent riders." Where had he picked *that* up, or the notion that she was an expert with firearms? Somehow, in the ebullience of the interview, Quincy's mantle of experience had been stretched to cover her lack of it. Her marksmanship depended actually on a few sessions of target practice, her riding on less than a dozen excursions, years ago, astride a sore-footed plug. But it was too late to protest. What she didn't know about guns and horses she would have to learn by experience, if in no other way.

The snow flurries slackened, the wind blew colder.

"You can wait in the office," said a grizzled hostler, coming up behind Ella. He motioned to a cubbyhole beyond a partition.

"No, thank you. I'd rather watch what's going on outside."

"Well, then, don't go farder'n the doorway, else you'll ruin them shoes." With a leer at Ella's black kid slippers, he shouldered past, leading a mare.

"Is that one of the horses you're showing my husband?"

"Yup. And he better not be too choosy."

The mare, a dispirited roan, clomped over the sill and down the short ramp into the yard.

With each "clomp" Ella's confidence quaked. Though she stoutly held to the certainty that they would start for Seattle tomorrow, the question of what they would start *on* was becoming more and more acute. A respected horse dealer in New York had told them they could buy mounts for seventy-five dollars apiece. Out of the two hundred and twenty-five she and Quincy had in their pockets, that would leave an adequate margin to pay for the rest of their equipment, their hotel bill, and what food they might have to buy during the first month. But yesterday a canvass of the sales stables midway between St. Paul and Minneapolis had turned up no riding horses priced lower than a hundred and fifty dollars each, and this market in South St. Paul was not much more promising. Saddle horses were scarce in Minnesota. The few good ones brought a rich man's price; most of the cheap ones were not fit to ride.

The roan mare, for instance. Her front legs looked as if they had been borrowed from an abused Steinway grand. Even a kind face, if she had one, wouldn't compensate for that.

Out in the yard Quincy was trying to keep warm by jogging back and forth between the stables and the exercise barn. Ella's confidence steadied as he came toward her. Broad shouldered, lean and tall in the gray Norfolk suit, hat cocked at an impudent angle above his intent blue eyes, he looked to her all that an adventurer should be. Living with Quincy Scott, she had discovered in the eight months of their marriage, was in itself an adventure—of mind as well as body. Ella had noticed that whatever their group of friends, young artists and newspaper people, set out to do Quincy usually ended up the leader. No one else could contribute as many interesting ideas about how to carry out whatever the project might be. He had the kind of bubbling energy that drew others into the current of his enthusiasms. Parallel to his gift of fantasy and roving speculation lay a deep sense of responsibility and an inventiveness directed to solving practical problems. And through all these varied strands glinted his delight in the comic. Even at the moment, though the jut of his chin signaled his determination to come out on top of this horse-buying contest, she knew that a corner of his agile mind was taking note of the preposterous angles of the game and composing a humorous account for letters home, and for the book he planned to write about the trip. That was one of the endearing and occasionally exasperating things about Quincy— he could find something wry or ridiculous to say about almost any situation.

The roan mare, hoofs planted on the frozen pudding of mud and manure, swung her head around in Ella's direction. Yes, she did have a kind face, that poor old horse, but you couldn't ride to Seattle on a kind face. Ella hoped Quincy would notice the Steinway legs.

Evidently he did, for he waved the hostler away without even inspecting Steinway's teeth or crinkling her tail. Already he had turned down a mouse-colored mare (too expensive) and a little bay pony with one eye wicked and the other eye gone.

"Mr. Scott, I'm afraid you're too pertic 'lar." Rollins, the salesman, came up from the exercise barn slapping a whip against his spattered boots. He was heavy-jowled, lumpy and corpulent. A remnant of cigar sagged from the corner of his mouth. "We haven't got much more on hand. You'd better make up your mind to buy the tall black."

"You mean Washboard-out-of-Stepladder?" Quincy jerked his thumb toward the stable. "That all depends. If you have anything else to show me, I ought to take a look."

With a slight backward tilt of his head, the lumpy Mr. Rollins gave some sort of signal to the hostler. The unshaven old man shrugged, grinned, and led the roan mare back up the ramp into the stable.

Ella beckoned Quincy closer. "What's wrong with the little bay pony?" she whispered.

"I caught a glimpse of him as I went past the exercise barn. He was bucking the living daylights out of a stable hand while our gallant Rollins stood by cracking his bullwhip. My guess is Little Bay had never been ridden before."

"And they're trying to foist him off on us as a *saddle* pony?" Ella's trust in horse dealers went down another two or three degrees. She peered over her shoulder into the shadowy cavern of the stable, toward the stall where the big black was tied. "That one you called Washboard-out-of-Stepladder. He's aristocratic, anyhow."

"Well—" Quincy looked down at the purpling bruise on his right wrist. He and the black horse had circled the yard twice, bouncing and bucking all the way. Only the wrist, hooked under the saddle horn, had prevented an unseemly parting of company. "I concede he has a beauty all his own, in spite of his intermittent mane and accordion-pleated sides. His eye is bright, his nostril red, and he had spunk enough to try and toss me. There's more horse inside of him than outside. I'd say he's a good nag gone wrong. But I hate to take a chance on him. Getting through this trip alive will depend pretty much on our horses, and Washboard just isn't built for what we'll be demanding of them when we hit range country. No, I think—"

"Now how about this one, Mr. Scott?" interrupted Rollins with a carefully manufactured smile that almost dislodged the cigar.

The hostler had appeared in the yard from a farther doorway, hand on the halter of another black horse, all black except for a wisp of white on the near front foot. Short-coupled and sturdy, with a clear and knowing eye. He was branded "16" on the left hip.

"Saddle him," ordered Quincy.

Ella could tell, from the decision in his voice and the confident way he swung aboard, that this cow pony was promising. They went three times around the yard, first at a walk, then at a trot and a lope. The pony handled his feet with precision and seemed responsive to the rein. Quincy pulled him in beside the ramp, and patted his neck.

"You know a good horse when you see one," drawled Rollins. "He's yours for a hundred and fifteen."

Quincy got off and walked around the horse for a critical once-over. He ran his hands down the well-boned legs, inspected the hoofs, pried open the mouth to scan the teeth. Ella wanted to shout, "Take him, take him! We'll manage somehow about the money." But Quincy stood back, shaking his head. "That's more than I figured to pay. Remember, I have to buy two horses."

Rollins took the tattered cigar from his mouth and rolled it slowly between his stubby thumb and forefinger. "Well, possibly I could shave the price to a hundred and ten, but I'd be losing money on him."

"You're losing money on feed every day you keep him."

"A hundred and ten, then?"

Ella began to understand what was going on. Somewhere in the rank raw air of the stable yard a deal was in the making, to be determined as much by the zest of combat as by the quality of horseflesh or the leanness of purse. A deal on which her life might hang.

Quincy pressed his one slim advantage. "Let's see first what you can do for us about another horse."

"You looked at the bay pony, but you ain't rode him yet. Plenty of vim, that boy." Rollins gestured to the hostler with his cigar. "Go get him."

The old man sluiced out an amber arc of tobacco juice. "Sure, Mr. Rollins!" he cackled.

Ella glanced toward Quincy with concern. Why hadn't she been sensible and waited in the office? Now, because she was watching, he would climb on that murder-bent one-eyed devil and get his neck broken. She knew Quincy's pride, his drive to measure up to the highest mark anyone set, and nobody set the mark higher than he pegged it for himself. He would not be shamed before his bride.

She started to turn back into the stable. But it was too late. The gleeful hostler had already brought out Little Bay.

Quincy slid two fingers under the girth to check its snugness, and helped the old man let down the stirrups. Little Bay's ears flattened as Quincy eased himself into the saddle, letting his weight come down slowly. Ella shut her eyes and steeled herself against the shouts, the thuds, the crunch that would end it all.

Silence.

She risked a glance, and saw Little Bay poking along sedately, his one good, and wicked, eye rolled back at Quincy. Horse and rider finished the turn and stopped at the ramp.

"For a green pony, his gait's not bad, but he doesn't have

much skidoo left in him. Besides, he's too small for me. What else have you to show us?"

"Young feller, you do know something about horses," said Rollins, with a hint of respect in his voice. "Not everybody comes in here could handle this pony like you done. But I ask you to believe me, you've seen everything I got that could be called a saddle horse. So it's choose your second one between them four—the bay, the tall black, and the two mares."

Ella knew without doubt which of the four *she* liked. She walked down the ramp to stand beside Quincy.

"What do you think, Bunny?" he said, using his special nickname for her. "We're not going to have time to look any place else, even if there is any place else."

She tilted her face up to his, taking a quick breath. "I don't pretend to be a judge of horseflesh, but you said that there's more inside of the tall black than shows outside. Wouldn't you say he's preferable?"

Quincy pursed his lips and stroked one cheek and then the other with the palm of his left hand. "Hmm. How much did you say, Rollins, for the scrawny black?"

"Seventy-five."

"All right." Quincy dropped his hand and straightened his shoulders. "I'll give you a hundred and eighty for the pair, that one and the black cow pony."

"Now, now, Mr. Scott! That's allowing me only a hundred and five on the cow pony. You know yourself he's worth more'n that."

"A hundred and eighty for the pair, Mr. Rollins. Divide it up any way you like."

Anxiously Ella tried to guess the outcome from the expressions on the faces of the two men. To bluff, browbeat or cajole a customer into parting with an extra dollar was Rollins' daily measure of success. But for us, thought Ella, every dollar we *don't* part with adds to our margin for survival this summer, and Quincy knows it.

His eye was steady on Rollins.

The salesman threw down his cigar and pulped it under his bootheel. "I ain't in business for my health, you understand. But since you're buyin' the two of them, we'll call it a deal at a hundred and eighty."

Only a wife—or a horse trader—would have noticed how Quincy's shoulders sloped with relief. The tense, stern set of his mouth broke into a friendly smile. He reached for his notecase. "Fine. Here's your money. Now if you'll just make out the bill of sale, we'll leave the horses here overnight and come back tomorrow morning to load our gear and start for Seattle."

Quincy and Ella sat close to each other on the streetcar that took them back into downtown St. Paul. They were no longer just a couple of tenderfeet with some luggage and a wild idea. They were horsemen, owners of two broncs, picked out, bargained over and paid for.

"Dear, I couldn't bear to look when you climbed on that one-eyed horse. However did you keep him from bucking?"

Quincy twisted around to look directly at her. "It's a temptation to say that I employed a secret power known only to gifted horsemen. But the truth is, I think that bullwhipping Little Bay got in the exercise barn took all the gumption out of him. He didn't even try to toss me off."

"But if he had tried?"

"Oh, then I would have employed the secret known only et cetera, et cetera." Quincy grinned and flipped his notecase into her lap. "How much money do we have left?"

She counted it, together with the contents of her purse. Forty-five dollars and small change. Plus the fifty that would be awaiting them at the Western Union office.

"It's a good thing you telegraphed Wallace this morning for the extra," Ella said, handing Quincy the bills and scooping the change into her bag. After the discouraging experience yesterday in the midway horse markets, Quincy had reluctantly asked Wallace Charters, engaged to Ella's older sister Jessie, to wire fifty dollars, and had mailed a check to cover it.

"Even though we don't have to use the extra now to help pay for the horses, we did have to plunk down thirty more for the pair than we planned," Quincy acknowledged. "What we've got

left, with the fifty, gives us a pretty good cushion to travel on—
till we run out of money."

He put his arm over the back of the trolley seat and pressed
Ella closer to him. She glanced around to see if any of the other
passengers were scandalized. Nobody was paying attention and
she relaxed gratefully against his shoulder. She knew he was saying, without explicit words, that he had forgiven her for urging
him to send the telegram to Wallace. Quincy would far rather
grant a favor than ask one, and though he wasn't borrowing, but
merely requesting the cashing of a check, it had troubled him
to trouble Wallace, and to admit in so doing that he had not
planned ahead realistically.

Ella laid her hand on his knee, smoothing the finely-woven
wool fabric beneath her fingers. She forgave him for forgiving
her. They both understood that it was by luck, or by the Providence in whom they both believed, that they had come out of
the horse deal with forty-five dollars left. Even Quincy's brass
in facing down Mr. Rollins would not have availed if the selec-
tion of horses had been any more limited. Ella felt a rush of
gratitude for those two black broncos, the ribby Washboard with
three white feet and the sturdy cow pony who stepped so neatly.

"Quincy, do you remember if the horse you bought for me is
marked in some way besides the '10' branded on one hip?"

"Hike has a touch of white on his near front foot."

"You've named him already?"

Quincy smiled. "Well, we had already decided, hadn't we, that
no matter what names they came with, we'd call our horses Hike
and Hobo. The chunky one's going to be a pretty good hiker.
And the tall one looks like a half-starved hobo. So, if it suits you,
they're named."

She tried the words on her tongue. "Hike. Hobo. All right, that
suits me. Oh, honey, I wish we were on our way!"

Some of the chill had gone from their bones by the time the
streetcar trundled into the business district of St. Paul. Quincy
helped Ella down the steps and across the slippery pavement.
Within a block they found a store where he left Ella to buy
gloves and a wool shirt apiece, while he collected the fifty dollars

from the Western Union office. Next they went to a camera shop. Quincy bought a 3¼ x 5½ Premo.

"We'll be taking pictures to illustrate a book," he said to the wispy, gray-haired man behind the counter. As expected, back came the properly curious questions. When Quincy and Ella had outlined the projected trip, the clerk asked, "Why Seattle?"

"That's home town to me," explained Ella. "My mother and brother live there. And my sister will be in Seattle for the summer, before she leaves in August."

"But if you folks have been in New York, why are you starting your trip from St. Paul?"

"Is there a better place to start from?" said Quincy innocently.

"No-o, I guess not."

Quincy leaned on the counter. "Look at it logically. We don't have the time or money to ride from ocean to ocean. But we have to start someplace, and you just agreed there's no better place to start from than St. Paul. So that's where we start."

They left the clerk shaking his head.

The sunshine lasted long enough for Quincy to snap a couple of pictures of Ella, posed beside a lamp post in her long-skirted serge suit of navy blue, her brimmed hat pinned atop her *pouf* of dark brown hair. A policeman with a morose Scandinavian face and drooping mustaches almost got himself included in the shot; Quincy shifted the camera at the last moment. Ella couldn't decide whether to lounge against the post with a sportswoman's carelessness, or to try for an air of prim sophistication. She ended up, Quincy said, just "looking like Bunny, cute enough to kiss." Which he did, on the tip of her diminutive nose. The policeman moved suspiciously toward them.

"It's all right, officer," Quincy beamed. "We haven't been married very long and I need the practice."

Back in their steam-heated room at the Hotel Ryan—one of the best in town, and six dollars for two nights—they unpacked the telescope suitcase and spread their gear out on the bed. It was a frugal assortment.

Early in their plans last winter, they decided to travel without a packhorse. The main reason was economy. In addition, Quincy thought of horse and rider as a self-contained unit, stripped of non-essentials, traveling free. The decision had been hardened by his father's flat statement that it couldn't be done. The Rev. Dr. Walter Quincy Scott, one-time president of Ohio State University and principal of Phillips Exeter Academy, had ridden with Sherman in the Civil War. He knew a thing or two about horses and logistical support. He was appalled at Quincy's rashness.

So was Ella, but for a different reason. She conceded that a man might get along for four months with no personal baggage except a razor and a change of underwear, but a woman? Where would she stow hand lotions, face creams, shampoo, soap, combs, brushes, perfumes, nightgowns, dressing robe, extra shirts, and a "dress up" dress to say nothing of the kitchenware and supplies she would require as official camp cook?

"Quincy, I can't *possibly—*"

"Oh, yes, you can."

And he had patiently won her over to his point of view, emphasizing not only the initial cost of buying a third horse, but the extra forage and oats the packhorse would consume, and the time they would lose every day just handling the additional equipment. He had continued crossing items off lists until he was satisfied that what went on two horses' backs would be compact enough to carry, yet adequate to get their riders across the West.

The saddles and blankets were to be shipped direct to South St. Paul tonight. But here on the bed lay each rider's outfit: a pair of canvas army breeches, side-laced leggings, dark blue flannel shirt, black wool jersey with short sleeves, two suits of long cotton underwear, four pairs of dark cotton socks, one pair of army shoes, a campaign hat, a bandanna kerchief, and a large square rubberized poncho which could be worn as a slicker or used as a ground cloth. For Ella there was also the khaki divided skirt she had made to button over her riding breeches when modesty demanded. (No nightgown or pajamas, no extra shirts or shoes, no coat or jacket.)

Also on the pile went the new camera, a compass, pedometer, small hatchet, hunting knife, two messkits, sewing kit, canteen, ropes, spurs, boxes of cartridges, the few necessary toilet articles, and a cotton bag holding a small supply of flour, baking powder and salt. Because both adventurers were artists, and hopefully the journey would eventuate in a book, there were pencils, sketch pad and a loose-leaf "journal."

A Savage carbine and a shotgun, smelling of fresh gun oil, leaned against the foot of the bed, each in its leather boot. The revolvers were laid out on the pillows, with holsters and belts—a Colt .45 for Quincy and a Smith and Wesson .38 for Ella.

"Let's see what kind of bandits we'll make," said Ella with an excited laugh. "We ought to try on the new flannel shirts anyway." She slipped off her skirt and turned to let Quincy unfasten the hooks at the back of her embroidered blouse.

Ten minutes later they stood hand in hand facing the mirror which was over the heavy, ornate bureau.

"Oh, Lord," snorted Quincy in disgust. "You're very fetching, but both of us look like city dudes!"

A fair-complexioned young fellow with blue eyes, bold nose and a clean-chiseled, sensitive mouth. The rich dark blue of the shirt brought out the original auburn lights still glinting in his sandy hair. Beside him, five feet seven to his six feet two, stood a rosy-cheeked young woman with brown eyes, small pert nose, dark brown hair parted in the middle and twisted into a simple knot at the back of her neck.

Ella regarded the mirror critically. Settling the divided skirt lower on her slim hips didn't help to make her appear any less the tenderfoot.

"Maybe this will do it," she said suddenly, unbuttoning the skirt and tossing it on the bed. She swung back to the mirror and stood with feet apart, hands thrust into the breeches pockets. She wished the reflection showed below the knees. Did her leggings and army shoes *look* as enormous as they felt?

"It's the clothes, Bunny, not us," Quincy sighed. "They're so new, it's a dead giveaway."

Ella glanced at the floor. "We could scrabble around on the carpet. Mabe that would stir up enough dust and rumple up enough wrinkles to make our duds look used."

"Let's try!" Quincy flopped on the red and pink Brussels roses and rotated briskly between the bed and the window. "Come on!"

She lowered herself gingerly to the floor. It was silly, but fun, and she couldn't help giggling. A vigorous twist brought her hard against Quincy. For a second they lay still. Then he put his arm gently across her breast and drew her tight while he kissed her.

"Quincy!" she protested when she could catch her breath. "We're not supposed to be spooning. We're supposed to be—"

He put his finger over her lips. "We're supposed to be on a honeymoon, Mrs. Scott. Remember?"

SATURDAY, MAY 4. *Cold, gray, gusty.*

Quincy and Ella breakfasted early in their room and sneaked out of the hotel as unobtrusively as they could. Ponchos and breeches seemed out of place in the Ryan's stately corridors. Not until they had deposited their city clothes at the railroad office for shipment to Seattle and ridden the trolley across the river could Ella feel that she and the surroundings matched. South St. Paul was the city's back yard, a place of railroad shops, foundries, stock pens and packing plants. From this clutter, rows of dismal houses stretched along the streets and unpaved alleys that ended either abruptly at the Mississippi River or petered out into the farmlands to the south and west.

A sizeable crowd of men and boys was waiting at the South St. Paul freight station. Mr. Rollins had spread the news about those eastern honeymooners buying horses for some tomfool trip, and the onlookers were obviously expecting something out of the ordinary. They got it. The couple's quasi-military appearance, even though slightly softened by Ella's divided skirt, delighted their impromptu audience.

"Are they sojers or cowboys?" squealed a young voice.

"Not neither," answered one of the men. "A couple of artist folks bent on ridin' across the country, just for the hell of it." His tone was contemptuous, but there was enough envy behind the contempt to make Ella straighten herself under her poncho and lengthen her stride until it almost matched Quincy's. Just wait until they jumped on their horses and clattered off into the West —that would give these staring fellows even more reason to pop their eyes and drop their jaws!

Ella somehow had the idea that packing would be a matter of a few minutes: saddle up, toss the gear on the horses' backs, and Seattle, here we come!

But the day went very differently, partly because of the cluster of admirers, which gradually grew in numbers as the time wore on. Each man and boy in the crowd was eager to assist and show how much he knew. Every time Quincy reached for a strap or a buckle, another hand was in the way, usually picking up the wrong piece of equipment.

The chief setback, however, was caused by the discrepancy between army horses and range horses. The McClellan saddles Quincy had chosen at the surplus store in New York came with girths to fit the big-barreled mounts of the U.S. cavalry. When Quincy boosted one of them over Washboard's bony back, no amount of tugging on the latigo would tighten the cinch. Hike, though better fed, was smaller than the average cavalry horse in all dimensions, and the problem with his saddle was the same.

Quincy returned to the station platform across the street, where Ella had remained to guard their pile of belongings. "Mr. Rollins says there's a hardware store about a block away. I've got to have the spider straps shortened. Shouldn't be more than a half-hour job."

A husky young man in the crowd offered to help carry the saddles and a few other onlookers trailed along. The rest of the group closed in around Ella, who was perched on the end of a baggage wagon, and plied her with questions and advice.

"Ain't you gettin' froze, missus?" yelled the freight agent from the shelter of his office.

"I'm all right, thank you." Ella hugged her arms more tightly under the clammy protection of the poncho. Her canvas riding skirt, over the breeches and leggings, kept her knees warm, but there was no comfort in the hard felt army hat that left her ears and the back of her neck vulnerable to the gusts whipping across the outdoor platform. Clouds bellying with their weight of un-fallen snow released a few sleety flakes every now and then as a warning of worse to come.

A long hour passed before Quincy returned. "You okay, honey? That fellow at the hardware store did a good job of sewing and riveting, but he was darned slow. Now let's get all this stuff over to the stable."

"It's nearly noon," Ella reminded him.

"Then we'd better eat before we saddle up. I noticed a little hotel where we can get some stew and a piece of pie."

The gallery of self-appointed assistants reassembled after lunch, this time in the stable and augmented by Mr. Rollins, the hostler—and a reporter from the St. Paul *Dispatch*.

"Wire service alerted us, Mr. Scott," said the reporter, pulling a notebook from his overcoat pocket. "You've had quite a bit of coverage in the eastern newspapers. I tracked you here from the Hotel Ryan. Now if you'd be kind enough to answer a few questions. You have a route all mapped out?"

Quincy laughed. "There aren't any detailed maps for much of the country we'll be traveling through. I tried to locate some in New York and then when we got to St. Paul. Just say that in general we'll be following the line of the Northern Pacific rail-road."

"Where's the rest of your equipment?"

"That's all there is, on the floor in front of you. That's as much as will go on our two riding horses."

"Holy S. Moses! No wagon, no pack mules? How will you eat after you leave the settled parts?"

Quincy reached out his foot to touch the carbine in its leather case. "We'll live off the country."

The reporter's pencil covered several pages of the notebook before he was through.

"One last question, sir. I take it you are both experienced riders?"

Ella answered that one. "My husband is an expert, but I know hardly anything about riding. You might say I can't tell one end of a horse from the other." There! Quincy would wince at her admission that she was anything less than rough, tough and ready, but she wanted the matter put straight. She gave the reporter an impish smile.

He smiled back approvingly. She had just furnished him a nugget for paragraph seven. "Well, thanks, folks. The story will be in the paper tonight. If you haven't ridden clear out of *Dispatch* territory by that time, ha-ha, you may want to buy a dozen copies to send to your friends. Goodbye, and good luck." He tipped his hat to Ella, shook hands with Quincy, and went whistling out into the windy street to wait for the trolley back to the city.

Quincy had been trying futilely to sort out equipment while he answered questions. Now he turned to the job with new determination. "Come on, Bunny. If we don't get this stuff packed, we'll be in *Dispatch* territory, ha-ha, forever."

Hike and the bony horse they had named Hobo suffered patiently in the confusion that followed. So many helpers took part in the packing that Quincy gave up order in exchange for speed. The saddlebags were jammed full. The remaining gear was bundled into the pup tent halves and tied, rather lumpily, back of the saddles. Carbine, hand axe and picket ropes were strapped below the pommel. The riders buckled on their revolvers. Quincy fastened his spurs and helped Ella slip her black poncho over her shoulders before he put on his own.

Through the open double doorway she could see that the weighted skies had made good their threat. It was snowing hard. The drab buildings across the street were nearly hidden in the storm. But this was no time to falter.

The tobacco-chewing hostler who had leered at Ella yesterday stepped forward to hold Hike's head while she scrambled into the saddle. It was an awkward business. She was encumbered with the poncho, and the saddle was bulwarked fore and aft with impedimenta. But she found her seat, settled her hat firmly over her forehead, and took the reins.

"Got to admire yer grit, missus," said the hostler. "But this ain't no weather fer a honeymoon."

A well advertised honeymoon can't be postponed because of a little snow. First day out of St. Paul.

Quincy mounted and motioned Ella to bring Hike up alongside. "All right? Then here we go."

The onlookers let loose an explosion of cheers. "Good luck! Take care of yourselves!"

Hoofbeats changed from hollow clopping on the wooden floor of the stable to squishing in the roadway slush. Ella looked back at the group strung out in the wide doorway and managed a half-staff wave from under her poncho.

A minute later the snow had dropped a swirling curtain between her and the stable. Faintly through the whiteness came a boy's shrill cry: "Ride 'em, cowboy!"

No sunshine, no larks, no soothing zephyr. But they were on their way. Quincy had said they would start May 4. In spite of the disappointments and obstacles, they had done it. That, Ella decided, was a better augury for the trip than if all the preparations had galloped along without a hitch. Her exultant pride in Quincy blotted out her fatigue, as the snow blotted out the line of buildings on either side of the street. Holding on to both his temper and his purpose during all the delays, he had pressed steadily toward the moment of departure. And she—well, at least she had kept quiet and out of his way, most of the time. That had not been easy, for she was just as determined as he to leave on schedule. But it had become clear early in the day that the effort required of her was simply that of letting Quincy handle the situation.

Her congratulatory mood ended almost as soon as it began. Hike had not gone more than a hundred yards from the stable when he began to spook, snorting uneasily, stopping every dozen steps to cast his eye back at her. At first, Ella was too busy to take in the warning signs. It took three hands to hold the bridle, hang on to the pommel, and keep the poncho clutched around her ribs. No matter how she shifted, she was continually one hand short. The wide black poncho went flapping out this way and that.

Hike put up with the commotion for about a mile. Then, abruptly, he started to spin. Rearing up, pivoting nearly full circle on his back feet, coming down to hit the ground stiff-legged. Then up and whirling and another pile-driving jolt. Ella lost her balance on the first spin. On the second, she grabbed Hike's mane as she slid sideways. With the third jolt Hike flung her loose. She catapulted into the road, striking her head.

Sparks flashed. Gongs rang. That warm stuff trickling from her nose was blood. She sat up gingerly, picked her hat out of the slush and staggered to her feet. Quincy had jumped off his horse, and came running to her.

"Bunny, Bunny! Oh, you poor kid." He put his arm around her to steady her, then checked carefully to see how badly she was hurt. A sprained finger, a nosebleed, and a lump beginning to swell on her head.

"We'll go back and make Mr. Rollins give you a different horse. And you can stay in the little hotel nearby until you feel all right."

Ella loosened the bandanna from her throat and wiped her face. She looked over at Hike, who was snuffling for grass in the roadside snow as unconcernedly as if nothing had happened.

"No, Quincy, we're not going back."

"Then we'll at least switch horses."

"No. I'm going to ride Hike if I break every bone in his body."

Quincy touched the lump on her head. "Haven't you got the pronouns reversed?"

"Well, maybe." She managed a faint grin. "But really I don't think he bucked me off out of meanness. That rubber poncho made him just too nervous, blowing and billowing around."

Quincy hesitated. "You're sure you want to try him again?"

"Of course. But I'm going to take off the poncho. I'd rather get soaked than croaked."

Reins in hand again, Ella rode warily in Quincy's lee, alert for any hint that Hike might be planning another rebellion. She didn't feel nearly as bold and insouciant as she had tried to sound in announcing that she would stick with this cow pony. Her head ached, her finger throbbed with every movement, and her sense of propriety had been shaken up even more rudely than her bones. To be thrown within the first mile of the starting point! Suppose it had happened just as she was leaving the stable. Suppose that nice reporter had still been there to write it all down for the paper! In a perverse way she was grateful to Hike for sparing her that humiliation. She took her hand off the pommel long enough to pat his snowflecked mane. "You old reprobate, you. At least you waited until we were out of sight."

They were reaching the outer fringes of South St. Paul by now. The street had dwindled to a country road, flanked by a thinning hodgepodge of workmen's homes and small farms. Somewhere to the right lay the river bluffs and the Twin Cities. Somewhere ahead were the ruins of Fort Snelling, high on the cliff whose prow jutted into the confluence of the Minnesota and the Mississippi, with the town of Mendota on the near bank, and the bridge they must take to cross the smaller river westward. Somewhere ahead—but everything ahead and behind and around was hidden by blowing veils of snow.

"What time is it?" Ella called out.

"About four-thirty."

"I'm hungry." Also wet, cold and tired, but that could be taken for granted.

Up to this point Ella and Quincy has been intent only on getting started in the general direction of Seattle. Now new uncertainties loomed. Where, in all this stormy countryside, would they eat and sleep tonight? And what, actually, *was* the general direction of Seattle?

A fork in the road emphasized their quandary.

"Quincy, I think you'd better dig out the map of St. Paul and Vicinity."

"It's wrapped around the extra piece of pie I smuggled out of the restaurant at lunch. I hate to have to rummage through four saddlebags looking for it. Let's see if this fellow coming along can help us."

Quincy rode toward a man approaching in an open wagon. "How do we get to Seattle?" he called.

"Vo oop!" The man tugged on the reins. He looked as German as his accent, round cheeks and nose almost lost in a tide of yellow whiskers. "Vat iss it you ask?"

"Which road do we take for Seattle?"

The German shook his head, dislodging a heavy bead of moisture from his nose. "Ver he lives I don't know. I ain't so acquainted around here myself yet."

"Well, do you know of any other place west of St. Paul that we could head for?"

"*Ja*, sure, you iss vest by St. Paul."

"Shall we go by this road?" Quincy pointed to the left fork.

"*Ja*, it iss a goot road."

"How about this one?" Quincy pointed to the right.

"*Ja*, that iss a goot road also."

"Thank you very much."

"It iss all right. Goot-bye." The man slapped the reins on his horse's wet rump and the wagon moved on.

"That wasn't a very enlightening conversation," observed Ella.

Quincy shrugged. "It told me as much as flipping a quarter.

All roads lead to. . . . . . .

Let's see—suppose we choose the right hand fork and try to get better directions from the next traveler we meet."

By the time they had ridden two miles farther, the snow was changing to an even more disagreeable rain. Underfoot, the slush softened into mud soup. Presently a horse and buggy came splashing up behind them.

Quincy simplified his question this time. Pointing ahead, he said to the driver, "Where will this road take us?"

"Oh, Ay tank dis road take you to Meeneapolis."

Sweden was no more help than Germany. Staring after the buggy, Ella said, "Maybe we'd better find the map."

"All right. I'm hungry enough now to look for the pie it's wrapped around, anyhow."

They dismounted. Quincy tied the horses to a fencepost with the halter ropes, and looped the reins over the post. After rummaging through three of the four saddlebags, he pulled out a squashy package, misshapen from jogging along under a box of forty-five-caliber cartridges.

Quincy and Ella had to eat the pie, taking turns with the hunting knife, before they could read the map. By the time they had scraped and licked up the last remnants of crust and filling, the map was reasonably legible.

As Quincy started to unfold it, a loose edge fluttered and crackled in the wind. That was all Hike needed. With an indignant jerk he flung himself back, head up and nostrils wide. Bridle leather went flying in all directions.

They had bought the headstall and reins second-hand, and now nothing usable was left of the rotten leather. Quincy held Hike by the nose and one ear. "Let's see what we can improvise," he said cheerfully. Using his spur straps to fasten the bit to a rope halter they had, Quincy put together a makeshift bridle. That done, he heaved the spurs over the fence.

"Not going to need 'em anyhow, and that much less to carry. Now we'll open the map carefully, behind a tree."

The map was eighteen inches square, "with lots of nice lines on it," as Ella commented. A few towns were spotted, most of them with names beginning "Minne—." But not a road was named. There were no compass points indicated, and nothing to show the scale of miles.

"So much for St. Paul and Vicinity," said Quincy in disgust. "We can't figure out from this where we are, much less where we ought to go."

"Then let's use our compass and just ride straight west over the fields," suggested Ella. "This is supposed to be a cross-country trip, isn't it?"

The first two barbed-wire fences they encountered were treated with respect. The riders went well out of their way to find a gate. But after that they took to using a handaxe to pry out the staple holding the fence's top wire. Quincy would spread his poncho over the lower wires and lead the horses across, then pound the staple back in. It saved a lot of time.

They rode on, facing into the rain, as dusk slowly closed in around them.

"Surely we'll find a place to stop pretty soon." Ella's voice was cheerful, but her resolution and hardihood were dissolving like damp sugar.

"The very first light we see, we'll head straight for it," Quincy promised. "Nobody can refuse us shelter on an evening like this."

Three miles short of Mendota they rode into a barnyard where a farmer was forking hay to his cattle.

"Not much room here," he said when Quincy asked if they might sleep in the barn. "You go on about a mile farther, a Mr. Brown will likely take you. If he don't, come on back."

It was a long mile, but at the end of it they found Mr. Brown grudgingly willing to accept two dollars to shelter them and the horses. "You can put the horses up, but you can't go in the house till my sister gets back."

By this time it was seven-thirty. The glow through the windows of the two-story farmhouse promised heat and light. There was neither in the barnyard. Quincy encouraged Ella to jog around with him in the drizzle to keep warm, but she preferred to sit inside the barn. The muscles of her thighs, cramped from hours in the saddle, made each step misery. At last Miss Brown appeared and the guests were permitted indoors. The Browns were a taciturn pair, which was just as well, Ella thought, for their voices were as flat and dull as their faces. Miss Brown was a trifle more friendly than her brother. She welcomed Ella's assistance in getting supper on the table.

Immediately after the meal Miss Brown showed the way upstairs to the "best room." Quincy carried up the saddlebags and one poncho.

"Why the poncho?" Ella asked as Miss Brown closed the door behind her.

"To keep the drips from our clothes off Miss Brown's carpet."

It was a sweet relief to peel off the heavy shirt, skirt, pants and leggings, and to exchange the soaking cotton underwear for dry long johns from the saddlebag. As Ella snuggled against Quincy in the feather bed she murmured, "I hope Hike and Hobo are comfortable, too."

"Mmmh, suppose so. By the way, we can't call my horse Hobo."

"Why not?"

"Tell you in the morning." Quincy was off to sleep, his hand resting lightly in the curve between her hip and her breast.

II It was broad daylight and Sunday morning. The banging of stove lids in the kitchen and the slam of the back door carried a clear message to the sleepy-heads above: Get up!

Quincy perched on the edge of the bed pulling on his khaki breeches. "The rain's stopped," he announced to Ella, who was still curled up under the feather comforter. "And our duds are almost dry."

He crossed to the window to lift aside the starched white curtain. A broken patchwork of gray and blue filled the sky, pushed into fast-changing shapes by a torrent of wind. Briefly the sun broke out to glint on the barnyard puddles. Quincy blinked against the brightness and drew in a great breath. This was a morning for rising spirits, and the road! Yesterday he had pushed on doggedly through the confusions and delays, the miseries of the weather, his fears for Ella. Yesterday it was no good thinking beyond the crisis at hand. But today his thoughts leaped forward in bounding exultation. He was heading westward, as a man should go—on horseback, to find the Old West of dream and history. The moment became a prism, collecting into itself a boyhood's turbulent longings to focus them in the steady beam of a man's reality.

"It's happening! I'm here, over the edge and into it. Please God I've got what it takes."

It was a prayer unuttered, half-conscious, and if his heart substituted "Whee!" for "Amen," surely the Almighty understood. They called the land out there God's country, didn't they?

Ella sat up with a little moan. Quincy came back to the bed. "What's the matter, honey? Saddlesore?"

"In every muscle, from my ankles to my neck, and that goes double for where I sit down."

He grimaced sympathetically, then bent over and parted the silky brown hair at the back of her head. "The lump has pretty well disappeared. No headache this morning? And your sprained finger?"

"Still swollen and hurting, but I can move it a little."

"Good." He drew her up to stand with him, and kissed her. "Do you have any idea how proud I am of you? You came through yesterday with flying colors, tenderfoot."

"You were no slouch yourself." She kissed him back warmly. "But may I remind you that it's not my feet that are tender. Honestly, I don't see how I'm going to sit on a horse *ever* again."

"It'll be cruel, but that's the quickest way to loosen up the kinks. Shall I help you get dressed?"

She managed it for herself while he shaved in cold water at the washstand. As she started with him down the stairs, she said, "Why can't you call him Hobo? I stayed awake all of three seconds last night trying to figure that out."

"I'll demonstrate it to you when we get out and going."

Breakfast was waiting for them at the kitchen table, where Mr. Brown was already halfway through his sausages and hotcakes. Miss Brown, her black Sunday dress protected by a bib apron, filled the coffee cups.

Quincy held the chair for Ella while she gingerly lowered her weight to the hard wooden seat. As he took his own place he smiled cheerfully at the Browns. "Good morning! My wife and I are surely thankful to you for a fine night's rest."

Miss Brown pursed her lips, her brother nodded curtly. The faint friendliness of last night had evaporated.

"You'll be making an early start," said Brown in his flat voice. "My sister and I have to leave for church as soon as you're gone."

Plainly the Browns were not going to stir until the strangers were safely off the property. "Serve 'em right if we puttered around all morning," Quincy thought. But he was in an even greater hurry than they.

After breakfast, while he and Ella saddled up in the barn,

Brown hitched his team to the carryall, delivering to his guests several hospitable admonitions such as, "Hurry up there, now," and "Better get a move on." Miss Brown appeared on the porch, making sure she was seen to lock the door and drop the key in her handbag.

Quincy boosted Ella up into the saddle, a maneuver accomplished with only one muttered "Ouch!" Brown looked back from the carryall, where his sister was now primly seated beside him, and motioned to the riders to precede him out of the gate. Quincy was equally gallant. He swept off his hat and insisted that the hosts go first. He didn't catch what Brown said under his breath, but there was no misreading the distrustful face turned backward all the way to the gate.

"He's probably disappointed that we didn't try to put the barn into our saddlebags," laughed Ella.

"Does that chuckle mean you're feeling more limber already?"

"No. I'm excruciatingly uncomfortable. But at least I've ridden the first hundred yards without screaming."

The Browns turned to the right at the end of the lane, Quincy and Ella to the left. The last of the clouds had blown away, and with the sun on their backs and the wind in their faces, they rode in what they hoped was the most direct route toward Mendota and the bridge that would take them over the Minnesota River. What they wanted was a road that would put them on the west side of Minneapolis, where they could follow the railroad line angling up and across to North Dakota. But Minneapolis, fringed with a sprawl of unmarked roads, seemed loath to let any traveler escape its web. Even persistent questioning of Mr. Brown had not been helpful. Most of his directions had ended up with, "But don't go that way, it'll take you to Minneapolis."

They had ridden about half an hour when Ella said, "If we're to keep track of our mileage, shouldn't we start using the pedometer? I think it's in one of the saddlebags on Ho—say, you haven't showed me why you can't call him Hobo!"

At the sound of his name, the big black horse stopped dead. Quincy recovered his balance and looked back at Ella. "There, see for yourself. Every time we say 'Hobo,' he thinks we're say-ing 'Whoa, bo,' and he obediently suspends all activity. At that rate we'll never get to Fargo, let alone Seattle."

Ella sighed. "Hike and Hobo made such a nifty combination. But you're right, we'll have to find another name. Let me think—" She tried out a string of names for their sound.

"Rogue, Gypsy, Wanderer, Tramp . . . No. How about Vaga-bond, and call him Vag for short?"

That was one name Quincy had considered. He leaned for-ward and thumped his horse's shoulder. "Suits me. Does it suit you, Vag old boy? And now while you're halted, I'll hunt for the pedometer. The problem is, Vag, where to tie it—on you, or on me."

It had been decided, while the trip was still in the planning stage, that part of each day would be spent on foot, to rest both the riders and the horses. Could the pedometer be fastened in such a way that would keep an accurate record of miles cov-ered, whether mounted or dismounted?

Quincy found the gauge in the first saddlebag he opened. He tied it to his ankle and walked until it registered half a mile. Then with it still attached, he picked a point a like distance ahead and rode Vag toward it, at varying gaits.

"What does it say now?" asked Ella, pulling Hike up beside him.

"Eleven and a half miles!"

"Eleven and—but I don't understand!"

"A pedometer records a unit of distance every time it's jarred. I guess Vag jars a lot more than I do. Maybe if we attach it to the old boy himself, we can regulate it according to his stride."

Vag didn't object to having the thing strapped to his left front foot, but as he picked his way along the stony roadway, he moved his front feet without any regularity.

"The place he seems to jiggle the least is his stomach," Quincy observed.

"Then why don't you feed the thing to him?"

"Great idea, Bunny, but I've got a better one." Quincy took the free end of the string, whirled the pedometer above his head

Neat barns and field were typical of the Minnesota country through which Quincy and Ella traveled.

and sent it in the same direction the spurs had gone yesterday—over the fence to oblivion. Mileage would have to be figured some other way.

Mid-morning and several turns in the road brought them to Mendota. Quincy dismounted in front of the only store they found open, a pharmacy, and came out with a copy of the St. Paul *Dispatch*, which he tied to the saddle. "Looks like we're going to be in *Dispatch*-territory-ha-ha for quite a while longer. The man in there says the bridge is about six miles south."

"Did you look to see if they got the story about us in the paper?"

"They did. You can read it when we stop for lunch."

"Quincy, don't make me wait that long!"

"It's worth waiting for," he teased. "Come on, the sooner we get out of town, the sooner we'll reach a farm where we can buy something to eat."

But the Sunday that closed stores in town was the same day that gave farm families the leisure to go visiting after church. Ella and Quincy, seeking a farm with someone on it, were riding up a small hill when they encountered a sulky on the way down. It was pulled by a large, fleabitten gray horse and contained a small boy, driving, and a smaller girl beside him.

At the sight of the two people on horseback, the big fleabitten gray reared up, snorted, and began a panicky jerking that threatened to overturn the sulky.

Quincy jumped off Vag and grabbed the gray's head. It took all his strength to lead the frightened old horse past the point where Ella held their own two mounts.

"Gee, mister," cried the boy, valiantly ready to take over again. "Don't know what about you scared him. Must have been them yaller pants!"

Quincy looked down at his breeches. In this country of faded blue "overhalls" and best Sunday black, maybe new khaki *was* bright enough to spook a conservative horse. The old gray plug did have about him something of the scandalized deacon.

It was noon, and still no sign of the bridge. On the far side of a hump in the road Quincy and Ella stopped at one more farmhouse door. Here they were able to buy a canteen of milk and a loaf of bread from two bachelor Swedes. Once again Quincy sought directions.

"Oh, best way to go 'round Meeneapolis is to follow t' river, yoost to Bloomington. T'en you strike up sooch a vay ven t'river bends t'at vay." The older of the two men swung his arm in a large gesture, from which Quincy gained the general impression that when the river turned west, Seattle-bound travelers should branch off north. It was all very vague, and strengthened his feeling that he was losing time on a foolish detour. Father Hennepin, who had shown the first white man's face in these parts two hundred and thirty years ago, probably had less trouble getting places.

Quincy and Ella made lunch off the bread and milk, sitting on the steps on the sheltered side of a lonely schoolhouse. Hike and Vag had their own fare, a neat pile of oats for each of them, poured out on the ground from the small sackful included in last night's lodging.

Before eating, Ella opened the *Dispatch* to the column headed "Honeymoon Trip of Couple in Saddle." At the last paragraph a glow of shy pleasure suffused her face.

"Oh, that *is* nice," she said softly.

Quincy took the paper. "'Mrs. Scott is very pretty and looked especially bewitching in her riding costume.' That may be news to the readers of the *Dispatch*, Bunny, but not to her husband."

"Thank you, darling." She reached for the paper again and he noticed with surprise that her hand was trembling. How much there was still to learn about this girl! Bunny had little vanity, spoke of her appearance seldom and then referred to herself as plain. She seemed indulgently amused when he lavished lover's compliments upon her. But now, in that slight tremor of her hand, he sensed that in spite of her modest self-appraisal, or perhaps because of it, she was moved by the generous words of the reporter.

She was glancing at Quincy now over the top of the paper. "The man wrote something nice about you, too. He says that Mr. Scott has a national reputation as a cartoonist."

Quincy threw back his head in a shout of laughter. "That's debatable, but I'm grateful. Now if you'll just slice me a hunk of bread, I'll uncork the milk, and we'll drink to the bewitching wife and the husband with the dubious reputation. *Skoal!*"

The wind blew harder during the afternoon. Hike and Vag stepped faster, ears pricked and nostrils flared to scoop in the stream of country sounds and smells. The grasses flattened under the gusts, and in the river bottom the willows, not yet fully leafed, tossed their branches like girls sunning cascades of tawny hair.

At length Quincy pointed to a dark line threading across a wider stretch of bottom. "The bridge. Or bridges. Looks like a series of them, from island to island."

"I'm going to lead Hike," Ella confessed as they struck the first span, "just in case he gets any funny ideas about jumping over the rail."

Quincy rode slowly behind her. Looking down into the current of the Minnesota, boiling and muddy-brown with yesterday's run-off, he tried to picture those other rivers to be crossed —the Red, the Missouri, Little Missouri, Yellowstone, Musselshell, Columbia. Dangerous rivers, whose names belonged in a litany of the West. Some were unbridged, some had only a railroad span. But swim, ferry or balance on gaping ties, he and Ella had to get themselves and the horses to the far side of every stream. He flicked the end of the rein against the protective railing beside him and thought, with disdain, "*This* one is no challenge."

They had covered about three miles since lunch when Ella discovered that the canteen had been left behind.

"No sense in our both going after it," Quincy decided. "If they'll take you in for a short rest at that farm just ahead, I'll chase back to the school."

A little sparrow of a woman opened the door as they rode into the farmyard. "Yes'm, you can come in," she said to Ella. "I got a dreadful toothache, but I s'pose it won' do no harm to set and talk a bit. I've had no company all day, and a Sunday too."

Quincy waited until Ella had tied her horse and gone inside. Then he turned Vag and trotted out to the road. Golly, what a rough gait to this bag of bones! But the old boy could travel, and seemed to enjoy the change from steady walking. Quincy admitted to himself that it was his own desire for a bit of speed, as much as the canteen, that prompted him to go back. All this bright windy day he had been spoiling to cut loose, to feel the muscles under him exploding into a dead run.

"Attaboy, go it!" Quincy pressed his heels, Vag humped his rangy frame, and they thundered away, clots of dried mud rocketing out behind the flying hoofs. A string of red-winged blackbirds, startled from their fence-wire perch, wheeled overhead in a wide parabola and lit a hundred feet beyond, to arc into the sky again.

Quincy let Vag run for about a third of the distance back to the schoolhouse. Then he reined down to a slower, jarring lope. A willing old horse, Quincy thought gratefully, St. Vitus jigs and all. It was a shame no one had ever taken the pains to gait him in his early years, or care for him properly in his later ones. But neither oats nor kindness could make him the right horse for this summer's gruelling marches. A year ago Quincy wouldn't have been caught dead hiring such a rack of bones, even for one afternoon's ride.

A year ago . . . that would be a little more than halfway between meeting Ella and asking her to marry him. It still gave him a dizzying, breathless feeling, a mixture of fear and marvel, to think of all the chance turnings that preceded the meeting. There was a girl, child of Mississippi and Kentucky parentage, but born in Texas where her father rode circuit court and died when she was two years old, a girl whose widowed mother moved to Seattle and taught school to put her children through college, a girl who began supporting herself as a teacher but turned artist, launched her career as an illustrator in Chicago, and then chose New York as a better place to study and to market her work. There was a boy, born in Ohio of New England-Pennsylvania stock, reared in New Hampshire, upstate New York, the Pocono mountains and the Jersey suburbs, who took his gift of caricature and political sense into Manhattan's newspaper world.

Their common profession accounted for that girl and that boy being in New York. But what celestial plot nudged the two of them to the corner of Fifty-seventh and Broadway at exactly the same moment on the first night of April, 1906?

Quincy was on his way to an early evening class at the Art Students' League. As he started across Broadway, he saw a girl ahead of him, walking with a free, natural stride, not the mincing step of city-bred young ladies. She was wearing a gray shepherd's plaid suit, sleek and close-fitting, with a black velvet collar. A black felt sailor hat was pinned to her dark brown hair. On an impulse, he quickened his pace to overtake her, and cast a darting look at her face.

If she was aware of his curiosity, she gave no sign. Her eyes (brown? deep blue?) were fixed steadily ahead, and he got no more than a brief glimpse of the soft rose of her cheek, the neat sculpturing of her nose, and a serious mouth. It was enough for him. "That's the girl I'm going to marry!" he decided before common sense took over. In New York's millions, only a fool would hope to see a passing face again.

At the Art Students' League he went upstairs to the sketch class, where he was a monitor. He was turning away from the door, when a distinctly un-New York voice behind his back said, "Here is something for you, sir."

He swung around. There *she* stood, a tiny smile parting those serious lips, soft cheeks glowing a deeper rose, and eyes not blue but deep hazel brown, looking up forthrightly into his. Her name was on the registration card she gave him. Ella B. Allen. And her address, only a few blocks from the apartment where he lived with his parents. She would be here, five nights a week, sitting at a drawing board only a few feet away from him. Common sense had said only a fool would hope. O happy, happy fool!

A year ago . . . he still could shake his head at how many

times it was a near miss, and acknowledge with inner trembling how bereft he would be without her.

As his thought rounded that dark corner, he put his heels into Vag sharply, swooped down on the schoolhouse steps to pick up the canteen, and galloped all the way back to Ella, to boast that Vag had done the round trip in thirty minutes!

III

JOURNAL ENTRIES

SUNDAY, MAY 5 . . . *Slept in barn of three bachelors who treated us well. Rather cold.*
MONDAY, MAY 6. *Early start. Breakfast scrambled eggs in woods. Turned north to Lake Minnetonka, which we reached in afternoon . . . Rode out west shore of lake, found deserted house where we camped. Slept in barn, with revolvers handy in case of hoboes disturbing us. Hay kept us warm.*
TUESDAY, MAY 7. *Woke up very stiff and cross. Lunched in woodlot by road with big campfire. Baked potatoes—began snowing before we had finished—saddled and started on. Rode till 4 in snowstorm. Stopped at Mr. Schlomer's and got shelter. Drew pictures of barn, comics, etc. Slept in house, very comfortably.*

Quincy did the comic pictures, surrounded by Schlomer's bright eager children. They hung all over him, watching the point of his pencil begin at a corner of the paper and produce, from the feet up, or the tail in, a carefully-proportioned but completely unexpected creature that sent them into stitches. They liked especially the curly-tailed piglet wearing a bib and eating soup with a dipper, and one specimen labeled "Seventeen-legged Bickersnoodle." As bedtime approached, Ella quieted the children with stories of elves and fairy kingdoms. Finally, for the parents, she sketched the neat farmyard and barn. "Ja, dot iss mein barn," Papa Schlomer conceded, "but vere iss mein bull?" She promptly added the prize bull to the sketch. This obligingness didn't prevent Papa Schlomer the next morning from charging two dollars for meals and lodgings, but she didn't begrudge him the price, for it had been the most restful night yet.

Quincy put "Becky Sharp" to work whittling shavings for a campfire in the Minnesota woods.

FRIDAY, MAY 10. *Had breakfast in the woods—
corncake, milk . . .*

It was nippy but clear, this morning at Annandale. Ella's high
spirits overflowed into the postcard she wrote to Daddy and
Mother Scott while Quincy was saddling up: "We've just been
eating breakfast around a campfire, after sleeping all night in a
barn. White frost on the ground last night but we're both fine.
Made 23 miles yesterday. Horses going well. Everybody treats us
nicely and we're well pleased with Minnesota. Will be in Fargo
in about ten days. Rations plentiful but limited in variety—milk,
eggs, bacon, potatoes, etc. Don't worry if you don't hear regularly as we can't always stop at P.O. Off for an early start at
7 A.M."

She wished there were space to tell more. Incidents like the
one at Delano when the horses, heretofore so good about standing that Quincy left the lariats off, lay down to roll and then
suddenly lurched to their feet and took off down the meadow
with what seemed like half the population of Delano running to
help Quincy catch them.

The weather was bleak one day, beguiling the next. Yesterday
the skies had cleared and the breeze lost its cutting edge. During the midday stop at a small lake Ella had taken a picture of
Quincy shaving, spraddle-legged in front of a mirror nailed to a
tree. Then she had carried a handful of underwear and socks to
wash at the shore. The sunshine lay like a scarf across her
shoulders, tender and protective. The mild air was freighted
with earthy odors liberated by the warmth of noon and promising summer in the smell of spring. Ella knelt there, holding the
dripping laundry poised for a final rinse, and let the air, sun and
earth surround her.

Early this morning, here at Annandale, it had taken more faith
to believe in summer. The rungs of the ladder leading from the
hayloft where she and Quincy had slept were slippery with frost.
Each ridge of farmyard mud was outlined in white. It wasn't

summer yet. But by the time breakfast was cooked, the sun had melted the rime, and her cheerful assurances on the postcard came naturally.

Trotting along beside Quincy the short mile into town, Ella's mood of smug confidence continued. Everything *was* going well. The saddle soreness had been jogged out of her muscles. The sprained finger no longer ached. Hike had a new bridle. The capture of the horses after yesterday's escape proved that a runaway was not an irreversible disaster. And though Minneapolis had finally been put behind them, flattering remnants of publicity still floated about. Hadn't a woman brought her children across the fields to the campfire yesterday evening just so her little Elvira and Benny-Benny could say they had seen "them people who was written up in the paper"?

Before Ella and Quincy finished tying their horses to the hitching rail in front of Annandale's general store, the usual crowd of men began to collect around them. By now, Ella understood that the chief magnet was the novelty—and impropriety—of a woman riding horseback astride. *My God,* the eyes said, *what kind of a girl is this?* Middlewestern farm wives did their outdoor chores in housedresses. When they rode anywhere, it was in a buggy or wagon, legs modestly covered. If an occasional newspaper illustration showed a society woman on horseback, she was mounted side-saddle, wearing skirts to the ankle. Ella was aware that she didn't fit either picture. Though she had designed her free-swinging divided skirt in deference to convention, under it was a pair of men's khaki breeches, finished off with canvas leggings that showed a good eight inches below the skirt. Her dark blue woolen army shirt, bandanna neckerchief and wide-brimmed felt campaign hat added to the unsettling effect. The revolver at her hip took care of anything further needed to mark her as a very odd, possibly immoral, and potentially dangerous woman.

Let the men stare. Ella knew she was sensibly dressed (except for the bothersome skirt). Her morals were stiffened with Victorian and Cumberland Presbyterian principles, and she wouldn't hurt a fly. Yes, let the men stare. After the first shock their mis-

When Middlewestern farm women rode, it was in a buggy or wagon, with their legs modestly covered.

givings about her respectability would be diluted by curiosity about the trip. Where were they headed? Why did they both carry pistols and saddle guns? How in the world did they manage without a packhorse?

Quincy, still worried over Vag's inadequacies, would ask about a horse trade; the question would draw every bystander into the conversation, whether he knew of any trades or not. The men pressed in to inspect Hike and Vag minutely. That bolder fellow there might be speculating about running his hands appreciatively over Ella's leggings instead of over Hike's fetlocks, but she was sure he wouldn't go beyond speculation.

Ella left Quincy to answer the questions and went into the store to buy steaks. While she waited for the meat to be wrapped, she saw a row of small faces pressed against the window. Elvira and Benny-Benny had walked into town for a second look at "them people," and brought along their playmates.

Ella waved, and the children scattered in giggling embarrassment.

The best moment always came when it was time to leave. For all his ungainliness, old Vag had style. As soon as he felt the weight of Quincy's foot in the stirrup, he would begin to move, a quick turn that swung Quincy into the saddle just as Vag shot away with a thunder of hoofs and an impudent swirl of his black tail. It was in the finest cowboy tradition, and today it brought the usual whoops and whistles from the onlookers.

Beyond Annandale the small towns were beaded along the tracks of the Soo Line—South Haven, Kimball Prairie, Watkins, Eden Valley, Paynesville. Quincy was in quest of nosebags for Vag and Hike; with oats so scarce, it seemed wasteful to throw the feed on the ground. But there were no nosebags to be bought —and nothing to put in them. "There ain't a oat in town," said one feedstore owner. No farmer would sell from his own scanty supply, and no householder was willing to take the gun-toting travelers into his home.

"I don't suppose we can blame them," Quincy said ruefully after the eighth try. "Practically all these folks are immigrant families. Everything is strange and threatening to them. You and I must seem especially suspicious. No wonder someone pointed us out as bank robbers in Buffalo yesterday!"

"It *is* kind of funny," Ella said, "wearing these revolvers to protect ourselves, when we must look more alarming than the hoboes *we* worry about!"

They bedded down for the night on a layer of corn husks in an abandoned settler's cabin, grudgingly turned over to them by a chisel-chinned farmer west of Watkins. The man had steadfastly refused to part with either hay or oats for Hike and Vag.

SATURDAY, MAY 11. *Horses shivering with cold and hunger. Man repentant, brought armful of hay and we let them eat till late while we wrote journal around fire. No breakfast but piece of corncake and ½ a microscopic frankfurter . . .*

Ella sighed as she rubbed a wisp of hay over the skillet. A meal like that left little grease to scour out.

The weather shifted again as they rode through Eden Valley to Paynesville, and men were out in the fields with teams and plows to take advantage of the break. Near the farmhouses, women in cotton sunbonnets stooped along the rows of the vegetable gardens, planting corn with a hand-stabber. It was like a ritual dance, slow-paced and bobbing. Each woman performed at her own rhythm as she bent down to plunge the stabber into the moist earth, pulled it out, dropped the seed corn into the hole, covered it, straightened up partially, and took a step to the next position.

"It makes my back ache just to watch them," Ella said.

At a yellow clapboard house close to the river Quincy and Ella stopped to ask about staying over the weekend. The owner here was a widow, Mrs. Rhodes, who kept house for her middle-aged son Ab and the hired man. Ella liked the big, slow-moving woman on sight. Above her rugged, weather-worn face and intelligent eyes, Mrs. Rhodes' gray hair was crimped into ruffles prim as the gingham curtains that framed her kitchen window.

"You say you're from New York, and you're riding horseback to Seattle?" She hesitated, holding the door half-open while she looked over her callers thoroughly. Then she swung the door wide. "Oh, you can come in. I don't see as if you're old enough to be any harm."

It had become a kind of game for the travelers. A bed in the house, meals at the table, a stall and feed for the horses, and some provisions to carry along on the journey counted as a big win. All this offered graciously, and free or with only a nominal charge, would be a double win. (Thus far they hadn't hit that jackpot.) At the other end of the scale was a flat refusal even of space to sleep on the ground.

Once Mrs. Rhodes had made up her mind to take the ruffianly pair in, she treated them well.

"You might as well sleep in the house. And if you want to cook your meals across the river, that'll be all right. It's turning off warm for a change, and it'll be nice over there in the woods. The horses? Ab will show you where to put them in the barn."

Preparing a dinner outdoors was always a major accomplishment, considering the miniscule size and general tippiness of the Preston mess kits. The saucepans were so small that each person's food had to be cooked separately. But the marvel of the utensils was their determination to upset. On a solid flat surface they were unreliable. On the uneven, shifting embers of a campfire, the pans teetered constantly at the brink of disaster. Quincy said the Army should have issued a suitably profane vocabulary to go with its unsuitable saucepans. But Ella was learning to outwit them, and tonight, with milk, eggs and bread from Mrs. Rhodes' larder and store meat, she served up a hearty camp meal without accident.

Before sundown Swenson, the hired man, shouted across the bridge, inviting Ella and Quincy to the farmhouse for a concert of phonograph records.

Ab Rhodes was fond of a record called "Love Me and the World is Mine." Mrs. Rhodes and Swenson agreed that "Goodbye, Little Girl, Goodbye" was *their* favorite. When both sides of every record had been played on the golden oak phonograph with its flaring black horn, Mrs. Rhodes announced that it was time for bed.

The next day was seductively mild. Ella wrote letters while Quincy went for a swim in the Crow and caught enough "croakers" to provide a gourmet luncheon of frogs' legs fried over a small fire of twigs. Afterward, Ella stretched out limply on her poncho and let the noontide heat lull her into a delicious nap.

A soft nudge of Quincy's toe wakened her hours later. "I hate to disturb you, Bunny, but it's going to storm. We'd better get back to the house."

The air was hot and motionless, a burden on her flesh. Southwest of the woods, the blue-black thunderheads were crowding toward the zenith. In a slow daze Ella began collecting the mess kits and rolling up the blankets.

Mrs. Rhodes seemed almost glad of their company when

Quincy and Ella reached the house, and invited them to have supper with her.

The storm broke before the meal was finished. While the lightning lit up the landscape outside with eerie flashes and thunder rattled the windows, Mrs. Rhodes reminisced about how she had come, during the Civil War, to a Minnesota where most of the prairie was untouched.

"Springtimes, there were flowers, like parti-colored quilts spread out for miles and miles. Puccoons, wild roses, bird'sfoot violets, prairie phlox—you'd see a bit of it even now if you weren't so early and the season so late. And water lilies in the ponds wherever there was a hollow in the prairie. Yellow and white water lilies."

"It must have been heavenly," Ella sighed.

"Humph! And hell too. All us settlers were plagued with prairie fires and Indian troubles. Why, during the first year we came, we had to carry our quilts every night to the blockhouse and sleep there for fear of Sioux raids. I can tell you, bringing up nine children was no easy job." She pointed her heavy forefinger at Ab. "That one doesn't recollect, because he was born after things began to quiet down a bit, but all the rest of my brood can testify that Minnesota was real frontier."

Ab looked slyly at his mother. "She claims she used to carry an umbrella every time she went outdoors, to keep off the arrows. I don't know whether to believe her or not."

"I've got the bumbershoot with holes in it to prove my story," said Mrs. Rhodes calmly.

Swenson pushed back his chair. "You never ban showin' it to me, missus." He rose from the table, wiping his long fair mustache with the back of his hand. He gave Ella an elaborate wink, as if to let her in on a venerable family joke. She smiled back, then exchanged delighted glances with Quincy. Whether the umbrella story was "tall" or not, she knew she would never forget the quick picture that had flashed into her mind of this sturdy, wise-faced pioneer woman going resolutely about her farmyard chores, protected by a black umbrella bristling with spent arrows. What an illustration that would make!

A biting wind blew head on, and the roads were so muddy that Hike and Vag could move only at a slow walk. Ella and Quincy huddled over a cold lunch in the lee of a few scrubby elder trees in a hollow. It was the only shelter in sight, for they were reaching the transition belt between hardwood groves and prairie. The snow began as they finished eating, and their flannel shirts and jersey pullovers were no match for it.

"Better wrap up in all we've got," Quincy advised. He helped Ella swathe herself in two of the saddle blankets with her poncho over it all before boosting her up on Hike. Somehow he got himself aboard Vag, wrapped in tent halves and poncho. There was no shying or rearing—the horses by this time were fairly blasé about flapping gear.

Heads down against the wind and snow they went, horses and riders, looking as Ella said, "like a fine Remington composition." She remembered how often she and Quincy had proclaimed in New York that they were taking this trip for the hardships as well as the fun. Well, she wasn't complaining or quitting. But that didn't keep her from being cramped, cold and thoroughly disgusted with the climate.

They were looking for Lintonville. Late in the afternoon it materialized out of the woolly whiteness, a thicker blur that sorted itself gradually into a cluster of houses and barns and a row of business buildings, topped by the grain elevators.

Ella said, between chattering teeth, "Do you think we would be too sissified if we put up at a hotel tonight?"

"We'd be crazy not to. I've never felt so cold in my life."

The hotel-keeper met them at the door, thumbs jammed into his vest pockets, elbows wide to bar the entrance.

"Sorry, folks. Got no more room. Try at the Bauers' farm across the tracks."

That evening, warmed in soul as well as body by the merry hospitality of Bauer and his large family, Ella sat in a rocking chair and cuddled the youngest, a two-year-old boy, in her arms. Across the livingroom, Quincy had been conducted with ceremony to the organ, and was tossing off minstrel songs to his own sketchy accompaniment. Ella pressed her cheek against the little boy in her arms. Some day, when this journey was over and money had been saved up again, she would have a child of her own to hold—a child with red-gold hair like Quincy's. Outside, the snow piled in clumps against the narrow windows. What it threatened for tomorrow she didn't want to think about. Enough to be welcome, well fed, and part of a scene that could serve as a postcard: "A Happy German Family at Home on a Winter Night."

Bauer, as rotund and glowing as the airtight stove in the corner, stumped over to her and picked up the little boy. "Bedtime for this one now. We are having a real *gemutlichkeit* tonight, *nicht wahr?*"

Ella smiled back at him. "It hasn't been that way every place. We've been turned down flat at many a door."

"Ach, that's a shame. But remember, these are bad times. After such a long winter, the pantry shelves and the grain sacks are empty. The weather keeps so wet and cold the farmers can't get their new crops planted. Then they are gloomy and worried."

"That's part of the trouble, I'm sure," said Ella. "But how about at the hotel? I don't really think all the rooms were full, do you?"

Bauer let out a booming laugh.

"Who with? Who's traveling in such weather? *Nein*, I tell you, that fellow, if he doesn't like your looks, he turns you away, no matter how many rooms are empty."

Ella's smile became an impish grin. "Did *you* like our looks?"

"Ach!" Bauer swung the boy to his shoulder. "I use my ears as well as my eyes. You look like no-goods, *ja*, but your talk is all right. So *meine frau* and I let you come in, and now we have not only good talking, but good singing too! Another night, the same."

"Another night?"

"The road will not be fit to travel tomorrow. Too muddy with melting snow. You stay here. There is a minstrel show at the schoolhouse in the evening. Maybe Mr. Scott will sing. He has a fine voice."

"I know," said Ella, pleased. "His voice teacher in New York wanted him to audition for the Metropolitan Opera, but Quincy says he wouldn't want the life of a professional singer. He'd be very handsome on the opera stage, wouldn't he?"

"He is handsome even in *mein* parlor." Bauer's laugh boomed out again.

A little later, the children trooped obediently off to bed, each pausing to kiss their plump smiling blonde mother, and to murmur "Sleep well" to the guests. The last one out the door, a saucy boy, chose to be different. "*Schlafen sie gut!*"

Sleep well they did. The thick feather bed, standard in the farmhouses of the Minnesota prairie, would have smothered them in warmer weather, but this night and the next they nestled gratefully in its embrace.

The next day, Ella used her leisure to write to her mother at length. Quincy read her letter over and added a postscript: "Bunny has given you a pretty good idea of our progress up to date. She omitted to tell you what a good traveler she is, how thorough a sport and how genuine her grit. She is . . . as tough as nails."

She kissed him for that, glad that outwardly she was measuring up to his expectations. It was just as well her hero didn't suspect how far short of tough his heroine usually felt. Quincy had been cheerful enough for two during these early weeks of the trip. His optimism, she recognized, was part principle, part temperament. He was trying to accept as one big happy lark all the things that plagued them—chill soakings, bruises, hunger, scowling faces and slammed doors, the growing anxiety about trading Vag. Her own silence wasn't entirely out of consideration for him. A good part of it came from confidence that life wouldn't push her into anything she couldn't handle, no matter how unpleasant or demanding. She had agreed to cross the West on horseback, and nothing had happened yet to shake her certainty that she would do it—and in fitting style.

The next morning the snow was gone, and there was no excuse to linger with the warm-hearted Bauers. After an affectionate farewell, Quincy and Ella took to the doughy road. The horses mired down several times and had to be coaxed free with great tuggings on the reins and urgings from the rear.

News of strangers in town brought Editor Babcock of the Belgrade, Minnesota, newspaper to the general store for an interview while Quincy and Ella shopped for groceries. The first installment of his story came out in the Belgrade *Tribune* later that day. Babcock had added a touch of the humorous exaggeration that was admired in clever writers of the time. It was also quite in accord with Quincy's and Ella's own attitude toward their trip.

". . . They were both on horseback, their heads bared to the sun, each with a rifle slung to the saddle bow and revolvers in their belts. No little excitement was created on the streets by their sudden appearance, and when they dismounted and tied their horses to a convenient telephone pole people were rubbering out of windows and store doors . . . a few, with the dread vision of the Northfield bank robbery haunting them, feared that they were part of a band of desperadoes . . . who might appear at any minute yelling furiously, rush into the banks . . . and with a fusillade of shots, dash off with the loot. The editor, however, made bold by his keen desire for news and impressed with the fact that as an officer of the law (yours truly, J. P.—marriages and legal business performed with dispatch and at reasonable rates) he had a right to know a thing or two about the matter, put on his hat and with pencil and paper in hand resolved that he could brave instant death to get a 'scoop' on the other fellows and supply the readers of *The Tribune* with news."

At that point in the article the editor ran out of time and space, and had to leave the rest of the tale for the next weekly issue.

Toward sundown Ella and Quincy were glad to take shelter in the relic of a house that was being used as a granary. When they spread their blankets on the oats, making hollows for hip and shoulder, Quincy chuckled. "What luxury! After all the trouble we've had to find even a peck of oats to buy for the horses, here we are sleeping in a roomful! Wonder what a bed-room of grain would bring on the market? Let's see. This room is about ten by twelve, and the grain is piled up about four feet. How many bushels in a cubic yard?"

Ella was too drowsy to calculate. "Pay the farmer's wife a quarter in the morning, honey, and forget the higher mathematics." As a bedtime luxury, oats couldn't compare with Mrs. Rhodes' feather bed.

They had been riding all morning across flat prairie land where the towns were visible for miles ahead. But in the late afternoon Quincy and Ella topped a rise and looked down from its gentle height to see blue water, white cottages, neat rows of trees. There was even a "mountain" rising about ninety feet above the town.

"What a painting that would make!" Ella cried. She framed the scene with thumbs and forefingers. "When the leaves come out, it will look like a pretty summer resort."

This was Glenwood on the shores of Lake Minnewaska. Glenwood mustered the usual throng of curious townsfolk, including a stoop-shouldered youth who grabbed the rope coiled at Hike's saddlebow and proclaimed, "This here's the larry-utt. When they git further west, they'll use it to ketch wild horses to ride when these ones git tired."

Quincy went off to inspect two horses offered for trade. Ella snubbed Hike to the hitching rack, muttering in his ear, "Too bad it's not *you* we're going to trade off." Hike often displayed a willful, surly streak that angered her. He showed his ungraciousness by bucking when she first mounted in the morning, by sudden jumps for no visible reason, and by his disdain for ropes, hobbles, picket pins and anything else that prevented his abandoning his riders for good.

"What luck?" she asked when Quincy came back for her. He waited to answer until they were riding away. "Between them," he said, "the horses here have just what we need. One is well-priced and the other seems durable. But the cheap one's not tough enough, and the tough one's not cheap enough. First I looked at a sorrel stallion that's very inexpensive, but too light and dainty. Then I was sent over to see a young gray mare. She's strong and easy-gaited, a real dandy, but the skinflint who owns her won't allow me more than twenty-five bucks on Vag, and we can't afford a short-ended trade like that. Do you think I did right to turn them both down?"

It wasn't her judgment on horseflesh he needed, of course. It was her judgment on *his* judgment. It was true she didn't fully understand why he was so determined to trade off Vag. Even with sparse oats the rangy black had begun to fill out the cavernous hollows around his hipbones and, in some lights at least, the washboard ribs were barely noticeable. To Ella he looked good. Might he not be equal to those eight hundred miles of scanty forage that stretched from the Missouri River at Bismarck to the Missouri River at Helena? But though she questioned in her mind, she didn't pretend to *know*. She had to trust Quincy for that, and she said gravely, "I think you were wise. There are still plenty of towns before we get to the sagebrush. Somewhere along you'll find the right deal."

"Well, that's what I figured." His face brightened. He pulled his watch from his breeches pocket. "Five-thirty. What say we stop at that farm ahead to buy some oats and milk, then put up the tent over there on the shore?"

It was the first time, after two weeks' travel, that they pitched their pup tent. They were to find they still had a lot to learn about camping.

Within a mile and a half of town they found a fairly level spot under the bare trees that bordered Lake Minnewaska. Quincy threw his hat on the ground to mark where the tent should go. There they piled the ponchos, guns, blankets and saddlebags. Hike and Vag, relieved of riders and sixty pounds apiece of saddle and equipment, shook themselves mightily and dropped their heads to graze.

"Oh, Quincy!" Ella stood, hands on her hips, looking around with joy. "No farmhouses or musty old sheds for us tonight. We're camping out!" She saw that the tangle of barren maple branches overhead was outlined against a cloudy grayness where the sun had been a few minutes earlier. She could feel the saturated sponginess of the ground under her feet, and the chill edge of the wind freshening from the lake. But it didn't matter. She was alive to adventure, as exhilarated as when she and Quincy had first begun to talk about this trip. Just to be outdoors, homeless, hungry and happy—that was what Quincy planned to say, in the foreword of the book they would write, to explain why they had chosen to go West by trail. In this savored instant, the words expressed it exactly for her. She jerked off her hat and sailed it toward the saddlebags. "I'm homeless, hungry and happy! Let's pitch the tent."

"No, let's not," Quincy drawled. "We have very neatly and stupidly stacked all our gear on the precise spot where the tent should go. You scrub the potatoes and I'll tend to Vag and Hike. We can fix camp later, while the spuds are roasting."

When Ella came back from the lakeshore with the rinsed potatoes in her hands, Quincy was rigging a system for hobbling the horses. Having neither soft rope nor leather cuffs, he had fastened a bridle rein around each horse's middle, leaving the bit hanging underneath. Through the bit ring he passed the handwoven army lariat, doubled, with the loop end secured by one of the saddle coat-straps to the horse's left pastern, and the double ends tied to the chin strap of the halter.

"Very ingenious," said Ella. "Will it work?"

"Well, I've been studying the actions of a walking horse. The tension of those lariats is such that every time Hike or Vag takes a step, the movement of his hind leg will pull his head down and stop him. It *ought* to work."

Next in order of business was making a fire. Quincy whittled shavings from the drier sticks they had picked up under the trees, piled on small twigs, then larger ones, and finally got the blaze started, after many matches and much blowing. The damp wood gave off more smoke than heat, but Ella hopefully buried the potatoes under the coals.

Quincy began moving the pile of equipment from the tent site.

"Bunny, this ground is awfully wet to sleep on."

"What else can we do, unless we make a bed of that old prairie grass, there across the fence?"

He climbed over the barbed wire and brought a handful of the bleached limp stems. "It's wetter than the ground."

"But softer. And it will at least protect us and the blankets from the mud. I'll pull a few poncho-loads of it while you cook the steak."

She snatched up a poncho, giving him no time to object. As she gathered armfuls of the wet grass and tossed them onto the poncho, she kept looking back to see how the cooking was coming along. Quincy was not a swearing man, but she heard imprecatory mutterings, and saw him leapfrogging to this side of the fire and that, trying to keep to windward of the smoke without losing the meat from the pronged stick.

She was about to call out some encouragement but changed it to a shriek of warning. "Vag! Look at Vag!"

The old horse was down, balanced on his withers, alternately pawing the air and flailing the earth with three legs. Quincy left the steak and sprinted to the rescue. Before he got there Vag had managed to heave himself upright, furious and frightened. His right hind leg had tangled in the lariat loop and was caught up against his shoulder. But even with only three legs at his disposal he could still kick. It was several minutes before Quincy was able to ease in close enough to cut the rope.

Ella swung her last ponchoful of grass over the fence and came to help him. They tied both horses to a tree. By now Ella could make a quick job of the hitching knot Quincy had taught her, explaining, "The harder the horse pulls on the rope, the tighter the knot will draw. But you can give one tug on the loose end of this loop and the whole thing will come free, very important in a crisis."

A sudden odor tainted the wind. "Where did you leave the steak, Quincy?"

"I don't remember precisely. I just sort of let go when you yelled."

"Then it must be the steak I smell."

The meat was a charred lump among the embers. Ella sighed. "Anyhow we still have the potatoes, and we can make tea."

Quincy boiled the unpleasant-tasting lake water in the tippy saucepan. He put in a spoonful of tea leaves and set it on the ground to steep. As he straightened up, his heel caught the handle of the pan. Over went the tea. Ella, perched on one of the saddles, said nothing. Quincy said nothing. He refilled the pan and soon had another supply of tea. He raked the potatoes out of the fire, pulled his saddle companionably close to Ella, and invited her to feast with him.

"Do have some tea, Lady Scott."

"Thank you. But do you mind straining off the grounds first?"

"Not at all, m'lady." He held his fork at the lip of the saucepan and tilted it carefully . . .

He stared at the ground, which was soaking up the tea while the leaves remained sedately in the pan.

"Expletive. Ex, ex, expletive!"

"Expletive? Is that the word you were muttering when you were trying to cook the steak?"

"Yes. I was brought up not to swear when there's a woman around, so I had to invent something to air my feelings. But it doesn't work nearly as well, so pardon me if I say hell and damnation, would you like me to make some more tea?"

"Don't bother. Just pass me a potato. It's almost dark and I want to eat while I can still tell the white inside from the black outside."

The burnt crust was gritty, the cores were not cooked, and the mealy mouthfuls in between were hard to swallow without tea to wash them down.

When Ella had gagged on the last bite, she saw Quincy lying on the earth, feet toward the fire. "Whatever is the matter? Are you sick?"

"No, just measuring. It's going to be a matter of nice calculation where to put the tent. If we put it too close to the blaze, the blankets may catch fire. If we don't put it close enough, what's the use of having a fire, after all the trouble I went to, getting it started? Now, Bunny, you stand there and fan the sparks toward me with your hat, and I'll inch away until I get just beyond their reach. Then we'll have to allow for my toes sticking out another foot or two beyond the open end of the tent."

He was half-pranking, to make up for the disasters of steak and tea, to coax a smile so that he would know he was forgiven. She allowed him the ghost of a grin, the most she could do just then. Night was thickening under the clouds and there was a smell of more rain in the wind. She wanted to get under cover in a hurry.

They arranged the hay, and erected the tent over it. The rubberized ponchos went down first on the hay. Then the outer saddle blankets, still damp and reeking with horse sweat. Last, Ella spread the inner saddle blankets, only slightly less moist and fragrant.

Undressing was a civilized indulgence not to be considered. Ella kicked off her muddy shoes and crawled between the top two blankets, wondering why she hadn't thought before to use a loaf of bread for a pillow. It was softer than the canteen. She tried to shift her hip off a lump in the ground. The grass padded the smaller countours beneath her, but it was uncanny how the weight of her body brought into high relief every major protrusion.

Quincy squirmed in beside her and twenty minutes went by peacefully. Then rip, crash, stomp! Vag came blundering at the tent, hind end first. Hike, annoyed by the campfire, had bullied Vag over toward the tent in order to take the less smoky quadrant for himself. Quincy led Vag around to the head of the tent, tied him to a tree there, and wiggled back into bed.

"I think I fastened him far enough away so he won't step on us but it's hard to tell in the dark."

Peace this time lasted less than ten minutes. Vag, startled, perhaps, by the swoop of an owl or the skittering of a rabbit, plunged backward to the full length of his hitching rope and thumped his great hoof down on the closed end of the tent. Ella heard the crunch.

"Quincy, did he step on you?"

Quincy groaned. "Matter of interpretation. I guess the metal

*Ella cooked breakfast in the
"tippy" saucepans at Lake
Minnewaska, Minn.*

shoe missed my skull, but the fetlock didn't. There's no other
tree back there to tie him to, so I'll just have to set the saddles
where they'll protect our heads."

Once more he went hopping out, to move the saddles and
shorten the tie rope. On his way back to bed he kicked the fire
out. "The smoke's making Hike restless."

Just as Quincy wormed his way once more into the blankets,
the first drops of rain splattered on the tent. Ella turned over,
found a hollow for her hip and drifted toward the fuzzy edge of
oblivion. If the tent leaked, it leaked. Maybe those three words
of Quincy's should be "homeless, hungry and sopping."

The rain was only a passing shower. In the morning they
awoke to a twig pattern of sun and shadow on the tent. Killdeer

were calling from the shore, *dee-ee-killdee, killdee*. A red squirrel alternately scolded and scampered in the maple branches.

Ella emerged, rosy with sleep, and went down to the lake to wash her face and hands in the chill water. How good a nice steamy tub bath would feel right now! Would she ever get another one before Seattle?

She cooked breakfast without burning or scorching anything, and smiled cheerfully for Quincy when he snapped a picture of her kneeling at the fire.

Even Hike was in a tractable mood this morning. He and Vag stood patiently while the blankets were folded and smoothed over their backs, and the McClellan saddles boosted up and cinched. Two weeks of practice made packing a very different operation from the confusion in the livery barn at South St. Paul. Mess kits, sketching case, saddlebags, the rolled ponchos and tent halves—each had a spot where it was tied or buckled to the saddle. Some of the gear had acquired "Scott" names.

"Polly Betsy Patterson," called Quincy, and Ella handed him the milk canteen, named for a cow once owned by his mother.

"Frances Willard next." Up came the water canteen, honoring that champion of temperance.

There was a place for the axe, christened "George Washington," and the hunting knife, "Becky Sharp." Quincy put "The Coroner" into the carbine gunboot, slung on the off-side of his saddle. "Bloody Mary" hung in a holster at his hip, and Ella fastened the smaller revolver, "Willie," over her riding skirt.

After one last glance around to make sure that all the gear was aboard and the fire out, Quincy and Ella rode away through the sunny woods, singing "Under the Anheuser Busch" at the tops of their lungs.

It took seven more days to reach the western edge of Minnesota. Most of the roads followed section lines, which meant that to head generally on the northwest diagonal, they had to ride in a time-consuming series of right-angle traverses, alternating due west and due north. The seven days brought more snow, rain

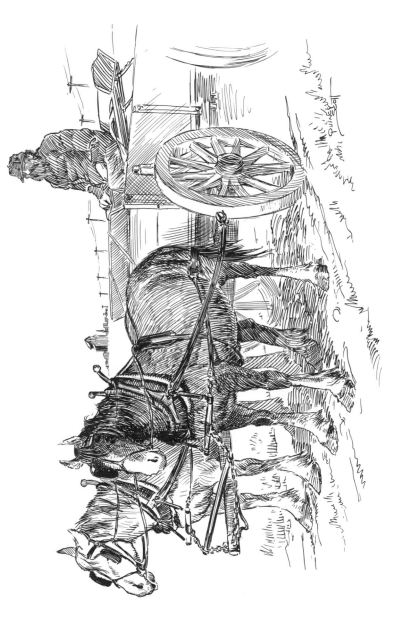

Riding horses were scarce in Minnesota, but there was no shortage of well-fed work teams.

and wind, broken only by a few bright warm hours. They slept in a dugout, in a granary, a barn. On four of the colder nights they pitched the tent. The horses ran away again and again. Quincy got sick on alkali water. Hike burned his leg badly on the picket rope. Ella risked a bath, making do with a pint of water heated in a saucepan. One morning they obliged a teacher who asked them to stop at her one-room schoolhouse. "I'd like the children to write a composition about you. You would be such curiosities."

Quincy looked at horses offered in trade at Barrett and Barnesville, and shook his head each time.

"No one here rides and there are no saddle horses," Ella wrote on a postcard to Mother Scott. "Nothing exciting happens, the monotony being broken only by not knowing till 6 o'clock where we're going to spend the night. Sometimes have to go for miles to find enough wood for a small fire."

Kensington, Fergus Falls, Rothsay—the prairie spread ahead of them flatter and more relentless at each mark of the journey. If the rune stone dug up on Olof Ohman's farm near Kensington has been read aright, Viking seamen breasted this grassy tide six centuries earlier, as alien in the prairie sea as these two travelers. Ella had encountered the plains before, but only from a train window, which was nothing like moving across them on horseback and afoot. Her girlhood had been spent in the Puget Sound country, dominated by the Olympics and Cascades, peaks snow-crowned and valleys deep in rain forest. Quincy had grown up among the Appalachians, where the earth leaped up to meet the sky close at hand in a ripple of hills and creases. If a village wasn't hidden in a notch, it was veiled by trees. The openness of the prairie continued to astound him. "Bunny, I can't get over this. We see a town for *miles* before we reach it!"

Yet, barely perceptible, the prairie had its ups and downs. Glenwood had been on the crest of a ground swell at fourteen hundred feet. From there the land had been tilting gradually westward, dipping across the bed of the prehistoric lake that stretched to thirty miles beyond Fargo. Barnesville, on the level of the eastern beach, was four hundred feet lower than Glen-wood.

The tilt bottomed out at the Red River, another hundred feet down. In a cottonwood grove, in the rain, on the muddy bank of that strange north-flowing stream, Quincy and Ella ended the third and final week of Minnesota.

It was Friday, May 24. The anniversary of their engagement.

Ella hadn't needed the extra fervency of Quincy's goodmorning kiss to remind her, and all during this damp dreary day she had been reliving in snatches of memory that magical spring evening in Central Park.

Now, as she squished around in the mud, dodging smoke, trying to boil potatoes over a grudging fire, with a gallery of farm folk who had come down the riverbank to "see what them Mexicans was up to," she caught the amusement and affection in Quincy's blue eyes, and knew that he was finding the contrast between recollection and reality as ironic as she did.

"Might as well give our onlookers their money's worth," he whispered, as she bent over the fire to dish out the potatoes. "Let's eat with our hands."

"Oh, honey! That may have worked all right this noon when those two women drove over from their farm to gape at us. Then we had bacon and cold cornbread. But these potatoes are *hot*. I won't burn my fingers just to scandalize our audience."

"All right," he chuckled. "I'd better indicate the show's over."

Quincy faced around to the half-dozen men and two small boys standing ten feet away. "*Amigos,* you have been indeed most gracious to sally forth in this inclement weather to make us welcome to your *haciendas,* but now as you see, we are about to partake of *les pommes de terre,* to—how is it you say?—eata da supper. So we must regretfully bid you all *adieu.* I hope you sleep well. *Bon soir, amigos.*"

He made a polite but unmistakable gesture toward the oozy path. After some murmuring among themselves, the farmers and the boys trudged away under the dripping trees toward their own suppers.

Ella wrapped her poncho around her shoulders, and sat down on her saddle with a plate of steaming potatoes in her lap. She poured tea into both cups and lifted one toward Quincy. "Well, my French-speaking Mexican with the New York Italian accent, here's mud in your eye. And aren't you ashamed of yourself?"

"Not at all. You wouldn't want them to go back and say, 'Yah, those two, they're yoost a couple of nice American kids.' Anyway, it's not my fault I wasn't old enough to enlist in '98, storm up San Juan Hill with Teddy and come back with a fine command of the Spanish tongue."

"I'm glad you weren't. You might *not* have come back, and then—"

"Then you wouldn't be squatting here on a hard saddle, feet wet, rain dribbling down your neck, nothing for dinner but boiled spuds and tea, and your only companions a couple of ornery hosses and a dim-witted husband who has no more sense than to go dragging you from one end of the country to the other. Bunny, what *were* you thinking of when you said you'd marry me?"

She set her plate in the mud beside the campfire and clasped her hands under the glistening poncho. She knew well enough what she had been thinking. She was thinking of May Herrick and the insistent advice she had offered when Ella arrived in New York with sixty dollars in her purse, and a determination to break into magazine illustrating. May Herrick was one of the two people she knew in the city, girls she had met during art student days in Chicago. May was now at the Art Students' League, the other girl at Chase Art School. Each had tried to entice Ella to her class, but it was May who prevailed.

"Ella, you're going with me to the League. No if's or but's about it. There's a student there who is just the right man for you. His name is Quincy Scott. Some of his cartoons are already appearing in the New York dailies. All the girls are after him, but you're the one he'd hit it off with best."

Before she could pay tuition at either school, Ella had to find a job. On her second day in New York she started at the Battery and walked north, showing samples of her work to illustrating and engraving establishments along the way. She had been doing professional assignments in Chicago and Louisville, and her portfolio was full of drawings. Stone-Van Dresser Company, at 23rd Street, offered her $17.50 a week. That was better than any salary she had ever received.

She took her time about choosing between Chase School and the Art Students' League. First there was the business of renting a tiny apartment in the mid-Fifties, getting settled, and devoting some spare hours to exploring New York.

It wasn't until she had been at her new job for a week that she put on her shepherd's plaid suit with the black velvet collar, settled her black felt sailor hat on her head, and started out to enroll in the evening sketch class at the Art Students' League. Crossing Broadway, she noted the nice-looking man, young and auburn-haired, who kept his blue eyes on her as he passed.

When she entered the sketch class fifteen minutes later, holding out her registration card, she discovered that the monitor was not only the "right man" of May's description, but also the man of the admiring blue eyes. My goodness, Mr. Scott was even handsomer at close quarters than passing by in the crowd! And his smile was unsettling, in a delightful way. Ella managed to keep her voice casual, but she could do nothing about the rush of color to her cheeks.

Neither could she do much about Mr. Scott's decision to do something about her. Within a few days his courtesy to a newcomer developed into a whimsically proprietary air. At the League's annual Fakers Ball, he assumed possession of her, preempting all the waltzes on her card and leading her off during intermission to a quiet corner to tell her how much her dress, splashed with white and pink roses, became her.

"But I'm surprised that a pretty girl can draw as professionally as you do, and toss out classical references besides."

That had puzzled her for a moment. Then she remembered. "The evening when you were doing quick sketches and everyone was standing around suggesting subjects?"

"Yes, and you said, 'Draw the Elysian Fields.' It would never occur to the other girls I know to mention the Elysian Fields—

even if they'd heard of them. I decided there and then to find
out more about you."

After that evening it seemed to be taken for granted that he
would walk her home from sketch class. If she protested that she
had promised one of the other young men to stop for an ice
cream, Quincy blithely joined the party.

He rowed her across the Hudson for a Sunday afternoon climb
up the Palisades, and on another weekend in May they took the
streetcar north of the city and did about fifteen miles on foot
along the country roads. It didn't dismay her to realize that he
was testing her against the out-of-doors. In her college years in
Seattle she had walked several miles daily through the forest that
lay between the University of Washington campus and her home
on Ravenna hill. At sixteen, on her way to a stint of school-
teaching in the northern Cascades, she had traveled all day up-
river in a canoe paddled by a strange Indian, and bicycled along
a trail overlooking a dozen bears eating salmonberries in the
meadow below. Could either the Jersey Palisades or West-
chester daunt her? The weight of a cumbersome skirt and the
pinch of city shoes made it hard for her to match Quincy's long-
legged pace, but she saw no reason to admit it if she kept up
with him and still had breath enough for some share in the talk
that went forward as briskly as the walk.

Quincy had not attended college. A newspaper advertising job
at seventeen had opened the way so quickly into cartooning that
he saw no need to go on with formal education. Through private
studies with his scholar father he had already gained what
amounted to a liberal arts education. Ella discovered that he was
well-read in history and philosophy and deeply interested in the
practical workings of politics. His ease with words more than
matched her own wide vocabulary, and he could use this skill
either in the flights of inflated rhetoric then fashionable as humor,
or in painstakingly precise statements of fact.

What a delight to be with this man whose mind ranged eagerly
to any subject that came along, who liked to speak of his ideas
and experiences, yet could listen appreciatively when she spoke
of hers! Perhaps that's what had been missing two years ago in

her brief engagement to Ned—the lively give and take of opinions, memories, dreams, speculations. Why, she and Quincy could talk till they were ninety and never come to the end of things they wanted to say to one another.

The days of that spring had piled up, charged with tantalizing whiffs of the season that blew haphazardly through the city canyons. Ella knew she was in love, a kind of love involving both her body and her mind, and going far beyond the placid pleasant feelings that she had taken for love before. The term at the Art Students' League was closing with the end of May—would Quincy find some pretext for seeing her during the summer?

When the sketch class was dismissed on Thursday, May 24, Quincy was in a hurry to leave. He cut short the usual bantering good-nights, and took her arm as they started along the street. "It's such a mild evening, would you mind if we walked through Central Park?"

The sheep pasture lay in tranquillity, away from the hot pavements, the clatter of carriages, the jangle of trolley bells, the sputtering of an occasional automobile. From the grass rose a fresh moist scent. The air touched softly her bare arms and throat. Quincy seemed distraught, alternating bursts of random comment with sudden silence. At the far side of the meadow he drew her down beside him on a bench and took her hand.

"Ella, I haven't anything worldly to offer, no regular income or position, no savings in the bank, or prospects of any family inheritance, but will you marry me? I offer just myself—and my love."

She put her other hand over his. "That's enough for me."

He kissed her. Tenderly, awkwardly, earnestly. It was their first kiss.

Ella had guessed that some turning-point in their relationship was approaching. She had considered what answer she should give. But none of those she had rehearsed fitted exactly here, and she hadn't even tried. Her answer had come spontaneously and sincerely. Quincy and his love were enough for her.

She gave him a fond glance now across the smoky campfire, and found him looking at her, a questing intentness in his eyes.

She had kept him waiting much longer for an answer tonight than he had waited a year ago. She unclasped her hands, stood up and walked around the fire to him. He pulled her into his lap.

"I asked you, what were you thinking of when you said you'd marry me?"

"I was thinking how much I owed to May Herrick's advice."

"Still feel that way?"

She relaxed contentedly into the curve of his arm. "Um-hmm."

"Rain, rubber-necking farmers, and all?"

"And all."

IV Fargo was the first city of any importance they had reached. Mail should be awaiting them there, and they'd have a chance to do some necessary errands. Quincy urged Vag to a quicker pace along the road that led into town from the Red River bridge. He was planning a surprise for Ella, one hour of creature comfort to lighten this dismal day. For it was still raining, the same cold drifting drizzle. The weathered buildings that huddled close to the west bank, relics of Fargo's frontier days, showed dark and glistening wherever the rain blew against their unpainted wood. Vag and Hike were making better time in the mud than the old Red River carts that had creaked over this trail, laden with furs or provisions or buffalo bones, but even so it was tedious going, and Quincy was impatient.

In the newer part of the city he and Ella turned north from Front Street into Broadway, a main thoroughfare paved with cedar blocks and divided by trolley tracks up the center. Business buildings of brick and stone, two to five stories high, lined both sides of the street. It was Saturday. In spite of the rain, the side-walks bustled with shoppers. "Hey, kiddo, some city!" Quincy called out to Ella.

He was conscious of the holes in his socks, the sodden leather of his shoes, the muck splashed shoulder high over Hike and Vag. He had been trying, ever since leaving St. Paul, to keep the horses decently groomed, rubbing them down at the end of each day's ride, cleaning manes and tails, checking feet for stones and loose shoes. From his cavalryman father he had absorbed enough wisdom to know that the outcome of this trip depended as much on the care he took of the horses as it did on his care of Bunny

In this portrait Ella caught the humor and strength of the Dakota pioneer woman.

and himself. He thought he had done a pretty good job so far, though it would be hard this morning to say which *looked* more bedraggled, horses or riders.

"Where first?" asked Ella, urging Hike alongside.

"Livery stable. We can leave the horses there for shoeing while we take in the town. And by the way, Bunny, there's a gob of Red River mud bedecking your nose."

She brushed her hand across her face in annoyance. "In respect to gobs, sir, you're even more generously adorned than I am."

They put the horses in a livery barn a few blocks off Broadway and walked on to the postoffice. Quincy didn't realize until he went up to the window how eager he had been to hear from home. The clerk, an inordinately thin man with sprouts of sandy hair shooting from his head in all directions, thumbed slowly through the General Delivery mail. He doled out two envelopes on the first time through, and three more on the second shuffle.

"That's all?" Quincy scooped up the precious pile.

"All?" The clerk eyed him disapprovingly. "Aren't you satisfied to get more letters than anybody else is liable to get all week?"

"I'm delighted. Just wanted to make sure, because we probably won't be back this way for several years."

Quincy drew Ella over to a corner of the postoffice lobby. "Here's one from your mother, and one from your brother. Mine are from my mother and dad, and Edith. We can't take time now to read them. Just skim through to see if there's anything we have to respond to while we're in Fargo."

He was opening the letter from his father when Ella gave a little gasp. "Oh, honey, look! My mother's sent a bank draft for fifty dollars!"

Quincy whistled softly. "Golly, she's too generous. Should we accept it?"

"Of course," said Ella practically. "It ought to get us pretty well across Montana."

"Maybe, unless we have to give too much to boot when we find a trade for Vag."

Ella put the bank draft to her lips and kissed it. "Thank you, Mother dear!"

Quincy hesitated. Certainly he would pay back the fifty dollars at the end of the summer, but it hadn't been part of his plans to depend on relatives even for a loan, and he felt uncomfortable as Ella pushed the draft into his hand, saying, "Now we don't need to wire today for money from New York, and that will leave more in our account there for emergencies."

She was right. Anxiety over money was one of the burdens that weighed him down this morning, heavy as the rain-soaked Dakota sod. Looked at from New York, a thousand bucks had covered the miles to Seattle without much stretching. But at the rate the dollars had been dribbling away during the first month, the extra fifty might be crucial. He tucked the draft into his shirtpocket. "Wait here a minute."

Quincy stepped back to the sprout-haired clerk. "Can you recommend a restaurant where a gentleman can escort a lady and be sure of a good meal in pleasant surroundings?"

The clerk eyed him even more disapprovingly than before, taking in the dripping poncho, the mud-caked shoes. "You could try the hotel on the corner, though you'd feel more at home at one of the family restaurants back on Broadway."

"Sound advice," conceded Quincy.

When he returned to Ella, she looked worried. "Were you serious just then, about eating lunch at a nice restaurant?"

"Yes. That's my little surprise for you. Remember, a year ago, the day after we got engaged, I took you to dinner at the Cafe Boulevard?"

"Of course. That was a very special evening, almost as special as the evening before. But—" she held her hands out at each side, palms forward, inviting him to judge for himself. "How can I walk into a dining room in Fargo looking like this?"

"Simple. While I go to the bank and the barber and try to locate a place to buy some more film, you toddle into a hair-dresser's. Along with whatever needs doing to your hair, you can wash up, and brush off your skirt. I'll meet you in forty-five minutes."

She was late reaching the restaurant they had decided on, and as she came toward him across the street, he was glad she was, for it gave him a chance to admire all over again the way she carried herself, the blend of confidence and unselfconsciousness that had caught his attention when he saw her as a stranger in New York, crossing that other Broadway.

The rain had tapered off momentarily. She was walking bareheaded, her folded poncho over one arm, her hat swinging from her hand. She lifted her face toward the shaft of pale sunlight that broke through the overcast. It shone on the glossy brown of her hair and brought out the warmth of her round face above the blue army shirt. Quincy was thankful he had squandered four bits on his own improvement, a shave and a haircut. He took off his hat and offered Ella his arm as gallantly as though she were stepping in silken skirts from a millionaire's carriage.

"My charming wife," he murmured, and pushed open the door of the restaurant.

They ate enormously. Roast beef and gravy, stewed corn, pickled beets, hot biscuits and honey, followed by thick squares of dried apple pudding topped with heavy cream. They let the waiter fill and refill their coffee cups, drawing out this luxury of warmth and good food until Quincy sighed, "Well, Bunny, I guess we'd better leave before they bring around a second bill. You ready?"

It was raining again and she prepared to drop her poncho over the army shirt. "This has been a lovely time. I feel so replete. Thank you."

The horses were shod and waiting when Quincy and Ella walked into the livery stable half an hour later, carrying the small supply of groceries they had bought after they left the restaurant. They saddled up, mantled themselves in their ponchos, and moved out into the steadily-falling rain. As they crossed one of the streets west of Broadway, Quincy saw to the northward the clock in the tower of the Agricultural College. The hands pointed to one-thirty. Involuntarily Quincy's heels prodded Vag to a splashing trot. The sight of the clock renewed his impatience and the anxieties he had repressed during that leisurely noon hour. Time! Like money, it was shrinking faster than he had anticipated.

This morning, clumping into Fargo, he had done some arithmetic and the result dismayed him. During the first two weeks, from St. Paul to Glenwood, he and Ella had covered 160 miles in ten and a half days' riding. From Glenwood to Fargo, 110 miles in seven days' riding. That averaged about fifteen and a half miles a day. Figuring 2000 miles all told, including detours and misdirections, that rate mean 130 days of actual travel. Adding 14 days of rest would bring them to Seattle September 25, a month behind schedule! Their money would run out—their time, too. Crossing the Cascades that late in the season meant the risk of snow and freezing nights in a wilderness. They *had* to make better mileage. Could Vag stand it until he could be traded off for a sturdier horse?

Today they must try to keep going as long as daylight prevailed. If only the blasted weather would give them a break!

It didn't. By four o'clock Quincy and Ella were soaked to the skin, and when he saw a farmhouse at the end of a short lane on the other side of the Northern Pacific tracks, they crossed over and were thankful to be invited in by its widow owner, Mrs. Mitchell, and her solemn button-nosed little boy.

"Put the horses in the barn, then come and dry yourselves off. I got a fire going in the kitchen stove." Mrs. Mitchell, whose square face matched her squarely-built frame, seemed actually pleased to have company.

They brought their letters to the kitchen with them. Wet shoes propped on the stove rail and wet shirts steaming on their backs, they plunged into the news from home. The envelope from Ella's brother Riley contained a clipping about the trip that made Quincy laugh till his sides ached. It was taken from the Seattle *Post-Intelligencer.* The text was reasonably factual, but the staff artist assigned to do an illustrative sketch had ignored everything in the story about camp outfits, army saddles and weapons, and had drawn a picture of a gentleman and lady in Eastern riding togs. The lady perched on a sidesaddle, attired in a striped blouse with leg o' mutton sleeves, a long flowing skirt, and a

*Ella perched on a bridge
west of Fargo to display the
gobs of Red River Valley
mud festooning her feet.*

scarf-draped hat on top of her high-fashion coiffure. The gentleman was shown in a dark dress coat, stock, and what was meant
to be a derby hat.

Quincy held out the clipping to Mrs. Mitchell. "Would you say
we bear any resemblance to that elegant pair?"

She wiped her hands on her apron and went to the kitchen's
one small window to study the clipping.

"Good land, no! Is that the way you looked when you started
out?"

Quincy began laughing all over again. "We started out in the
same clothes we've got on now—that's what's wrong with them,
and they're going to get more so."

"My brother, Riley Allen, is a reporter for the *Post Intelli-*

gencer," put in Ella, "but I'm sure he never had a chance to pass judgment on that sketch before it went to press. He'd know better."

"Anybody ought to know better," snorted Quincy. "But we'll save the clipping anyhow, just for laughs."

The other letters produced no surprises or alarms—just the tidbits of family doings he and Ella were so eager to hear. Quincy's older sisters, Edith and Cornelia, both married to doctors in Pennsylvania, were busy with their lives as homemakers. Quincy's father wrote of his church history lectures and translation work at the Bible Teachers Training School. Mother Scott's letter was filled with accounts of dinner parties and visits from friends, interlarded with admonitions to be very careful way out there in the Wild West.

News from Seattle was of much the same sort, in three short paragraphs from Riley, and six long pages from Mother Allen. Hers ended with the reminder that Ella's sister Jessie would have to leave Seattle in time for the beginning of her teaching job in Los Angeles. "So we are counting on your reaching the west coast by mid-August if at all possible."

When Quincy and Ella exchanged letters and he came to that final sentence, he felt once again the pressing sense of haste. If he were traveling alone . . . But hold on, he would only be traveling alone if he had not married Bunny, and if he hadn't married her, he would have no special reason to be hurrying toward Seattle. He looked fondly at her as she bent over the letter in her hands. He was not traveling alone, thank the Lord. And he wasn't going to spoil the rest of the trip by letting a demon deadline nag him. They would take each day as it came, do their reasonable best, and abide by the outcome. Only, they would have to upgrade their idea of what was their "reasonable best."

Mrs. Mitchell served a supper of the ever-present bacon and fried eggs, accompanied by a johnny-cake that Quincy pronounced glorious. The hired man, fat and whiskery, came in to join them. After the dishes were cleared away, Quincy entertained little Button-nose doing tricks with a knotted handkerchief.

But the small boy was interested in something else, too. "Mister, did you see any otty-mobiles in Fargo?"

"No," said Quincy. "I think there must be some there, but we haven't seen a gas buggy since we left St. Paul. However, I drove one through the middle of New York City a couple of years ago."

The boy's eyes rounded. "Did you, honest?" He leaned on Quincy's knee, staring up to see if this stranger was telling the truth.

Quincy fingered an "X" over his shirtpocket. "Cross my heart."

"Did you scare a lot of horses?"

"You bet I did. Kind of scared myself too!"

"Was it fun?" asked the hired man from his tilted chair on the other side of the stove.

"Almost as much fun as riding a good horse."

"Aw, horses." There was such disbelief and disgust in the two words that Quincy smiled. But before he could argue, Mrs. Mitchell said, "There've been automobiles in Fargo off and on, though p'r'aps there wasn't any on the street today. They had an auto race right in town for the Fourth of July seven years ago, and the boy saw it, because I carried him in my arms."

"What kind of autos in the race?" said Quincy with quick interest.

Mrs. Mitchell turned questioningly to the hired man.

"One-cylinder Oldsmobiles," he said. "Two of them. And a Cadillac from Minneapolis showed up for the contest. It had two cylinders and shot out ahead at first. Then danged if the driver didn't get lost, not knowin' Fargo streets, so one of them Oldsmobiles come out winner." He shook his head admiringly. "You talk about horses, mister, but for excitement, they's nothin' alongside them cars a-roarin' and bangin' along. Best Fourth of July we ever had!"

Button-nose began to cry. "I *saw* them otty-mobiles, but I can't remember because I was too little."

Mrs. Mitchell rose to alight a second kerosene lamp. "Yes, he was just a baby. P'r'aps I never should have told him. It makes him mad not to remember."

Quincy lifted the boy to his lap. "There's no need to cry, sonny. I'll bet that before you're in long pants, you'll see an automobile with *four* cylinders coming poppity-pop right down the road past your house."

Button-nose went off to bed comforted while Quincy took the proffered lamp and lighted Ella up the stairs to the room above the kitchen. She turned back the covers on the bed.

"Quincy, see here. Blankets and quilt. The first place we've stayed that didn't have a feather bed!"

"It's a sign," said Quincy jubilantly. "A sign we're getting West."

Eighteen miles short of Jamestown, North Dakota, Quincy sat in a little hollow between two snow fences paralleling the railroad, writing to his father and mother. It was the 29th of May, the sun was hot on his back, the wind cool on his face, and his appetite temporarily quieted after a pleasant lunch of milk, applesauce, toast and gingersnaps.

". . . So far we find the Wild and Wooly West about as wild as a fricaseed chicken and as wooly as a Mexican hairless dog. The farmers are for the most part Norwegian, Swedish or German.

". . . The horses are doing very well. Had them weighed today. Hike, Bunny's horse, weighs 845 lbs. He is very chocky and chunky in his body, and has shoulders that couldn't be beat. His feet are perfect, and his legs trim and strong. He is a great hand to pick grass at every infinitesimal ghost of an opportunity, and to lie right down on his side like a dog and rest. He is phlegmatic in temper, and saves himself. He hogs all the room when tied by the other horse. He will last out. Vag . . . weighs 920. He is too long and light, and I am going to trade him for a chunk. He has the frame for 11 or 12 hundred, if you could get that much oats into him. Through this flat country he has been going fine, outtraveling Hike, but he is too feety for the mountains. Nobody out here knows anything about weights in horses—

*Quincy gave Vag and Hike a "grazing break" in the sweet green
growth of North Dakota grass.*

they guess, but never seem to weigh them. They use very light
horses for everything except farm work, and so far we have
found ourselves to be the only equestrians, and curiosities on that
account.

"This morning we stopped (at Eckelson) to buy grub, and a
couple of gazeeks with store clothes and ½-inch wide watch
chains and a kodak wanted to take our picture. 'This is new to
me,' said one of them, a tall fellow with a black diagonal cut-
away and tobacco teeth. 'I am from way back East in Ottawa,
and I've never seen a real cowboy outfit before.' So we let them
snap us, they being particular to have us pose so that the guns
would show, and we rode away roaring, they knew not what at.

". . . We cover about 20 *railroad* miles a day . . . May 27th
we broke a crust of ice to get water in the morning. We have
not taken cold, although for a whole cold week my feet were
not dry for 5 minutes, except when in bed in a farmhouse . . .
The weather is now much better—we take off our flannels during
the day, and put them on at night. We sleep outdoors in our
little tent, or in deserted sheds . . . Though we have had some
fine weather, we have not had one single 24 hours of continued
climatic excellence.

". . . We have not taken very many pictures. We have only drawn a couple. Art doesn't flourish in a cold rainy climate . . . Your advice about eating moderately is good. As we divide all our work, I let Bunny do that. We find the alkali water question not difficult, as the water gets alkaline about in proportion as we get west. A half hour's discomfort is all we have found evil in it, as yet."

He ended the letter "With all the love in the world for the dearest home-folks in the world, Your tough-and-tan Quincella."

In truth, he was more sunburned and peeling than tan, and he had been thoroughly miserable after his first encounter with alkali water, but otherwise this was a reasonably accurate report. He would mail it in Spiritwood, next station on the line.

Ella was busy repairing rips in her army shirt, so Quincy spent another twenty minutes with his pencil, bringing the journal up to date. Behind him, Hike and Vag cropped the bluegrass along the nearer snow fence. He kept his ear attuned for any sound that would indicate trouble. He still hadn't figured out a fool-proof way to keep them close by without haltering them. On Sunday, the first day out from Mrs. Miller's, he had tried hobbling the horses together. They didn't like it, and had bedeviled each other with nips and jerks until he loosed the hobbles and tied them separately, as now, to a fixed object with the ropes left long enough so that they could forage. The rustle of the grass stems as lips and teeth twitched them loose, the rhythmic "chonking" of jaws that crushed each mouthful, the stamping hoofs and swishing tails dislodging pestiferous flies—all these let Quincy know without turning his head that everything was well, so far.

A dozen yards away, erect and poised for immediate escape into its burrow, a small creature with yellowish fur watched him, its liquid-bright eyes fixed on him alertly. Quincy raised his pencil in salute. "Hello, flickertail."

The ground squirrel dived and came out at another opening a yard farther away to resume his lookout duty.

These leisurely noonings were often the best part of the twenty-four hours for Quincy and Ella. If there was any warmth in the day, they got it then. They could stop at will. If the place provided grazing, so much the better, but there was not the necessity of water and feed that made the choice of a night campsite so critical. In the late afternoons, when they were hungry and footsore (for they continued walking about ten miles for every fifteen they rode), the search for an adequate stopping-place sometimes dragged on for several hours. Ella was not finicky, but he had more than once felt her disappointment when he had to pass up an inviting retreat in favor of one near water and grass. If the hunt went on into the dusk, she was ready to stop *any* place, just to stop. Her weariness added to his own, yet he had to say, "Not here" and "Not here," until at least they found water.

Yesterday evening, west of Sanborn, they had given up and decided to bed down beside one lonely post sticking out of the prairie sod. But a stormcloud curtaining the sunset prompted them to mount again and ride into the darkening evening. They found a deserted barn, large enough to shelter the horses at one end and themselves at the other. The rain had come just as Ella finished cooking supper.

Quincy recorded that fact under the dateline of May 28, and looked around at Ella.

"Ready to move on?"

"In a few minutes. I have another rip to mend."

"Then I guess I'll have a little session with Hike, bareback. Wonder if he's ever been ridden that way before."

Obviously, he hadn't. Or, if he had, his memories of the experience weren't happy ones. He began by jumping out from under when Quincy tried to vault to his back. Once Quincy had scrambled aboard, Hike exploded into the same kind of kines-thetics that had sent Ella sprawling into the mud in South St. Paul. But this time he carried a veteran rider prepared for fire-works. Quincy had one hand twisted in his mane. The other gripped the lariat snubbed around Hike's nose. Quincy hooked his toes under Hike's elbows and rode it out.

The bronco stood first on his hind legs, and then on his front legs. He bucked, whirled, bucked, slamming to the earth stiff-legged. "Lord, he's driving my spine right up through my skull!"

As suddenly as the explosion started it was over. Hike dropped his head and went back to grazing. Quincy slid off, temples pounding and knees gelatin-soft. But he was alive and triumphant.

Ella was putting her sewing kit into the saddlebag. "Well, I see Hike's learned who's boss."

Quincy flopped down on the ground. "Let's hope he remembers. That's one lesson I'd rather not have to give twice. Next thing I've got to teach these boys is not to be gun-shy."

"But not right now, Quincy. We really ought to be going."

"I know. However, we're reaching game country, and I can't hunt for meat if Hike and Vag spook off at every shot. Maybe we can find a camping spot early enough this afternoon so I'll have time to work with them awhile."

"Oh, we won't."

"Won't what?"

"Won't find a camping spot early. You'll look and look and look and it'll be dark, and we'll be as dead tired as we were last night."

Ella had her back to him as she began saddling Hike, but there was a challenging note in her voice that made Quincy answer recklessly. "Honey, I promise you we'll stop at the first adequate place we find after four-thirty."

She didn't answer except to say, over her shoulder, "Let's get going." She was in the saddle and moving before he finished tightening the girth on Vag.

Quincy was vulnerable to any hint of disapproval and could rarely rest content until he found out what was wrong and then explained, debated, cajoled or apologized to restore a comfortable relationship. But when he caught up with Ella she spoke of something else, and so matter-of-factly, that he decided he had imagined the disapproval.

"What did the feed store man in Sanborn tell you, that we'd have to cross the Missouri in a railroad car?"

"Yes. He heard that the ferry at Bismarck broke down because

With Quincy in the saddle, Vag struck one of his aristocratic poses.
If only his endurance had equalled his style!

of all the high water. Temporarily the N.P. is running a transfer car back and forth on the bridge till the ferry can be repaired."

"Will that be safer than getting the horses over on a ferry?"

Quincy shrugged. "It all depends. Main thing is, it'll put us on the other side."

The other side of the Missouri! How far away that had seemed last week, dogging along with miles of Minnesota still between them and Fargo. But now Fargo was behind. At Valley City yesterday they had crossed the Sheyenne. Tomorrow it would be the James River. So they could at last let themselves think, even talk, about the next beyond that, the Big Muddy. With luck they would reach Bismarck in another four days, not counting Sunday for rest. They were rolling up better than twenty miles a day, easy to compute because the road roughly followed the railway and at each town they could check how far they had come. It was well they didn't have to rely on the people encountered in between stations—local estimates of distances were wildly differing.

This was still the farmer's prairie. After the gentle tilt into the Red River valley and up its western rise, they were back at the same elevation as they had been in west central Minnesota, fourteen hundred feet. All around them stretched the level monotony of the drift plain, broken here and there by the isolated thrust of a poplar windbreak sheltering a house and barn. Gray-green winter wheat was well up in the fields that flowed away on either side of the railroad. Other acres beyond would be blue with blossoming flax in early July. Only about half of the early pioneers had stayed with the land, but the hardy farmer who had survived the homestead years now possessed something besides land to show with pride: harvesting machinery shipped all the way from Chicago, and a new frame house, severe but ample, built a little distance apart from his original sod house or pine shanty. Rewards for sticking it out through blizzards, drought, grasshoppers, and prairie fires. Good times or bad, the farmer of the eastern Dakotas was a partner of the soil and the prairie belonged to him. Beside each station on the railway rose the temple of his faith, the grain elevator.

Yet as Quincy jolted along to the rise and fall of Vag's rough gait, he was aware of alterations in the "feel" of the country. If this was not the High Plains, neither was it a replica of Minnesota. In the older state, most of the farms had been conspicuously neat—no heaps of weeds, no cattle running loose. North Dakota, one row of states farther from the East coast and a generation nearer the frontier, would get around to those niceties in due time. Meanwhile the imprint of the Wild West was fresh and vivid here. Ruts of the early wagon trains still scored the banks of the Sheyenne River. A scant twenty-four years had passed since the last big buffalo hunt, seventeen since the final Sioux uprising.

Quincy had been eight when that fighting burst out. His father had read the story to him from the newspaper, trying to help him understand the Army's maneuvers against the tribal "ghost dancers." A little chill of awe cooled the sweat on the back of Quincy's neck as it was borne in on him once again that he was here, *actually here,* riding the same earth, scanning the same horizon, as the soldier and Indian heroes of his boyhood.

Another pleasant shiver had rippled up his spine when he asked the man in Sanborn about wild game.

"Well, not much of the eatin' kind this side of the Missouri, except jackrabbits and ducks. But it wouldn't hurt to have your gun handy. Some folks say a wolf's been seen over beyond Windsor."

That was fine with Quincy. So far there had been occasional hardship and plenty of discomfort on this horseback honeymoon, but scarcely a whiff of danger. Was it the threat of boredom that had prompted him, back there, to leap on Hike without the saddle, just to see what would happen?

He kept his promise about a campsite. He stopped at the first adequate place they came to after four-thirty, having passed up a shed standing alone in a barren farmyard ("You can see, Bunny, there's no water or forage here") and a shallow draw that offered privacy and grass but nothing else. It was well beyond five o'clock when they reached a thicket of willows and chokecherries bordering on a small slough. Quincy said cheerfully, "This will do. We probably can't drink the water, but it'll be all right for the horses, and there's good grazing on both sides of it. Okay?"

Contrary to her usual lively interest, Ella took no part in the decision. She slid off, tied Hike to one of the stouter willows, and began loosening the girth.

Making camp was a familiar routine by now. When the horses had been unsaddled, Quincy watered them and left them to graze, picketed. Next he started a fire with the wood Ella had been gathering. There was plenty here—no need tonight to "sliver" the snow fences. He made the bed on the ground and set the pup tent over it. Ella went about cooking supper.

It was potatoes again this evening. She put them to boil in

their jackets, then started rummaging in one of the saddlebags. Quincy was watching her, uneasily aware that she had neither spoken nor looked at him for the last half-hour.

"What are you hunting for?"

"I just wanted to see if there were enough gingersnaps left to qualify as dessert."

As she turned to go back to the fire with the cookie box in her hand, he saw that she had been crying. In two long jumps he reached her. His arms went around her tight.

"Honey, honey, what's the matter?"

She ducked her head away. "Nothing. Please let me go."

"Are you sad because you'll be twenty-five years old tomorrow and I can't bake you a cake or buy you red roses?"

She tried to loosen his hold. "My birthday has nothing to do with it."

."Ah, then, there *is* something!"

"Quincy, let me go. The potatoes are about to tip over."

"This is more important than potatoes." He spanned her chin with thumb and forefinger, bringing her face around squarely to his. "Now, out with it. Somebody or something is making you unhappy. I can't do anything until I know who or what. Am I the villain, pushing farther and faster in a day than you can handle?

"No, not that. It's—oh, you big galoot, you take so much pains to find a camp the horses will like, and pay no attention to what would be comfortable or pleasant for your wife!"

She was half-laughing now, and he knew from the "big galoot" that she was not deeply angry with him. But she had been crying minutes ago, and Quincy's hands were gentle as he drew her down to sit beside him on the trampled grass. He brushed a strand of hair out of her eyes and kissed her. "Bunny, for a highly intelligent girl, you are sometimes a blithering idiot. Listen, it's not only that our getting to Seattle requires the endurance of the horses. There'll be moments when your very life may depend on Hike's stamina, on some last ounce of energy he's got because he's had the best fare we could find, day after day. Do you understand? It's because I love you more than anything in creation that I have to provide those animals enough to eat and drink."

He'd had an impulse to make a joke of the matter, to follow the cue of her half-laughing outburst. But he sensed, in the tears and the silences that preceded them, something demanding a reasoned answer along with an assurance of her worth. Was it to counter-balance the irritations and miseries of the trail? She'd been unbelievably uncomplaining for three weeks and more. Perhaps that was why she had let her feeling of injustice build up into a thundercloud today.

He smudged away the last trace of tears from her sunburned cheeks. "You do understand?"

"I guess. Anyhow, I'm glad you explained. Maybe I should have known, but you see, things got so—" She was just about to melt, but whether into his arms or into fresh tears Quincy never knew, for Ella suddenly cried, "Oh, the potatoes!" and scrambled to her feet.

At roughly the same moment a band of wandering horses, attracted by Vag's shrill whinnying, came thudding up to the verge of the thicket to see what was going on. Quincy scooped his hat from the ground and sprinted off, whooping and waving. There were about twenty head. Before they had crashed more than a few yards through the trees, they took alarm at his gyrations, snorted their astonishment, and whirled away down the prairie a hundred yards. There they slowed and milled around uncertainly. Two of the bolder ones started back toward the thicket, still curious.

"Whoo! Get on!" Quincy pranced out from cover, shaking his hat. That was enough. The whole band swung and galloped away in close formation, manes streaming in the wind. It was as beautiful a sight to Quincy as any he had seen so far on the trip. Individually they had not been much to look at, assorted farm horses turned out to pasture. He hadn't noticed any that appeared as a suitable substitute for Vag. But his fingers itched to capture on paper the lines of force and flight, and the play of sun on the shifting mass of color—chestnut, bay, sorrel, blue-black. He waited, trying to fix the details in his mind against the time when he would be back at his easel in New York. Which was the highest pinnacle for the artist, the moment of perception or the moment of its re-creation? Either way, he thought, it was double joy, and he whistled happily as he circled around to the slough to check the picket pins and give thanks that Hike and Vag hadn't pulled up stakes and disappeared with the running horses.

On the way to camp he saw a cluster of harebells, their delicate blue almost hidden in the grass.

Ella was on her knees by the fire, feeding small sticks into the coals with extreme care so as not to disturb the balance of the saucepan. He knelt beside her and offered the flowers.

"Not exactly long-stemmed American Beauties, darling. But happy birthday, with love from the big galoot."

"How pretty they are!" She took them and held them against his cheek. "What's more, they just match the eyes of a sensible and forgiving husband. What blithering idiot would want roses?"

JOURNAL ENTRIES

THURSDAY, MAY 30 . . . *Rainy and cold. Jamestown at 10:30 . . . Windsor at 6:30 . . . Bought can of peaches in honor of E's birthday, also cookies. Camped near slough between snow fences. Slept on dried bushes (Russian thistles) without tent. Much dew. Very comfortable.*

FRIDAY, MAY 31. *Awoke at 5 A.M. Two "great big gray wolves" fifty feet away. Gone before could get out rifle. Q followed over hill and saw ducks. Went after ducks. Shotgun no earthly good . . . Stopped to look for horse at LaBorde's camp.*

From a distance LaBorde's showed as a tiny cluster of dots against the prairie's green-brown tweed of new grass pushing up through the old. As Quincy and Ella drew nearer, the dots separated into a work wagon, a loaded hayrack, a buggy, a tent

Horsetrader's camp on the North Dakota prairie between Cleveland and Medina.

with stovepipe jutting through the top, and a sheep bed—a tall narrow canvas-roofed wagon, the movable home and symbol of the western sheepherder, though this was in fact a horse trader's camp.

Learning that the trader had nothing that interested them, Quincy and Ella were about to leave when LaBorde's wife came out of the tent and invited them to look inside. The noonday stew was simmering on the small castiron cookstove. Mrs. LaBorde, so tall and uniformly stout that her checked apron encased her from shoulders to feet with scarcely a wrinkle, gestured toward the quilt-covered mound of hay that served as a bed, and to the boxes drawn up for seats around a small wooden table. "It's not like home, but we make do."

> *. . . Medina late noon. Paid like smoke for bread, beans and milk (40¢) and oats (25¢ for 10¢ worth) . . . Late camp at Crystal Springs. Sand flies. Beautiful*

water to look at but couldn't drink it. Red scum on it
when boiled. Couldn't buy milk. Very dry that night.
Slept on leaves without tent. Saw prairie fire. Seemed
very wildernessy.

Relaxing on the leaf bed, Quincy wondered what gave him
such a sense of wild country tonight. What made him feel the
lonesomeness of the land, the unreachable distance between the
predictably familiar surroundings of the East and this patch of
prairie where he and Ella lay curled together?

Part of the feeling, of course, was the wolves. For honesty's
sake he was going to put quotation marks around that journal
note. He wanted so much to believe that he had really been face
to face with wolves that he might have deceived himself. Yet he
was reasonably sure those two great gray shapes had been
neither coyotes nor farm dogs.

Part of the feeling was the prairie fire, seen as a mass of omi-
nous brown smoke roiling along the horizon, low and to the southwest. It was far enough away not to threaten them tonight, for
the wind, blowing all afternoon from the northwest, had dropped
to a light breathing of airs after sundown. Still, the fire was there.
Tomorrow they would have to pass close to it, and where would
it stop?

Part of the feeling was the sudden abundance of game birds,
flying the great migration corridor that crossed east central North
Dakota. For the last two days the sloughs on either side of the
road had been clamorous with pintails, mallards, redheads and
canvasbacks, feeding in the wind-riffled waters before continuing
their flight to Canada, a month late because of the prolonged
winter. Roast duck would completely outclass broiled gopher as
a supplement to beans-and-potatoes, and Quincy had been disgusted when the shot from his new bird gun scattered so errati-
cally that he returned empty-handed from each of his forays. But
at least he had hunted. And knowing, since his training session
with Hike and Vag two evenings ago, that they would hold
steady when he was firing on foot or from the saddle, he was

sure he could properly acquit himself in game country as soon as
he got a better gun.

More than anything, though, the feeling of wilderness came
from the place itself. With nothing but a blanket between him
and the stars, the prairie night pressed in on him through every
sense. The hemisphere of blue-black sky rested on his open eyes
and swung as he moved his glance. From beneath, the earth
pushed hard against his tired body. The air stroked his face with
a touch that was cool when it skimmed toward him from the
pond, or faintly warm when it blew over the sod. It brought to
his ears the gentle rasping of the reeds, the rustling of the grass,
and smaller rustlings *in* the grass where the white-footed mice
ran their nighttime errands. He heard the whisper of wings and
saw a darker shape against the dark sky—a burrowing owl on
the hunt for unwary errand-runners. The wind also brought the
prairie smell, salty from the drying alkali flats, rich with the
nutrient odor of bluegrass, and streaked with the tang of
meadow parsnips, squareweed and wild parsley. And in his
mouth was the taste of prairie thirst, lip-cracking, throat-scraping
thirst.

He welcomed it all, the wolves, the distant menace of the fire,
the lonesomeness, even the elusive ducks and the undrinkable
water. Good copy for the book. Signs he and Bunny were prob-
ing deeper into the West. And each experience provided a test
of themselves, though as yet at a kindergarten level, against the
hardships that lay in wait on the High Plains.

Hike could be sulky and stubborn, but this day he looked as if he were enjoying a good laugh with Ella.

JUNE: *The cowboy's prairie*

God forbid that I should go to any heaven in which there are no horses.

R. B. Cunninghame-Graham
IN A LETTER TO THEODORE ROOSEVELT

V "Ho! Ho, there. Steady, boy!"
Ella's arms were jerked to full stretch as the lurching transfer car sent Hike scrabbling rearward. Another lurch threw him forward again, and she barely got her feet out of his way. His eyes rolled wildly and she could feel the tremor of his muscles.

"Quincy, I don't know how much longer I can hold him."

"Want to trade off?" A gleam of mischief took away for an instant the lines of weariness and strain in Quincy's face. "I'd be very happy to accommodate you."

"No, I don't want to trade." She could see he was having even more trouble keeping Vag upright. "I just thought you should know—whoa, easy, boy!—that I may give out."

The Northern Pacific transfer car consisted of two boxcars hooked together. The adjoining ends had been knocked out and a circular table built into the floor over the couplings. A team hitched to a large hack occupied the front section of the double car, and a team and buggy the opposite end, leaving Quincy and Ella to stand in the center holding their horses as steady as they could. Vag had to rest his forefeet on the constantly shifting table.

"Only takes five minutes to cross from Bismarck to Mandan," said the brakeman when Quincy had questioned the safety of the arrangements. What the brakeman had neglected to say was that there would be a half hour of shunting and switching on either side of the Missouri. The transfer car had been bumped, tugged, slammed and jammed back and forth for more than twenty minutes already. Ella's arms ached and her heart was pounding. Even more frightening than losing her grip on Hike's bridle was the chance of being crushed against the side of the car. *Just hang on,* she said fiercely to herself. *Just hang on tight.*

The driver of the hack, an old man in a mustard-colored overcoat, was having less difficulty with his team. Chocks fore and aft of the wheels held the hack steady, and the horses could brace themselves in the harness.

"I'm on my way to Dickinson," he told Ella, half-screening his mouth with his puffy hand to indicate that this information was confidential, though he had to shout to be heard above the clomping of hoofs and the screeches of the jouncing car. "Used to drive for hire in Valley City, but too much competition. Trolley car and two other hacks. Den me and Ned and Bill here—" he nodded toward his team—"we set up in Carrington. But we wasn't makin' a livin'. So I says I'm leavin'. De people wanted my coach and horses to stay in town. But I say, 'Why don't you patronize 'em den?' And dey say, 'Where you goin'?' And I say, 'Dat's none of yer biznesss.' But I don't mind yer knowin', missus."

Ella noticed that Quincy, in the short lulls between lurches, was getting advice on horsey ailments from the bucktoothed young man standing at the head of the buggy team.

"Now suppose your horse gets a dust cough, best thing I know is to put pine tar on his tongue. Yessir, pine tar."

Before she could hear any more good remedies, the transfer car was sent into its place in the line with a kick that pushed Ella so far off balance that she nearly went down under Hike's plunging feet.

The old man shook his head. "Don't look as if yer horses ever been in a railway car before."

"Well, I've never been in a railway car *with* a horse before, and I don't like it any better than they do."

Ella swung suddenly with Hike's weight, then righted herself. If he lost his footing completely and came smashing down . . . *Don't think about it!* She willed herself to think instead about the earlier hours of this long day, as exasperating in its delays as it was threatening in its conclusion. To begin with, it had taken her and Quincy twenty-four hours longer to reach Bis-

Near Tappen, N.D., Quincy snapped Ella galloping against the backdrop of smoke from a prairie fire.

marck than they had planned. After the night at Crystal Springs they had passed the prairie fire, close enough to use its tower of smoke as a background for a dramatic snapshot of Ella at a gallop on Hike. They had spent a restless "rest day" camped astride the hundredth meridian, beyond Steele. The following morning was lost in chasing their runaway horses for several miles after Hike snapped his picket rope, enticing Vag to careen after him, pin, line and all. Vag tripped on the rope and went end over end in a somersault that knocked him flat. The fall didn't keep him from tagging Hike over the next roll of prairie, where they were caught, but it caused Vag a limp that slowed down the afternoon's ride considerably. A day of bad weather followed. Consequently it was not until this morning—Wednesday, June 5—that Quincy and Ella came trotting to Bismarck on the banks of the Missouri. It had been so cold at sun-up that they'd had to break ice on the watering trough in the farmyard where they had slept. But by the time they rode the six miles from camp to town, the air was bright and warm.

From the road that passed the penitentiary southeast of town they could glimpse the square, ponderous bulk of the state Capitol, commanding the slope to the north. They debated detouring for a closer view, and to see Teddy Roosevelt's ranch cabin which had been placed on the Capitol grounds, but decided against it.

"T. R. can wait till we reach Medora," Quincy said. "We have a lot of things to tend to today, so let's go straight on downtown."

Ella carried a list. "Mail. Trade shotgun. Lariats. Pants for Q. Shoes, E and Q. Premo film packs. Q—shave." She had underlined the last item, for she wasn't fond of the red bristles that had sprouted on his cheeks since he'd lost his razor at La Borde's camp.

It didn't look like a very long list.

"Oh, dear, how can we fill in the extra hours?" she asked when Quincy came back from scouting the railroad yards to announce that the transfer car wouldn't load until about 5:30 that afternoon. She needn't have worried. Bismarck on this June morning didn't display the bustle of commercial enterprise they had found in Fargo. The pace of life along Main Street was leisurely. The store clerks, who perhaps were also filling up a long day, moved without hurry, prolonged their chats with customers, and disappeared for minutes at a time in the back rooms, supposedly searching for requested merchandise.

The dicker over the shotgun didn't interest Ella. She went window-shopping. When she returned to the hardware store, Quincy proudly showed her a Stevens Favorite .22 rifle. "It cost six bucks, but I sold the shotgun for a dollar seventy-five, and the man threw in a box of cartridges. Here, heft it."

She picked up the Stevens. "It does have a nice feel in my hands. Light and well-balanced." She put it to her shoulder and sighted it at the ceiling.

"Like it?"

"Yes, I do."

"Good. I bought it for you. The man says there won't be much bird-hunting as we go west, so I thought a small rifle would be more practical."

There was only one letter at the postoffice. It was from Quincy's parents. Nothing from Seattle. Ella tried not to show her disappointment. There must have been some misunderstanding about dates or directions. She left a forwarding address with the clerk: Terry, Montana. She wasn't exactly sure where that was—somewhere between Glendive and Miles City, a pinpoint in a wide emptiness.

"How long will it take us to get that far, Quincy?"

"It all depends. If we're lucky enough to find a trade for Vag soon, we can push on pretty steadily. Should make it inside of three weeks."

Three weeks! She felt a pang of lonesomeness, sharp and bittersweet. But on its heels came, characteristically, a practical thought. If she had to ride to Terry for a letter from her family, the sooner she and Quincy were ready to leave Bismarck, the better. She looked at her list.

"Let's try next for the pants and shoes."

Bismarck couldn't scare up a single pair of khaki riding pants, although it was obvious from the shredded condition of Quincy's that he needed a replacement. As for shoes, the search for sturdy, comfortable ones took him and Ella into every footwear store in town. He finally settled on a pair of bluchers, in spite of their brilliant saffron color. Ella bought low-heeled calfskins with a sober Sunday-go-to-meeting look. Neither pair was a perfect fit, but they would have to do. Their old shoes were falling apart. Ella glanced at hers with a sigh. "Too bad there's no room in the saddlebags for the evidence. Those wrecks would prove that I really did walk 200 out of the 500 miles we've covered!"

Quincy had his shave before he and Ella ate a late lunch at a restaurant and did the rest of their errands. Then they rode to the end of the street, passing the old log building that dated from Bismarck's beginnings as Camp Hancock. They came out on the bank overlooking the Missouri. Here they had an unhindered view of the river in flood, spilling its yellow-brown waters over the flatlands that lay between the channel and the shale banks. Quincy reined Vag to a halt and pointed to the other side. Just north of where the Heart River emptied into the Missouri, Mandan squeezed itself along a narrow shelf of ground bordering the water. Behind the town the land rose in a sloping facade of knobby bluffs. Sunlight, shafted between gathering clouds, gilded the crest of the facade and accented the vertical lines of shadow where the bluffs folded into one another.

"Hills," said Quincy. "Hills!"

Ella nodded, savoring with him the upthrust of the earth. There had been days and days of flatness and straightness, when it seemed that the only change in scene was the slow moving of her shadow from directly in front of her at six in the morning to directly behind her at six in the evening. Now she was refreshed by the thought of following a hill road that could slip around a turn or over a hump.

She shifted her eyes to the big river, letting herself feel for one frightening instant its merciless drive. Against that force the roalroad bridge looked frail and presumptuous. Someone had told her today that the bridge was built at an Indian ford, known as the narrowest and safest crossing, and she had been over the span more than once in a railway passenger car. But that assurance didn't help much as she looked upstream and pictured, bearing down on that bridge, the melted snows of half of Dakota, two-thirds of Montana, and corners of Wyoming, Alberta and Saskatchewan.

She shuddered and turned Hike with the rein. "Let's board the transfer and get it over with."

"Wait." Quincy reached for Hike's bridle. "Bunny, do you realize we're looking directly across at what's left of Fort Abraham Lincoln? That was Custer's headquarters, and he rode out of there on his way to his death at Little Big Horn. Do you realize that Lewis and Clark wintered not many miles north of here, and that yesterday we crossed the trail of Sibley along Apple Creek?"

"Who's Sibley?"

"General Henry H. Sibley, sent out to bring the obstreperous Sioux into line in the 1860's. Didn't you ever read about Indians?"

"Read about them? In Seattle, all I had to do was get on a streetcar and ride downtown to Pioneer Square, and there was Princess Angeles, daughter of Chief Sealth, sitting where anybody who wanted to could look at her. I didn't need to *read* about Indians."

Quincy laughed and let go of Hike's bridle. "All right. But please be a little impressed by the history of this spot on the continent."

"I am impressed. But I'll be happier about it on the west side of the Missouri."

So they turned back from the turbulent river, found the transfer car waiting in the N. P. yards, paid two dollars, and coaxed Vag and Hike aboard. And now here they were, at nearly six o'clock in the evening, arms aching from the pull of the fractious horses, legs trembling with the effort to brace both themselves and the horses against falling—and not yet out of Bismarck!

"Quincy . . ." Even in her own ears her cry sounded plaintive, and Ella bit it off. "Never mind, I'm all right." She took a fresh grip on the sweaty leathers of the bridle and waited for the next bone-jarring crash.

Instead, there came a sense of sustained forward motion. Not smooth—Vag must still constantly shift his feet to compensate for the bobbling of the loose center table—but the car was on its way. The random creaks, rattles and squeals settled down into a rough pattern, punctuated by the quickening rhythm of the metal wheels on the track. Ella thought she detected a change in sound that meant they were starting out on the bridge. She ducked to the other side of Hike and peered through a crack in the side of the car. Yes, there was a slice of half-cloudy sky and below it a slice of *cafe au lait* river. She drew back hastily.

"You can be glad de ferry broke down," said the old man behind her. "Bumps and all, dis train beats buckin' de river in flood."

The actual crossing proved to be the easiest part of the hour. Ten minutes after the engine pulled out of the Bismarck yard it chuffed onto a siding in Mandan and the long process of switching and kicking began all over again. The transfer car was finally nudged up to a platform where hack, buggy and horses could unload.

The transfer car had done more than bring them across the Missouri river. It had brought them out of farmer country to cowboy country. It had brought them to *the* West. Ella saw this as soon as they turned from the railroad yard into the main street. Men in broad-brimmed hats. Saddled ponies tied in front of every store. Indians sauntering by, dressed in a mixture of tribal and town clothing. The wooden false-fronts of pioneer days intermingled with the ornate brick buildings of the 90's. Though it was after six in the evening, business houses were doing a brisk trade. Screen doors slammed, people shouted across the street to one another. A man came at a gallop behind Quincy and pulled in his buckskin horse to walk in step with Vag. Ella was fascinated with the rider's muttonchop whiskers and the sweeping curve of his hatbrim.

"Saw you was strangers and thought I'd say howdy," he said. "Stopping in these parts or just going through?"

Quincy explained briefly, and then asked about possibilities in Mandan for a horse trade.

The man combed his fingers through his muttonchops. "There's a big sale barn here in town. You might also try the Indian camp out along the Heart River. And then I heard Mr. Gowan has a fellow visiting him who's got a horse to trade."

Quincy had been eyeing the buckskin. "Not interested in a deal yourself?"

"Nope. I farm, punch cattle, and run the Mandan town hearse, all with this one horse. It sure knocks hell out of him, but I can't get along without him. I wish you good luck!" He whooped at the buckskin and galloped on down the street.

Exhilarated by the livelier pace on this side of the river, Ella and Quincy forgot their weariness. They tied Hike and Vag in front of a general store, bought grub, new hobbles and a hobble chain, and then followed directions to Gowan's house. Neither the guest nor the guest's horse was there, but Gowan promised to bring both along the next day. "Best place for you to camp, Mr. Scott, is a mile out of town, on the Heart River. I'll see you there first thing in the morning."

Quincy and Ella found a campsite. It was across the railroad track and about four hundred feet from the Sioux tepees. The sky, which had turned sulky with sundown, threatened in earnest now, so they put up the tent. Then the wind shifted and blew into the open end. They had to take the tent down and set it facing in another direction. They were too tired to bother with a fire or to hunt for the candle stub they carried in a saddlebag. In the dark they ate a can of beans, cold, and squirmed into the blankets.

But Wednesday, June 5, was not through with them yet. Just before midnight they were wakened by a series of weird shouts. After listening for an anxious moment, hands on their guns, they decided that the noise came from the Indian camp and was no concern of theirs. But it was fortunate they had been startled awake. The storm had broken in fury, the wind had shifted again, and in through the open end of the tent funneled a blast of twigs, sand, mud, pebbles and rain, straight into their faces. There was something else out there in the night too, silhouetted against succeeding flashes of lightning—something black, massive and topheavy, swaying toward the tent on a long tapering stem.

Quincy grabbed Ella's arm. "See that? A twister, coming straight for us!"

"Where? I don't see it."

"Wait till the next flash lights it up . . . There, right in front of your eyes!"

"Oh, *that*." She laughed with relief. "That was there when we went to bed."

"Get out! I guess I know a twister when I see one."

"Get out yourself, and see if you do."

He crawled to the edge of the tent just as another revealing discharge crackled across the sky. He gave a grunt of disgust and acknowledgment, and crawled back into bed. "You have to admit it looks like a twister."

"But it's a tree?"

"Yes, a tree. Or the only tornado ever discovered with bark on it."

They were through breakfast the next morning and nearly packed when Gowan and his visitor came splashing into camp. Introduced as Mr. Darcy, the visitor sat astride a big white horse that looked strong and hard. Ella hoped Quincy would approve an exchange, for she was fidgety about the prolonged search. But there was no deal. Darcy, after some sneering comments on Hike and Vag, said he was interested only in a sale, not a trade. He went away grumbling at Gowan for wasting time on a wild goose chase.

Ella stood with her hands on her hips, frowning as she watched the two men ride off. "After those disrespectful remarks about our horses, I'm glad Mr. Darcy didn't want to trade! I couldn't trust a thing he said about his white monster."

"Don't worry, I wouldn't have taken the white monster anyhow. By the looks of him, he's a heavy feeder, what we've got to avoid. We need a horse that can keep fit on lean pickings. Shall we try our luck at the Indian camp?"

Luck was no kinder there. But they had some vigorous exercise scrambling up the muddy hillside, and a close view of an Indian camp on a drizzly morning. The tepees were closed tight against the weather, giving the place a deserted look. Gangs of mongrel dogs roamed the camp, sniffing for bones. Occasionally the younger dogs would leap toward the strips of jerky meat drying on cords strung from tall stakes, and fall back whining. Ella halted at a discreet distance while Quincy advanced to halloo at the first tepee.

"Anyone home?"

An old woman, her thinning white hair in pigtails, stuck her head out from the nearest tepee. To all of his questions she answered with the same vague monosyllable, forcing him to decide that either she couldn't understand English, or was under instructions not to talk horse trading in such miserable weather.

He and Ella slid in the gumbo back to level ground, scraped the worst of the mud off their new-only-yesterday shoes, and rode once more into Mandan. Here Quincy had to turn down two offers: a magnificent big bay at $200, and a pair of inferior bays at the same price—in either case, $200 more than he thought he could afford. At the general store Ella bought a loaf of bread and cans of corned beef and peas. Clinking the change in her hand, she stepped over to examine the candy case. Considering the state of their finances, even a small bag of horehound drops would be an extravagance, but didn't they need something tangy after the flat taste of the morning's disappointments? She paid out the extra five cents happily.

"Bless you!" said Quincy when she held out the open bag to him. "One piece now, another for dessert at lunch, and the rest as long as they last."

The road to New Salem began with a long pitch around the courthouse and to the top of the bluff. The clouds were beginning to break away, but there was not enough sunshine to dry the mud, and Hike and Vag made heavy going of it. Still, the novelty of hill-climbing compensated for the lack of speed. From near the top Quincy and Ella twisted in their saddles to look back at a broad vista. Mandan at their feet, Bismarck sprawled on the opposite bank, the glint of sun on the wet roofs, and the N. P. bridge still looking frail and presumptuous as it marched stiff-legged across the Missouri, up to its hips in the rushing brown water.

Ella drew a deep breath and let it go in a silent prayer of thankfulness. Safely across the Minnesota, the Red, the Missouri —wait, wouldn't they have to find a way to get over the Missouri again, in Montana? She thought she remembered, from the hours she and Quincy had spent poring over the none too helpful maps of the U.S. Geographical Survey, that somewhere just east of Helena and the continental divide, the Missouri would bar their path a second time. Well, safely across the Missouri *once*, anyhow.

The interval of sunshine lasted through their nooning beside the road, and a call at a farm to buy oats and turn down one more horse trade, a black mare Quincy considered too "grassy."

Montana jack rabbits grew a little taller than the cattle.

They rode all afternoon under gradually darkening skies, and were directed by another farmer to a creek and an empty barn "very nopotty vill hurdt you to gamp dere—it iss py de road, yust." They found the barn a mile across the prairie from the road. The creek was nothing but a series of alkali pools and red iron-tinted puddles. But in addition to the barn there was a two-room cabin, flanked by a big pile of hay. So it was easy to forgive that extra mile, especially since the farmer had sold them six eggs and three pints of milk for seven cents. In the cabin cellar they discovered a bag of oats. Rain came with dusk, but horses as well as riders dined well and slept dry. Afterward, Ella liked to remember that, for it was their last night in charge of Vag.

By following the telephone line over the hills the next day, she and Quincy cut four miles off the road distance and came to New Salem in a mid-afternoon drizzle. New Salem was the first of another string of "in between" towns, known first only as siding numbers on the Northern Pacific railway, then acquiring names and identities of their own as store, bank, church, school, elevator and livery stable were built along the siding. New Salem looked much the same as the other towns, but there was a difference, more noticeable in the rolling prairie around it than in the town itself. After some bitter years of crop failure, many New Salem homesteaders had turned from wheat to range and dairy cattle. It was a difference that proved favorable not only for the ranchers, but for Quincy and Ella, as they began to understand when they took Hike to the blacksmith shop and asked about horse trades.

"Yup, you come to the right town for that," said the smith. "There's dairy herds and some beef cattle raisin', and that means a demand for broncos. Guess that's why Gus Lowell runs his stable here. He owns ranches in Montana and drives horses east to sell. Just go along the street there and you'll find him."

They left the blacksmith pulling nails from Hike's old shoes, and took Vag to the sales stable.

There was nothing about the first sight of Gus Lowell's strawberry roan to tell Ella that the long search was over. To begin with, the roan was noticeably homely. No arching neck, no finely-modeled head or regal eye, no lustrous coat displaying a ripple of muscles. He came sauntering at the end of Lowell's lead rope, lipping the stems of a mouthful of hay, head down, tail indolently brushing away a few torpid flies. His nose bowed outward from brow to muzzle. There was a large kite-shaped white blaze on his forehead. His mane, forelock and tail were mahogany brown, his hind legs mud-flecked white from the hocks down. The rest of his body, as nearly as Ella could name the color, was pinkish gray liberally sprinkled with cinnamon. In the last month Quincy had been offered a dozen more promising-looking mounts and turned them down. She was sure he was going to make one of his polite excuses for passing up this specimen, too.

But if so, he was taking his time about it. From where Ella sat in the barn on a stack of dusty oatbags, she was too far away to hear all that he was saying to Lowell, but she could see the two of them pointing to successive parts of the roan's anatomy. Quincy examined the teeth, ran his hands slowly over the cinnamon legs, and picked up the feet for a closer view. She saw him slide a stick under the horse's tail, close to the root, and heard the sharp *snap!* when the tail clamped down hard and broke the stick.

Presently Lowell came to lift a saddle and bridle from pegs on the wall beside her. In spite of his brown wool business suit and collarless pink-and-white-striped shirt, he looked to Ella more like her idea of a cowboy than anyone she had met so far in North Dakota. His hawk face was deeply seamed and weathered. There was a tilt to the crumpled brim of his Stetson and a roll to his bowlegged walk that set him apart both from dirt farmers and eastern horse traders.

"Your husband is going to take the roan for a little test. Do you want to try him out too?"

"Oh, no, thank you. The horse is for Mr. Scott, and I'd rather leave the decision to him."

"That's smart, ma'am. But I'll tell you, Mr. Scott can't go wrong on this one. Plenty of bottom, yet easy-gaited and gentle enough for anybody."

"What's his name?"

"Name?" Lowell's dark face split in a smile that showed four gold teeth. "Ma'am, I've got hundreds of cayuses going through my hands every year. I don't take time to think up names. This one's never been called anything printable, so you can pick any monicker for him you want." He swung the bridle over his shoulder and went off, carrying the heavy stock saddle by the horn.

Ella noted that the lean and weathered Mr. Lowell, for all that he had praised her intention of leaving Quincy a free hand, had used his opportunity to influence her attitude. Well, she wasn't going to indicate, even by the set of her mouth, that she was displeased by Quincy's decision, whether it was to trade for the strawberry roan or turn him down. Impatient as she was to have the matter settled, she had been trying for days not to hint at her edginess, lest she jostle Quincy into a hasty, ill-considered choice. And when he did choose, she would have to accept his judgment. He knew what made a horse right for their purpose, and she didn't.

The roan stood placidly while Lowell threw on the saddle and Quincy slipped the bit into his mouth and adjusted the headstall over his ears. There was no nervous sidestepping when Quincy started to mount. They were out in the street in a moment, minus balking or bucking. So far, so good. Ella gave Lowell a more approving glance when he strolled over to her. He made a cigarette, pulling the drawstring of his sack of Bull Durham with his teeth and neatly licking the paper to seal shut the cylinder. It was the admired ritual and she had seen it done hundreds of times, but never, she thought, as quickly and tidily as now. After he had struck a match and drawn in a deep lungful of smoke, Lowell began asking questions. Why didn't they have a packhorse? How many miles a day would they be averaging? What route would they follow? What about feed?

She answered as well as she could, explaining Quincy's confidence in their system of traveling light, with almost daily replenishment of food for themselves and oats for the horses. "We've been making better than twenty miles a day here in Dakota. We try to walk about two miles out of every five, to rest the horses, and part of each day we usually change off, to give Vag a lighter weight to carry."

"I can see from the old black's condition that your husband knows how to take care of horses on the trail."

"He's very careful to camp only where there's the best water and grass available."

Lowell brooded down at her, his eyes half-concealed by drifting smoke. "You realize, don't you, that the best available isn't going to be very good in eastern Montana? Specially if you try to save distance by cutting pretty straight toward Helena. Ranches are a long ways apart. It'll be late June, early July by then, water holes will be going dry. Little creeks drying up too. Unless you know just where to look, you might ride two-three days and not find a drink."

"We can stand it," she said firmly.

"Maybe, but can the horses? You and your husband better figure things ahead very carefully once you leave the Yellowstone. Myself, I'd advise you to stick with the river."

"That would take us too far out of our way. We want to reach Seattle by the third week in August. Mr. Lowell—" She stopped, a plea on the tip of her tongue. This man seemed to be a different breed of horse dealer from the Mr. Rollins of South St. Paul. Under that striped pink shirt, wasn't there a heart that could pulse to some other rhythm than the clink of dollars streaming into the cash register? Maybe . . . but she had better not count on it. She held her tongue.

As if Lowell had guessed her mind, he leaned forward and gave her a touch on the shoulder, not exactly fatherly, but not exactly anything else, either. Just a light pressure of the fingers that saluted her as another human being with problems.

"Don't you worry, ma'am. Treated right, that strawberry roan will get your husband through Montana if any horse can, and we'll work out a fair deal."

But he laughed when Quincy returned with the roan and offered to trade Vag even-steven. "Mr. Scott, I just told your wife I'd make a fair deal, and I intend to. Maybe weight it a little in your favor, since I'm interested in what you kids have set out to do. But don't expect me to make you a present of the roan. Your horse is old. Whether or not he used to be a game one, he soon won't be good for much of anything. Now my horse, he's younger. He's tough. His legs are sound. He's used to keeping fit on grass alone, what we out here call a real 'liver.' He's easy-riding and has a decent disposition. You've just seen that for yourself, haven't you?"

Quincy admitted the roan behaved civilly.

"Well, then," continued Lowell, "you and I could dicker for half an hour and not come out any better than I'm going to put it to you now, my lowest offer: for your old black horse and twenty-five dollars, you can have the roan. I doubt if you'd find as good a bronco for that price between here and Montana. I know you won't find a better one."

Quincy walked off to study the horse from a distance. Then he came back and worked his way along one side of the roan and the other, using hands to tell him what eyes could not. Ella watched, expecting Quincy to ask her opinion before the final decision as he had in South St. Paul. Wouldn't he at least send her a questioning look?

But as she was worrying about how to respond, she saw Quincy holding out some bills to the dealer.

"I'm satisfied, Mr. Lowell. Here's your twenty-five."

In the weeks since he had negotiated for Hike and Vag, Quincy had evidently learned some new things about horses, horse traders and himself. Ella was relieved that he hadn't sought her opinion, and proud of the self-confidence he showed in closing today's bargain. She hopped down from the pile of oatbags and rubbed the roan's whiskery nose. To own him didn't make him any more handsome, but she was ready now to believe in all those sterling qualities he must possess if Quincy thought him worth twenty-five dollars more than Vag!

Tucking the money into his shirtpocket beside the Bull Durham sack, Gus Lowell waved toward the small office partitioned off at the front end of the barn. "You folks are welcome to spend the night here, if you haven't any better place in mind."

"We don't have any place at all in mind," said Quincy with a grin. "Your offer is gratefully accepted."

They brought Hike over from the blacksmith shop, unpacked, and spread their blankets on the office floor, on top of several armfuls of clean bedding straw. The drizzle stopped, allowing them to eat supper in the stable yard, over a small campfire.

"The ways and beans committee will come to order," said Quincy, spooning up a last mouthful of the latter. "It takes money to buy beans, and we've just made such a Grand Canyon-sized hole in our exchequer that we'll have to wire for another draft on our bank account. How much? Twenty? Thirty?"

Ella poured herself a second cup of tea. "Let's make it thirty. Now that we're not stopping at farms so frequently, we have to buy a larger proportion of our food at stores, so it's costing us more to eat."

"All right, thirty dollars. Better have it sent to Dickinson, I guess. Bunny, I hated to let go of that extra dough to Lowell, but I thought we had looked long enough. This new horse is what I've been hoping for all along. Did you notice he's lower at the withers than Vag, by about a hand? Shorter in the back, too, and bigger around the chest, all advantages for endurance and weight carrying."

"Will he be comfortable to ride?"

"You bet. After a month of jolting along on Vag, the roan's gait seems as smooth as cream."

"Tell me, why did you put that stick under his tail?"

Quincy chuckled. "I used to hear my father say that a horse that clamps his tail down hard has a strong backbone. You noticed that the stick cracked."

Before turning in they took the kerosene lantern from its nail in the office and carried it down through the barn to make sure the horses were secure in their stalls. When they came to Vag, Ella moved in and laid her head against his mane, stroking him gently. Funny old Vag, still awkward and a bit ribby. Flighty old Vag, snorting at a train three miles away, shying at any round object. Proud old Vag, such a ham that no matter how tired he was, he would flare his nostrils and prance whenever there were onlookers to impress. Dear, funny old Vag.

"Goodbye," she whispered. "Good bye."

It was raining again as she and Quincy started out in the morning. The gray masses of clouds rolled eternally along from behind, pressing so low, Quincy claimed, that he could stand up in the stirrups and touch them. The next town beyond New Salem was Glen Ullin, named by a romantic railroader in honor of the Scottish ballad, *Lord Ullin's Daughter.* The scene might have been suitable to the misty Highlands, except that the rain came in cloudburst quantities, the two lonely shepherds encountered on the hills spoke a European tongue that was certainly not Gaelic, and the hills themselves were no kith to the bens of Scotland, but queer things, gouged into haphazard forms and sizes, topped with patches of red rock, and interlaced with a maze of gullies.

"Quincy, are we getting into the Badlands?"

Ella was uneasy. She had heard descriptions of the wild and foreboding country ahead of them, whose name itself gave her the shivers.

"Oh, no," he reassured her. "We won't hit the Badlands until near the western border of the state. But this looks like an introduction in miniature. I imagine the same general kind of geologic processes have been going on here, the softer soil eroding away from the prairie level and leaving these 'thumbs' sticking up all over the landscape."

Gus Lowell had suggested their following a shortcut about twelve miles out from New Salem. They had no trouble finding the place to branch off, but getting back to the main trail took them most of the day, with no help from the sheepherders. The men seemed to understand the name Glen Ullin, but their gestures revolved toward all points of the compass.

"We mustn't be too hard on the poor fellows," Quincy said as he led off in the direction in which the last shepherd had pointed most frequently. "A sheep is the most dotty animal of all, and has a very contagious personality. Every sheep *baas* about one-twentieth of the time, so that a man who is herding four thousand sheep has to listen to the concerted *baa-ing* of two hundred. Say *baa* to yourself and see how silly you feel. Then imagine listening to *baa, baa, baa* for ten years, going weeks on end without the sight of a human face, and you won't wonder that there's a law in Minnesota against one man's herding sheep alone."

The only offset against depression was the new member of the party. The easy-going roan had no difficulty in accepting Hobo as his name, the first ever bestowed on him. His ear was more discriminating than Vag's, for he didn't confuse "Hobo" with "whoa." During the morning's riding Ella cast anxious glances at Quincy, wondering if he felt satisfied with the trade. While they huddled over a cold wet lunch beside a creek, she asked, "Is Hobo working out all right on this rough trail?"

"He's working out fine. He hasn't got Vag's style or flashy temperament, but that's all to the good now. I like the solid feel of him. In fact, Bunny, I think you'd better take him for your regular mount, and let me cope with Hike. All right with you?"

"Either way. I'm just so relieved that we no longer have to keep looking and worrying about a trade."

"Oh, I wasn't—well, all right, I was worrying." Quincy changed his disclaimer to a wry admission. "It did seem as if we'd never find a decent horse that wouldn't bankrupt us. Monetarily, I guess we couldn't afford Hobo, but time was running short and he's about what I wanted, so let's say we couldn't afford not to take him. Too bad he's such a homely cuss."

The horses were browsing along the creek bank, stopping every few mouthfuls to fret at the new rope hobbles. It was strange to see that gray-and-cinnamon shape beside Hike instead of two familiar black silhouettes. Ella felt a twinge of disloyalty. For five weeks Vag had been so important to their journey—how could she and Quincy have gone off and left him this morning, knowing they would never see him again? It would have been no sorrow to part with Hike. Although he traveled well and kept in good condition, his sulky, obstinate attitude hadn't improved in the least. If their personalities had been reversed, she wouldn't be feeling so sad about Vag. Then she considered how comfortable the old horse must be at this moment, snug and dry in Lowell's stable. And she remembered the six or eight times when he had jerked up his picket pin and gone galloping away with never a backward look, leaving her and Quincy stranded miles from anywhere. Silly to twang any more heartstrings over the final parting.

She looked more particularly at Vag's replacement. "I don't mind Hobo's being homely," she said, getting to her feet and trying to wring out her rain-soaked skirt, "provided he's got the stuff."

It would have been sensible to go to a hotel in Glen Ullin. Just the thought of a hot bath, shampoo and clean sheets sent Ella into a swoon of longing. But even if they could have spared the price, it was too late to go that far by the time they picked up the main trail. Still, they were lucky. Just as the clouds let go with the hardest downpour yet, Quincy sighted a house.

They arrived soaked and shivering. Almost before they were

off their horses, the door opened and they were sucked into a maelstrom of Zopstrachs—thirteen of them, from Grossvater and Grossmutter to a gaggle of towheaded, barefooted children. Kathy, strapping, blonde and seventeen, who appeared to be general manager of the household, was the only one who spoke English. But words weren't necessary at the moment.

"I guess we look as forlorn in German as in English," Quincy whispered to Ella as the beaming grandmother beckoned them in.

One of the middle-sized boys was called to show Quincy where he could put up the horses in the cow barn. Ella was already sitting in front of the open door of the kitchen oven when Quincy returned, and she pointed to the chair waiting for him. They reveled in the warmth billowing from the cavernous oven, while all around them swirled a flux of Zopstrachs, curious, excited and friendly. Kathy, constantly summoned in and out to deal with small crises, had little time for interpreting, but Quincy did catch her on the wing long enough to explain that he and his wife were riding horseback across the country, and would be very grateful for a place to eat and sleep tonight. Kathy translated this to the elder Zopstrachs.

"*Ja, ja, der mann und seine frau sind wilkommen!*" Grossvater Zopstrach nodded benignly. He was about fifty, Ella decided, muscular and burly. Impossible to tell in the waning daylight whether his light-colored thatch and beard had started to go gray. He looked considerably younger than Grossmutter. But in spite of the lines in her broad cheeks and the stoop of her shoulders, she had a hearty, durable air about her—she would probably outlast Grossvater.

Kathy began preparations for supper by adding a cupful of fresh-ground coffee to the veteran deposit already simmering in the biggest coffee pot Ella had ever seen. In went more water, and the pot was left to boil for an hour. Next Kathy took twin iron skillets, each about two feet in diameter, and filled one with eggs and the other with a great mound of sliced potatoes, all to sizzle and sputter in a sea of bacon fat. While she tended the frying she shot intermittent salvos of commands at the younger children. "Scrape the mud off your feet!" "Wipe your nose." "Wipe Kah-tie's nose." "Feed the dogs." "Ernst, stop teasing the cat!" It was spoken in German, but by watching the results, Ella could guess at the orders. In between, Kathy switched over to English to recite the family relationships for the guests, who found them confusing even when sorted out into generations.

"Most of us come in 1905, from Austria," Kathy continued. "But mein brother und his vife yust now come last month mit der *kinder*, Emmi, Heinie und Katie—ve say Kahtie."

Namesake of her managerial Aunt Kathy, four-year-old Kahtie was the darling of the household, doted on not only by her grandparents and parents, but by all her aunts and uncles, some of whom were not much older than herself. It was "*Komm, Kahtie!*" "*Ach, Kahtie!*" "*Was willst du, Kahtie?*" When she put her little forefinger in her mouth, which was most of the time, they tried to shame her out of the habit with cries of "*Nein, nein, Kahtie! Schmoke, Kahtie!*"

But Kahtie got no favors when it came to supper. As there were only four chairs for the kitchen table, the meal was served in shifts. Kathy directed Quincy and Ella to sit along one side with Grossvater and the married son. The little barefoot children ranged down the opposite side, standing. No eggs, potatoes or bacon for them. Each had a soup bowl of black, unsweetened coffee with a thick chunk of bread dropped in the middle.

The food served the grown-ups was good, if greasy. Ella was so hungry that not even the bristles on the bacon rind lessened her appetite. She felt guilty about enjoying such rich fare while the children got only the bread and coffee. But if that was their usual diet, it must have had some mysterious nourishing power, for all the youngsters were pink-cheeked, plump and healthy-looking.

Tonight they were paying more attention to the guests than to their meal. Kahtie in particular was unable to take her big blue eyes off Quincy, who was making funny faces for her benefit. She stood stock-still, staring at him, spoon idle, one moist finger tucked into a corner of her pouty little mouth.

"*Iss*, Kahtie!" admonished her father.

Still looking at Quincy, she slowly dipped her big galvanized iron spoon into the bowl, brought it up brimming, and tilted it waveringly toward her mouth, which still harbored the finger. A few drops spilled on her apron.

"*Kahtie, mein Gott!*"

While Kahtie cast her blue eyes downward to view the small mishap, her right hand, poised in midair, gradually turned with the weight of the heavy spoon. Coffee and softened bread splashed to the floor. The other children sniggered, but Kahtie, after a thoughtful look at the puddle, turned her solemn glance once again at the funny man across the table.

Ella gave Quincy a nudge. "Stop clowning, honey, and let the children eat. There's another shift waiting."

The kitchen was the one warm sociable spot in the house. The two other rooms on the main floor, to be used some day as parlor and dining room, were as yet unfurnished except for a few packing boxes and a broken morris chair and a double bed. The upstairs was a slope-roofed attic, divided off by rough partitions into three sleeping rooms and a cubbyhole with a bunk. At bedtime this last was assigned to the guests.

Like every other farm family with whom Quincy and Ella lodged that summer, the Zopstrachs had an outdoor privy. Walking back and forth from the house, sometimes in full view of the back windows, sometimes unavoidably meeting the men of the family on the way, troubled Ella's modesty more than the primitive arrangements necessary when she and Quincy were camping out, for then at least they were alone, and the shield of a willow clump or a slight dip in the prairie was enough. She was glad tonight for the darkness und Crossmutter's protective company through the muddy farmyard.

During the evening Ella had been comparing the Zopstrachs with the Bauers of Lintonville, where she and Quincy had spent the jolly snowy evening. Both families were hospitable, optimistic and charged with energy. But whereas the Bauers lived well-dressed in a well-equipped house, showing evidences of education and some interest in the arts, the Zopstrachs existed on the raw edge. Scarcely enough furnishings even for the basics

Children in this ranch house west of Mandan, N.D., ate standing up because there were no chairs or benches for them. Their food was bread soaked in black coffee.

of eating and sleeping. Children barefoot in the mud. The plainest food—were bread and coffee *really* enough for those little ones? Only one family member spared from work long enough to learn English. Not a book, painting or musical instrument in sight. There were plenty of families like that in the western Dakotas, Ella knew, homesteaders struggling for a foothold on the frontier. Give the ambitious Zopstrachs another generation and they would catch up with the Bauers.

She wanted to discuss this with Quincy when they retired to the cubbyhole. But the peculiarities of the bunk under the eaves were not conducive to speculative conversation. First, it was irredeemably hard, a straw mattress on wooden slats. Second, it was exceedingly narrow. Ella got in and squeezed herself as close to the wall as she could. Third, it was disastrously frail. As Quincy followed, two of the slats splintered and sent him to the floor with a thud.

Hmm . . . what now? Quincy dragged an old trunk from the other side of the tiny room and shoved it under the broken section. Not high enough, but it would have to do.

"Quincy, I'm awfully cold. Can you find something to put on top of these thin blankets?"

Their own clothes were still too wet, and the saddle blankets hung dripping in the cowbarn. By the light of a candle stub he searched the closet and brought out a pair of pants, so ample of cut that they could belong only to Grossvater Zopstrach. They made a cozy coverlet, and after Quincy and Ella had developed a system of rolling uphill toward the wall to compensate for the steep outward slope of the disabled bunk, they passed a fairly comfortable night.

In the morning, having breakfasted on a repetition of last night's menu, they followed their usual procedure and requested some food to take along with them, before they asked for the bill (they wouldn't have the nerve afterward, if the host should say "No charge.") Kathy gave them half a dozen eggs and several potatoes. The going price of eggs was one cent apiece, ten cents a dozen.

"How much do we owe you altogether, for lodging and food?" asked Quincy.

Kathy consulted her mother. "*Ach,* she says you owe notting. It iss a pleasure."

"*Danke schoen.*" His accent wasn't perfect, but he had certainly said the right words. Grossmutter's ruddy face crinkled in a wide smile.

"*Bitte!*" She pressed Ella's hand warmly and called the rest of the family to say *auf wiedersehen.*

As she and Quincy rode away, Ella turned around for a final look, imprinting in her mind a picture of the unpainted house set in the miry farmyard without a tree or shrub to soften its bleakness, and nothing between it and the broken ranks of the hills except the cow barn, pigpen and windmill. But the whirling blades of the windmill caught the sunshine in a bright wheel of light, and the thirteen Zopstrachs, shouting their good wishes from the front steps, were smiling and undaunted. Kahtie, perched on Grossvater's shoulder, had only one fat little hand free to waggle. The other was in her mouth.

Ella whipped off her bandanna and waved vigorously. What kind people! She hoped they wouldn't have to wait a whole generation to catch up with the Bauers.

SUNDAY, JUNE 9 . . . *Rode 2 miles, found nice brook, good grazing, pretty thicket. Made camp for rest day. Rest day? Quincy put in time gathering brush for bed, setting tent, watering horses in hat, cleaning guns, cutting firewood. E darned socks, mended Q's rapidly disappearing trousers, wrote letter home, got dinner. Q rode Hike to ranch 1½ miles west for milk, bread and oats—paid 25¢ for same. After work was done, sat down to rest under trees. Thunderstorm pounced down immediately. We ran for tent. Hard rain. Tent began to leak in a dozen places. Rivulets on back of neck, under ponchos. E caught stream in hat, filled it twice. Began to soak up through the blankets from ground. When it let up just at sunset, we cooked and ate a hurried supper of bacon and coffee, and splashed through the mud to the ranch ... Good stalls for horses, hayloft for ourselves.*

No, Sunday wasn't much of a rest day. So on Tuesday, when they woke up in the sod house they had stumbled onto the night before, they debated trying again. They had made good distance on Monday, sixteen miles through Glen Ullin to Hebron in a little under five hours, then going on toward Antelope until they stopped at this deserted homestead with a slough, straw stack and plenty of wood.

"Let's stay," urged Ella. "We may never get another chance to play pioneer in a soddy. And besides, before I forget what they looked like, I want leisure to do a sketch of the Zopstrach youngsters lined up at the table, with Kahtie and her wayward spoon."

It turned out to be one of the happiest days. During its sunny, still hours, this was their private domain, hidden even from the nearest occupied ranch by the grassy swellings of the prairie. Ella took off her cumbersome skirt. She slipped the pins out of her dark hair and brushed it with long slow strokes, and left it free to sun awhile—she didn't want to risk a shampoo in the alkaline water from the slough.

It was like playing house to tidy up the blankets and stack the travel equipment on the hard-beaten earth floor of the tiny soddy. It measured only seven by eight feet, and a scant six feet high. The newspapers which had once covered the inside walls were hanging in festoons. The floor was cluttered with bits of straw and rubble, but it was "clean dirt." Compared with some of the rat-infested sheds where they had slept, downwind from a dead horse or a strewing of dead chickens, the little sod house ranked as fairly sanitary.

Ella got out the knapsack that held the pad and pencil, and looked through the drawings already filed away to serve as the basis for pen-and-ink and wash illustrations, among them

Ella sunned her hair in the dooryard of a deserted sod house in western North Dakota.

sketches of St. Paul's lugubrious cop, a team of fat Minnesota plowhorses, a mustached farmer smoking a corncob pipe, and his smug wife with a kerchief around her head. There was a silhouette of grain elevators against the evening sky, several views of the tent and campfire, and a dozen studies by Quincy of his favorite subject, horses. Today she would add two more sketches, the Zopstrachs and the sod house. A shame she couldn't make the finished drawing of the outdoor scene here and now, capturing the colors pulsing in the river of light that poured out of the clear prairie sky.

First, the house. She pencilled it in quickly, indicating the heavy wooden frame that held the door, the rough walls built of oblong chunks cut from the sod, and the ends of the cottonwood roof timbers showing between the wall and the mounded earthen roof. The bank had been dug out and the rear of the house set well into it so that only half of the sod wall showed above ground there. A few tangled clumps of grass sprouting from the roof added to the sense of this small dwelling as a natural growth, integral with the prairie. As she worked, Ella wondered if the woman who once lived here had come to feel part of the prairie too. Or had she looked out of the low doorway with the eyes of an alien? Did the sky beckon her forth to exult in its freedom, or drive her back into her burrow to hide from its enormity? From the sagebrush at the top of the bank a meadowlark was singing, its notes like a cascade of irridescent bubbles. Had the ranch wife once listened with joy to such bird-song, or had the music's crystal sweetness only made her more homesick for a place where there were trees for birds to sing in?

Speculations were interrupted by the crack of rifle fire. In a moment Quincy came long-legging over the slope, the Stevens .22 in his hand. "Those dratted rabbits! I swear I've shot at the same one fifteen times this morning. He always disappears just before I pull the trigger!"

Ella shook her head sympathetically and suggested a ride over to the nearby ranch to buy some supplies. She watched him go off on Hobo at an easy trot. She was glad of a little while to be alone. Now and then a break was needed—otherwise the many hours they had to spend together, day and night, could become too many. She had said in her latest letter to his parents, "If Quincy wasn't as amusing as any other four men, as patient as Job, as good-tempered as a summer day, as wholesome as a box of Grapenuts, and as altogether dear as only he can be, then it would grow terribly tiresome. But we are learning to understand and appreciate each other better every mile—and conditions are favorable for him to exercise all the virtues!"

While he was gone she did her sketch of the Zopstrach children, then packed away the drawing materials, pinned up her hair, and started a fire for lunch. Quincy returned with a news-paper parcel holding bread, eggs and potatoes, and a pail of milk from which a considerable amount had been slopped out.

"I brought you some highfalutin reading." He held out the wrapping from the parcel. "A snappy issue of the Sheboygan *Herald*, only a month out of date. Listen to the way things have been going in Wisconsin, according to the *Herald's* country cor-respondents. 'Wagner Bros. lost a colt lately on account of the botts, the animal's stomach was just full of the same . . . Marguerite and Neil Geolzer are getting along nicely from the effects of the measles . . . That dog which was kicked the other day nearly all over is going to come out all right just the same."

There were columns more to keep them chuckling through lunch. Afterward, Quincy tucked the newspaper into one of the saddlebags. "Got to preserve the evidence, otherwise nobody in New York will believe Sheboygan . . . Bunny—" As he turned back toward her, his face was sober. "Now that we're fortified with a little fun, I'd better tell you why our nice Mr. Lowell didn't ask for more than twenty-five cash on the trade. Hobo may be sound of limb, but not of wind. On my way over to the ranch, after he got warmed up, I galloped him full tilt to see about his speed. Well, he's a roarer."

"What does that mean?"

"He's wind-broken. Sometime in the past he's either been overworked or had a lung infection."

Ella was dismayed. "So we've got to start looking for another trade?"

"It all depends. If the problem isn't very bad, it won't bother him unless he's under a severe, prolonged strain. I think he'll work out all right at our pace. Have you noticed the distinction between him and Hike? Old Hike takes care of himself by sticking up for his rights and a little more, getting to the water first, picking the softest bit of ground to roll on. But you watch —Hobo's different. He takes care of himself by never doing a single darned thing he doesn't have to. He's a machine dedicated to the conservation of energy. He only galloped today because my heels gave him no peace. Maybe in a dim horsey way he knows his limits and wants to take no chances."

Ella scaled her opinion of Gus Lowell downward, though only slightly. He had said that, treated right, the strawberry roan would get them through Montana if any horse could. She still felt inclined to trust Lowell's assurance of the roan's general toughness. They would just have to treat him right.

They spent the afternoon napping and loafing. Quincy brought the journal up to date. Supper over, they let the campfire die. No need for extra light or warmth this bright June evening. Quincy, bemoaning having to leave his banjo in New York for lack of room on the saddlebow, pulled a strip of loose planking from the platform of the disabled pump, and pretended to be strumming the notes as he wandered from song to song. Sometimes Ella sang with him, sometimes she fell silent, listening half to him and half to the protesting chirps from the prairie dog village a hundred yards away. About a dozen plump gray burghers were alternately frisking and freezing to attention at the burrow door-ways. Then one by one they dived below to join their fellow villagers for the night.

The sun dropped behind the breast of the prairie. With its going, a small cool wind ran through the sage. Quincy leaned back and stared up into the sky. "Look! Isn't he glorious?"

A golden eagle, high enough above them to catch the last of the sun on his wings, was soaring homeward.

Ella watched until he was only a dot against the lemon-tinted west. "I hope he's happy with this day. I am."

In the night, stirring from a jumbled dream on the soddy floor, Ella heard the nervous yip-yip of coyotes nearby, and felt a thrill of kinship between herself, the passer-by, and the prairie wife who had been wakened nights on end by that eerie cry.

VI

"In all my traffels, I neffer seen no skeenery like dem Patlants. Id peets all."

A German homesteader, whose ranch beyond Belfield bordered the eastern edge of the North Dakota Badlands, was ready to oblige when Quincy and Ella stopped to ask his opinion of the topography.

"Hell with the fires out—that's how General Sully described it," said Quincy.

"Ja? Vell, nod all der fires iss out. Some of dem dark streaks in der hills iss coal, lignite. Maybe der lightning set it on fire a long time ago. Some places iss still burning. You vill notice der schmoke. Der pink color or der red color iss vere der clay next to der fire gets baked. From here a vays, id iss nod so spectacoolar. But after you cross der river id peets all."

The sculptor of the masterpiece was the Little Missouri, a stream whose tracings wrinkled across the map like fine accordion-pleating. Beginning eons ago as a small drainage rill in the high prairie, it had eaten its way down through hundreds of feet of earth and rock, drawing into its course the scouring tongues of tributary rills, and turning the southwest corner of the state into a phantasmagoria of domes, pyramids, ridges, mesas, canyons and cones.

Not far beyond the ranch the road began dropping below the level of the prairie tableland, twisting and looping to take advantage of the ravines that opened between the steep-sided buttes. It was a lonesome road—the "locals" went by train when possible.

"I suppose it takes a couple of Eastern romantics like us to

What Ella didn't know about horses, she was learning by necessity.

enjoy this," mused Quincy, urging Hike into a trot along one of the rare flat stretches. "Assuming you *are* enjoying it."

For himself, he found it exhilarating. But that was his mood anyhow on this Saturday afternoon in mid-June. He was fairly sure his pants would hold together until he got the new pair his mother was mailing to Terry. And he had money in his pocket again. The thirty dollars had been waiting in Dickinson. After buying groceries, a new open-blade razor and another canteen, there was plenty left to give him a propertied feeling. He hadn't liked being quite so close to penniless as they had been between New Salem and Dickinson. Another day, and any offer he made to pay for food or lodging would have been pure bluff.

Presently he and Ella dismounted to give the horses a rest and themselves a break after several hours in the saddle. Footing it along the narrow stony road, they began to play a favorite game, choosing a color of the landscape and naming the pigments that could be mixed on a palette to reproduce it. In the Badlands, with the earth exposed in variegated layers, this was a pastime that could go on indefinitely. But it soon became difficult because Hobo walked more and more lazily, increasing the distance between Quincy and Ella until they had trouble hearing each other. Finally Ella called out, "This Hobo is no good at all! I'll bet if I yelled at him suddenly, he'd fall over."

"Try it."

"BOO!"

Hobo promptly collapsed, landing on his back, legs cocked up at comical angles. They let him rest until they were through laughing.

When he was on his feet again they got into the saddles, for within the next few miles they would reach Medora, which could be entered appropriately only on horseback. It must have been through a sly jest of history that the rough-tough little cow town had been founded by a French marquis, named for the daughter of a Wall Street banker, and made famous by an Eastern dude in precarious health, Teddy Roosevelt.

As no man is a hero to his valet, so no great man is completely great to his cartoonist. Roosevelt was President now, and Quincy's political caricatures of him had been appearing in the newspapers for several years—the mustache and the "bully for you" grin, the pince-nez glasses rakishly astride the nose, the big stick carried behind the broad back. Somewhere in those years Quincy's adolescent admiration for T. R. had been diluted, and he had not expected to be impressed by the scenes where young Teddy had once played cowboy. But today, threading mile after mile of rumpled Badlands, he found himself thinking, "This is no sissy country. To ride and hunt here, even as a dude, would take grit and guts." Much of his early respect for Roosevelt was returning.

And there at last, around a bend where road and railway ran parallel, was T. R.'s town. Medora dozed in the late afternoon quiet, a handful of buildings on the flat, shaded by a scattering of lordly cottonwoods. The yellow-gray bluffs rose steep behind it, and steep again on the opposite bank of the Little Missouri. The Marquis de Moraes' dream of making this town the center of a great beef-raising and shipping industry had been a brief one, but the yellow chimney he raised for his packing plant still thrust up into the sky, a giant exclamation point at the end of his North Dakota story.

Quincy's pulse quickened and he pressed Hobo into a lope as they swung into town. Would it be standing yet, the wooden building whose name Roosevelt took for his troops in Cuba? Yes, on the corner. The Rough Riders Hotel, two floors high, with its pairs of narrow windows set along each side, and the front angle skived off so that the double doors faced diagonally across the street. Ella and Quincy tied their horses and walked in. Quincy found himself pulling his hat lower on his brow and fingering the handle of his revolver. So might he have swaggered through this doorway in the 1880's, a hard-riding, straight-shooting cowhand, thirsty from the roundup, equally ready for fun or trouble. It was a bit of play-acting not to be resisted, a moment of make-believe to make himself believe that he was really here.

He had come, however, not to stand drinks for the boys, but to buy a loaf of bread. The Rough Riders lobby now housed the general store. That brought him down to earth. Quietly he asked the young man behind the counter about the Little Missouri. "We heard back in Belfield that the bottom's shifty, and full of quicksand. How do we cross in this high water?"

"I'm new here. Ask Old Mac—Michael McDonald." The clerk nodded toward the cool interior of the room where a man sat in an alcoholic doze, his chair tilted back against the wall.

When Quincy spoke to him, he blinked his rheumy blue eyes awake and tipped his hat deferentially to Ella. It was a tan felt hat with a large, smooth, round crown, rather like a chamber pot, inverted. Beneath the wide brim showed a fringe of white hair. Old Mac had a straight neat nose, and a mustache, still with traces of its original fiery red color, that right angled down from each corner of his upper lip. His grimy shirt was collarless, and his dark worsted suit looked as if it hadn't been taken off night or day for the last five years. But none of that embarrassed Michael McDonald or lessened his childlike pleasure in being addressed by two young strangers.

"Crossin' the river? Now, look here, I donno ye, an' ye donno me. I niver see ye afore, an' ye niver see me afore, but—un'stan', I'm tellin' ye as a fren'—I'd niver go in the river!"

"Is it too deep?" said Ella.

"Well, ye're doin' it, 'tis yer business, but as a fren', go in if ye want to, but thin again, ye might not come out."

"Then how about the railroad bridge?" persisted Quincy. "Can't we get the horses across on that?"

"There's some has done it. There's some has done it. But here's the best thing to do, 'tis simpil. Ye walk down the track, and ye look at the bridge. Ye go down here, an' ye look at the river. Ye're doin it, young felly—I'm tellin' ye as a fren'—ye look at the bridge, an' ye look at the river. There's the bridge, an' there's the river. Take yer ch'ice, but don't ye go in the river!"

To his counsel Old Mac added an invitation to put up overnight at his cabin on the opposite bank. "Ye can cross afoot all right, seein' there's a plank and a railing to one side of the ties. 'Tis yer horses that'll cause ye trouble, the plank's that narrow."

Quincy left Ella to accept the offer while he went to the little railroad station to find out if any trains would be coming along in the next half-hour.

"Four overdue right now." The paunchy agent stopped riffling through his bills of lading long enough to stare out of the window as if he expected trains from both directions to be in sight.

"Well, if one came while we were on the bridge with our horses, couldn't the engineer see us in time to stop?"

"Not a chance. No, sir. Not coming from either east or west, because of the grades."

That was grim news, particularly about a piece of track that had a concealing curve at each end. Quincy silently debated the risks. The trains might be along in two minutes—or two hours. But there was a smell of thunderstorms in the air and he was anxious to reach the other side of the river and the shelter of Old Mac's cabin. When a bystander in the station, introducing himself as Drummond, offered to help with the horses, Quincy decided to go ahead. Drummond looked as if he could handle his share. He was a lean dark whip of a man in dusty boots and levis. High cheekbones and a wide firm mouth betokened a Sioux grandmother and perhaps a Scotch grandfather.

He and Quincy brought the horses to the near end of the bridge. Old Mac, who had trailed along, was given the job of holding Hike while Ella and the other men started across with Hobo. The bridge was single-tracked, with nothing between the rails except the cross-ties. At one side ran the plank footway, protected by a light handrailing. Quincy's practiced eye told him that the bridge was actually not very far above the river, but when he got out there, balancing on the ties, and looked down into the churning yellow current, he had a flash of vertigo that almost cost him his footing. He could sympathize with Hobo's trembling hesitancy.

Drummond, who had taken horses over before, gave the orders. While Ella inched along the footplank leading Hobo, Quincy and Drummond braced their feet against the track and leaned with all their force against Hobo's side and haunch to push him toward the handrail and keep his hind feet on the plank. Hobo wanted nothing to do with the walkway—it was too close to the fearsome edge. But he couldn't be allowed to shrink away or his legs would plunge between the ties.

About halfway across, Hobo's proclivity for doing things the easiest way took over. It was less effort to stay on the plank than to resist the pressure on his rump, and he followed Ella safely to the other side, where she was left to hold him.

Quincy took a quick look both ways along the track.

"No train yet. Let's get the other horse."

Hike had been snorting and rearing, giving Old Mac a bad time. Quincy arrived in a sweat of impatience tinged with anxiety. Hike, smelling it, turned stubborn with fright of his own when they finally pushed him onto the bridge. Since Old Mac, after his four-day binge in Dickinson, wasn't in shape to help, Quincy sent him on ahead and led the horse himself, leaving Drummond to keep Hike's hindquarters shoved close to the rail.

But Hike was too strong. A third of the way across he crowded away from the edge. His hind shoes clicked over the tracking and he went down to his stifles between the ties. My God, could they possibly heave him back on his feet before he broke his legs? And what could they do if a train came now? Quincy and Drummond exchanged desperate glances.

But Hike was cooler than either man. Carefully and gently he was pulling himself up, first one leg and then the other. Just as he stood tremulously upright again, bruised and skinned but ready to go, Drummond pointed back toward Medora. A stream of gray-white smoke trailed above the curving bluff.

Hike could be mulish and unpredictable. But he was smart enough to learn from his mistakes. From there on, he kept his feet on the planking. The train itself was visible now, snaking around the bluff at the far side of town. Quincy saw the plume of steam against the smoke before he heard the warning whistle, and increased the pace as much as he dared. Fifty feet to go . . . thirty-five . . . thirty . . . The steel rails whined, and Drummond was salting his grunts with curses. They got Hike off the bridge less than a minute before the train thundered by.

Ella said, "I couldn't bear to look, that last ten feet."

Drummond accepted Quincy's earnest thanks as if close shaves were all in his day's work. Perhaps they were. He touched his finger to his hatbrim and started walking back across the bridge to Medora. Old Mac stood silently watching until he made it to the other end, then waved his hand in the opposite direction.

"Now I'm goin' to show ye the goddamnedest shanty ye ever set eyes on, beggin' the ol' lady's pardin. I been to Dicki'son fer a few days—it's all right—I'm drunk, ma'am, if ye don't mind."

Even after pulses and breathing returned to normal, reaction to the narrowness of their escape persisted in Ella and Quincy as a kind of giddy light-heartedness. Funny things were funnier, and everything looked, sounded, tasted and smelled double strength. The hours with Old Mac that followed could never be forgotten.

Apologies notwithstanding, the shingled cabin was haven

enough to travelers who could see a blue-black thunderhead rising over the bluff behind it. Mac pointed out a makeshift shed where they could put the horses, but before they unsaddled, he conducted them to the well and drew up drinks all around.

" 'Tis the finest water in the state. Ye'll find no more like it, not between the Rocky Mountains."

After horses and humans had all they could drink—and Mac was right about its being fine water—the old man put his hand on the wooden curbing of the well. "Now, we're here. Ye're here an' I'm here, an' I'll answer any questions ye ask me, in a social way, un'stan'. Am I right?"

"Dead right," said Ella.

At the cabin door, Mac paused. "Well, here 'tis. Ye might say it's me home, but I call it—well, I live here, that's all. I live here."

"How long?" asked Quincy.

"Oh, dammit, twinty years, beggin' the ol' lady's pardin. But come inside an' we'll talk awhile an' have some supper. An' we'll fix ye up fer a place to sleep. There's me ol' bed. Ye wouldn't be wantin' that—more bugs than blankets. I'll make ye a shakedown in the little room back there. Go in an' look at it. Say, ye're man an' wife, ain't ye? Shure? I took ye so—it's all right."

In the kitchen he continued. "Now, there's the cubberd over there, an' there's the stove. I ain't hungry meself. Nothin' ever sets on me stomach no more, only whiskey. I can't ate. The dishes ain't washed—I have only meself to ate after—but there's water in the pail, if ye're patic'ler. Set down, Mr.—?"

"Scott."

"Mr. Scott, set down, an' we'll talk, an' watch the ol' lady do the cookin'."

"How do you make out for your cooking when you're here alone?" said Ella.

"Oh, I'm a ol' lumberjack. I used to cook all me life. I cooked fer the big lumber camps in Minnesoty. I got childer there in St. Paul now. I try to get me daughter to come an' live wid me, but she won't do it. I run away from home whin I was a kid in Ireland. Yes, I ain't a bachelor. I'm a widdy man. I had a wife died on me, an' two babies, in the Eighties. She was good to me.

"Well, here 't is. Ye might say it's me home." Old Mac posed in front of his shanty on the Little Missouri River at Medora, N.D.

If she'd a lived, I wouldn't be like this now. But I'm lonesome. A man shouldn't be livin' by his goddam self—beggin' the ol' lady's pardin. Now, if I could only get someone to have me—"

"Why don't you?" suggested Ella, who by now was sudsing off Mac's dishes and kettles and laying out food for supper.

"Well, there was a widdy woman around here onct awhile back, an' she was all right too, I guess. But she moved away, an' negoshiations kinda dropped. Will ye have whiskey, Mr.—?"

"Scott."

"Mr. Scott. No? Ah, ye're damn right. Now, if I'd a let it alone, I'd give a dollar. It's hell, beggin' the ol' lady's pardin."

Presently Ella announced that supper was ready. At first Old

Mac would have nothing, but after a few minutes he took a cup of tea, and then accepted a slice of bacon and small helpings of canned corn and mashed potatoes. Ella tried to press more upon him.

"Don't crowd me, don't crowd me! I'm doin' first rate, don't crowd me. 'Tis the first I've ate hardly anythin' fer a long time. 'Tis not the same when ye don't cook it yerself. Och, a man shouldn't be livin' by himself, an' that's the truth."

There was a sadness in the old man's voice that moved Quincy as much as the reeking brogue delighted him. But as Mac responded to the pleasure of having someone to talk to, the sadness was absorbed into his rising humor, and he didn't let his respectfulness to Ella hamper his style.

Quincy asked him if he had known Teddy Roosevelt.

"Him that's Prisidint? Shure. Ate off'n the same damn plate wid him, as the felly says. We niver knew in them days where he'd be gittin' to. Am I right?"

He was much interested in Quincy's plan to write a book about the summer's journey.

"Och, writin', that's a rale accomplishmint. Puts me in mind of a lad we had around here. They made him clerk o' the county, he could write that well. He was dead on one side—you know, paratic—had to write wid his left hand, but my God, how he could scratch! If ye're goin' to be writin' now, jist tell them ye saw Old Mac at Medory. They'll know."

"Have you lived in this cabin ever since you came out west?" said Ella, filling the teacups all around.

"Shure, except I've traveled some. I was to Hunter's Hot Springs where all the rich wimmin goes to git themselves patched up and pickled. They got waters there, ye know, an' medicine mud. Och, I felt sorry for all the ol' ladies, rollin' around in that stuff! Their back is give out, belly give out, legs give out, an' they goes there to git mended. Fine wimmin, some o' them. Diamin's up one finger an' down the other. I used to be great fren's wid them. Och, I'd go talk to them when they was a-drinkin' their waters. One o' them says to me onct, 'What's yer name?' 'McDonald,' I says, 'an' what's *yer* name?' She laughed—

she didn't think I'd be askin' her—but she answers, 'My name's Drinkwater.' 'Well,' says I, 'ye fill the bill.' Yes, good times there, but it's all changed. Everythin's changed. Even this goddam town, beggin' the ol' lady's pardin."

Mac pushed back from the table and took a very small sip of tea, shaking his head. "Medory used to be on this side of the river. Begun as a camp for sojers who was a-keepin' the Injuns from pickin' off the track-layers for the N. P. They called the town Little Missouri then, which was proper, it bein' on the river o' that name. But where is it now? On the other side, dammit. Am I right? That's the truth. It all moved over there when Markis de Moraes put up his packin' plant. An' there niver was hardly a critter killed in the plant, ye might say, but the damn town didn't come back."

Quincy offered to wash the dishes, but Mac dissented. "Look here," he said, pointing an argumentative finger at Ella, "ye know yer own trough, don't ye?"

"Yes," she smiled.

"Well, then, why be wastin' time washin' when we're jist goin' to turn around and ate breakfast out of the same in the mornin'?"

The electrical storm blew on to the northeast, treating the cabin in passing to a dozen deafening booms of thunder and a brief rain squall. By bedtime the sky was clear. The evening star winked down on Quincy from the western bluffs as he walked through the wet grass to the stable to check on Hobo and Hike. On his way back to the cabin he glanced across the narrow flat to the river and the bridge, still visible in the late dusk. He shuddered. Merciful God, that had been a close thing this afternoon! Ella had been apprehensive about what might happen in the Badlands. Well, it had happened. She could rest easy. Or was there something else waiting?

In the morning it was hard to leave, so earnestly did Old Mac plead with Quincy and Ella to stay. He sat on the bench outside his door watching them pack up.

"Dammit, I'll be as lonesome as hell when ye're gone. Ye don't know how it does a felly good to have someone to talk to—some-one, that is, as'll listen to him. I don't know what, after ye're away from here. I suppose I'll go an' get drunk again, dammit. But if ye must be on, why, ye're doin' it—I'm yer fren'. Good luck to ye, as the felly said."

He insisted that they help themselves to potatoes from his root cellar and canned vegetables from his kitchen. "I can't ate anyhow, and ye'll be hungry. 'Tis a long ride to Sentinel Butte. Ye go up through the notch there, and folly the damn road." He walked with them to the gate. "Hell, now, I wisht ye would stay wid me. But if it's ye're business to go, good luck to ye.'

He stood aimlessly about for a few minutes after they rode away. Then habit came to his rescue. The last they saw of him, he was starting across the railroad bridge toward his chair in the Rough Riders Hotel.

Quincy couldn't figure out where or why he had branched off on the wrong road. They has passed the cellar holes that were the only remaining evidence of Little Missouri, the original town, and glimpsed the Chateau de Moraes, the twenty-eight-room ranch house built by the Marquis atop the western bluff. They had walked the horses between hillsides spiked with yucca, and then trotted for awhile as the road began its intermittent twisting climb toward the far edge of the Badlands.

There were places where the track dwindled to no more than a pair of ruts, and it wasn't until the pair they were following petered out completely that Quincy realized they were lost.

"I remember several forks, and at the last one we bore to the right. That means the main road is south of us, so we'll just zig across country until we intersect it." He took a compass reading— on this brilliantly sunny day he could have done about as well with his watch and a matchstick shadow—and they launched out through the nearest gully that headed south.

R-r-r-r-r-r!

Hike sprang sideways on three legs. The forefoot that had been about to come down on a rattlesnake hit a clump of harmless bunchgrass. Quincy was jounced to his back teeth. The snake lay tensely coiled, half-hidden in the mouth of a prairie dog hole. Quincy pulled the .45 Colt and put a bullet neatly through the triangular mottled head. When Ella was sure the snake was quite beyond doing any damage, she dismounted to count the rattles.

"Fourteen. Sounded more like forty! Lucky for Hike they were working. I suppose we'll have to be on the lookout from here on, especially when we make camp."

Over a ridge and down another gully they passed a hot spot where an exposed bed of lignite burned with a yellow-white flame licking between cracks in the glowing coal and sending up wisps of the "schmoke" the German rancher had predicted they would see.

"A perfect place to broil our steak for Sunday supper," said Quincy, "except that it's not suppertime and we have no steak."

Beyond the third ridge they came to the railway. After following the track for a couple of miles without finding any sign of the main trail, they took off southward again. Presently they reached a creek bottomland varying in width from a hundred yards to a mile. The stream wandered half-underground, surfacing in long narrow pools bordered by spring-green grass and slender cottonwoods. A woodpecker was beating out a tattoo at the top of a splintered tree. Swallows pirouetted in an airy ballet. Quincy called Ella to show her the creekside paw-prints of a raccoon. But the riders had to choose their way carefully through this pretty place. Some of the alkali mud, sun-dried to a white crust, had formed deceptive patches over quicksand.

Ella was in the lead when they came to a narrowing of the valley that forced them to cross the creek. The stream was only ten feet wide here, and the banks looked solid. She urged Hobo into the water, Quincy following. On his second stride, Hobo began to sink. Quincy reined Hike short. Only his front legs were in and he pivoted back to safety. But Hobo was in with all fours, unable to turn. His vigorous plunging mired him deeper.

"Whip him across!" yelled Quincy.

Ella laid on the quirt. Hobo was belly deep but still moving his legs. The quag clutched at him with greedy sucking noises.

Quincy, unconsciously straining his own muscles to impart extra push to Hobo, saw the mud closing over the horse's rump as he bogged down to the left.

"Jump, Bunny, jump!"

She hadn't waited for the cry. As Hobo tilted, she threw herself into the creek, still holding the reins, and floundered toward the farther bank. Quincy frantically loosened his lariat to throw to her, but before he could get it free she had reached solid ground and was tugging with all her might on the reins.

Freed of her weight and aided by her pulling, Hobo righted himself and came lunging out with great snortings and splashings. Except for his head and saddle, the evil-smelling gray mud covered him completely.

The crossing had taken a few seconds over a minute, but Quincy felt as shaken and weak as though he had been through an hour-long crisis. Yesterday it was Ella who had to wait while disaster rumbled toward him. This morning it had been his turn to watch in aching helplessness. He damned himself for letting her go into the water first, for not testing the crossing before committing the horses, for not paying out a safety line, and for general inexperience. Some of his inexperience had just been abruptly cured.

Now, here they were, Ella and Hobo on one bank, himself and Hike on the other, with ten feet of quicksand in between.

"Let's go a little farther down the creek," he said after some thought. They found a place about as wide, but shallower. Ella threw her lariat across. He knotted it to his rope and tossed one end back to her. The other end he put around Hike's neck, secured with a bowline hitch so it wouldn't act as a slipnoose. Using the rope for a handline, Quincy waded out to test the bottom. The mud was belt-deep, but it held his weight. Hopefully it would support the horse.

Having looped a knot in Hike's tail to give a firm grip, Quincy signaled Ella to start hauling. Into the water they went, Hike first, and Quincy hanging to his tail with one hand and applying the quirt with the other.

It worked. Though Hike's struggles left them both liberally

decorated with slime, they got across to Ella without stopping.

None of the other three could compare with Hobo for the hand-dipped look. His tail was reduced to clothes-pole size and hung heavy and stiff. Everything tied to the saddle below the level of his back was coated too. As the hot sun dried the plastering on the horses, their body movements cracked it off in heavy flakes. But Hobo's tail was too heavily encased to switch itself free. The cast baked so hard that eventually Quincy had to knock it loose with the revolver butt.

He said little to Ella as they scraped some of the mud from their clothes and equipment and started on, walking to give the horses a chance to dry. Twice death had brushed close, and this morning Quincy felt none of the exuberance that had followed the escape at the bridge. There he had taken a deliberate risk, hustled like mad to pull it off, and felt entitled to cheer when he beat the odds. But the quicksands had menaced in a different way, sly and devouring in their treachery. He didn't want to talk about it, not yet. The stink of the slime on his clothes was too strong a reminder of his heartsick impotence in that moment when Ella seemed trapped beyond rescue.

Where the valley merged into another run-off system they came to an abandoned ranch and stopped for a trail lunch. Three men on horseback, driving a herd of range cattle, moved into sight half a mile ahead. Quincy rode out to ask directions.

"You come to the right spot," said one of the men, grinning. "This here's the main road we're on. You just follow it up west and it'll bring you to Sentinel Butte in about three hours."

It took them nearer five. The afternoon was oppressively hot and the horses sluggish. But the leisurely pace was all right, for the Badlands, as if to atone for two near disasters in twenty-four hours, staged a panoramic picture show.

During midday, with the sun nearly at the zenith, the "skeenery" had been more desolate than dramatic. But as the afternoon shadows began to spread and the leveling light reflected directly off the steep-sided ravines, the colors warmed to life: yellow, lavender, umber, olive, magenta, ocher, gray, and white, layered with brown lignite and the pinks and reds of hard-baked scoria.

Cedars, growing in the clefts, provided a contrast of dark green. There was bright new green grass in the gully bottoms. And over the flanks of the buttes and pillars and mesas, myriads of erosion channels forked downward in delicate purple veining.

"Quincy, how are you going to describe all this in the book?"

"I've been worrying about that. It will use up an awful lot of adjectives. Maybe I'll just have to quote our rancher and say, 'Id peets all.' "

They halted on the last hundred yards of grade and looked back. They had now climbed flush with the main sweep of the prairie, and what they saw, except for the gulches at their feet, was thirty miles of plain, criss-crossed with long, rock-edged streaks, all that was visible of the deep-slashed canyons scoring the Badlands from one end to the other. Quincy found it hard to realize that, concealed in one of the distant streaks, the Little Missouri stormed along past Medora, four hundred feet below the prairie top. And that equally well hidden, somewhere between here and there, a pretty little valley lay quiet in the evening shadows, innocently reflecting the still-bright sky wherever the stream surfaced to cover the quicksands of a shallow pool.

VII

Montana!

Five hundred miles of it, rolling out ahead of them sky-wide and handsome. At the far border they would be across the High Plains and the Continental Divide. For Ella Montana was the heart of the journey, on the map and in her mind. The cachet to pit themselves against it had been bestowed yesterday by a photographer at Beach, the last town in North Dakota. "It's not often I see real cowboys—let me take your picture for my souvenir postcards." If they looked as trail-hardened as all that, Ella thought, maybe their six weeks in the saddle had toughened them enough to meet Montana's hazards.

The first thing the state taught them was that the Badlands didn't end with North Dakota. Glendive Creek had gouged out the same kind of landscape on a smaller scale. The stream doubled back on itself so many times in the day's ride that Quincy was reminded of the question asked by the old lady who was serving at a church pancake supper. "She tilted the syrup jug over each diner's plate in turn and said, 'Will you take it crinkle-crankle or poured all over?'"

The quicksand was as tricky here as on the Dakota side. With Sunday's experience still sending warning shudders along their nerves, they tested out each ford cautiously. At a place where the crinkle-crankle had left a stony beach shelving firmly into the water, they made a noonday stop and peeled off their clothes to take the first all-over bath in three weeks. What pure pleasure to soap away the grime and sweat and mud, to splash and shout, and wade back to dry in the sun! Ella let the breeze define the contours of her flesh as it divided and flowed around the solidity of her neck, her breasts and waist and hips. It stirred the faint hairs on her legs and forearms, outlining with cool fingers the edges of her body.

"Bunny—" The fingers that touched her now were warm and firm, Quincy's mouth was eager on her lips. Edges blurred, dissolved, blended . . .

The afternoon's riding repeated the morning pattern, except that as the creek broadened toward its confluence with the Yellowstone River, fording became more risky. Near suppertime Quincy and Ella came to a great looping oxbow. Rather than wade it twice and cut across the intervening neck of land, Quincy suggested it would be safer to stay on the same side and follow around the curve. But at the far end, when they had plunged down the rocky bank and scrambled along its base, a barricade of fallen cottonwoods stopped them. It took half an hour of perspiring persuasion to coax Hobo across. He had to climb up over a tangle of roots, jump a log, slide with sprawling hoofs over a steep boulder, and land in a pile of stones. It was done with no grace, but Ella gave him an approving pat for doing it at all.

Hike absolutely refused to try, even for a bribe of oats. Quincy put a rope around his neck, took a half-hitch on a tree, and inched him up to the barrier, but he fought so hard that he had to be eased off for fear of breaking his legs in the crisscrossed logs. Ella saw that Quincy was near exhaustion, and was relieved when he finally shouted, "We'll have to tie Hike and leave him here to think it over."

They took the other horse to the top of the low bluff and picketed him in the grass. There was water and forage, and now that Ella had become as particular as Quincy about those two requisites, she wasted no time wondering if there were a prettier or more comfortable site nearby, but started cooking supper. While she washed up afterward, Quincy went down to the creek for another session with Hike. He came back alone.

"That goldarned bronco's still determined not to join us. He's feeling deserted and abused, and he knows the oats are on this side, but he won't surrender. You've got to admire a horse with a will, or a won't, like that."

Hike's forlorn nickering continued long after Quincy and Ella settled down on the cut sagebrush that cushioned their blankets and pungently scented the dusk. About three o'clock the next morning, as moonlight was fading, Ella awakened to the yipping of a coyote. Quincy fired his pistol into the air to scare him off.

"Take another snooze, Bunny. I'm going after Hike." He carried a hatful of oats with him.

In a few minutes Ella heard a frantic, welcoming whinny. She stayed awake until Quincy appeared on the bluff-top, silhouetted against the graying east, Hike docile at his heels. When the horse had been picketed near Hobo and given another handful of oats, Quincy slithered in beside Ella with a sigh.

"The rascal had chewed the bark off the tree where he was tied, above and below, as far as he could reach. And he had pawed a hole in the ground bigger than a bushel basket. He was lonesome, cold, hungry and trembling. When I unfastened him and gave a tug on the rope, he went over those roots and logs as nimbly as a flea. I could almost hear him quoting Old Mac, 'Oh, well, ye're doin' it—I'm yer fren'.' "

This tussle of wills was the shifting point in the relationship with Hike. Previously he had been, if not an enemy, at least a very reluctant and often sullen co-traveler. Now they felt that he *was* their friend. Something happened down there in the shivery damp of the creek bottom to win him from rebellion into partnership. Quincy and Ella speculated about it during the day, as the change became more evident. "You faced him down," said Ella. "You made him climb over those logs, and he finally accepted you as the boss."

"That may be part of it," Quincy conceded. "But it's more than that. He's decided we're worthy of his confidence. I'm sure he thought—if horses can be said to think—that we had abandoned him permanently, leaving him in the fix his orneriness had got him into. When I came back in the morning, he was so surprised it was pathetic. 'By golly,' he says to himself, 'these people do have hearts after all! I've been a dodgasted fool not to trust them.' "

Just beyond the town of Glendive, Quincy and Ella passed

over the Yellowstone on a substantial bridge, and just beyond the bridge a thunderstorm drove them to a roadside cabin. The door was unlocked and nobody home, so they hitched the horses and went in. Ella noticed a pile of potatoes in the corner.

"Those are choice-looking spuds. When the owner comes back, let's ask for some."

"Sure, and if he doesn't come back, we'll just assume that if he had, he'd have been very generous."

The owner didn't return, but three of his neighbors, footing it out from town, came pouring into the cabin for shelter, shaking water from the coats they had been holding over their heads, and stamping the mud from their feet. In the presence of these witnesses, Ella was shy about expropriating the potatoes. She waited until the rain slackened and Quincy inveigled the men outside to look at Hike and Hobo and the travel equipment. Then Ella popped as many potatoes into her khaki breeches as she thought they would hold. The divided skirt camouflaged the lumps fairly well. She went out, moving with very short steps to the post where Hobo was tied, and beckoned to Quincy.

"You'll have to help me into the saddle," she whispered. "I took too many spuds."

The neighbors, unsuspicious, let them go with a nonchalant wave. Hike and Hobo set off at a fast trot, but after a couple of jounces, Ella reined in. She was half laughing, half moaning. "We'll have to walk the horses. I wasn't built to be a human potato masher."

"Just as soon as we get out of sight over that hill, we'll unload you."

Just over the hill, however, they were joined by a sociably drunk sheepman who insisted on keeping them company. Even at a walk, Ella was in acute discomfort. Some of the potatoes were under her in the seat of her breeches, some were lodged along the inside of her thighs and knees. With each motion of Hobo's, she winced. After three miles, when she thought she couldn't stand it any longer, the sheepman tired of holding to their slow pace and galloped on. Ella stood up in the stirrups, loosened her waistband, and fished out the potatoes one by one for Quincy to stow in a saddlebag. He was yahooing with laughter as he buckled the flap on the last potato. She looked at him reproachfully.

"All right, it *is* funny, and after my bruises heal I'll join you in a good long haw-haw. But don't you dare say it will make good copy for the book!"

Quincy atoned the next day by stopping in a small gully to carve on its sandstone bank his initials with hers, enclosed in the outline of a heart.

They were on their way up the Yellowstone, southwesterly toward Fallon and Terry. Once this had been buffalo country. But the men who spent their summers cutting wood to fuel the Yellowstone steamboats had to keep busy at something the rest of the year, and shooting buffalo for hides and tongues was profitable. When the 1880's were gone, so were the great herds. The cattlemen had already moved in, and after them came the sheepmen, and more recently the "honyockers," the land-hungry immigrants and Midwesterners who were dotting the landscape with their frail tar paper shacks and turning this into grain country. Cattle and sheep still cropped the grama and buffalo grasses and picked their way past the mounded burrows of prairie dog villages, but the range was being broken up by fences. All along the valley spread the wide counterpanes of greening wheat.

For Hike it was a homecoming.

"What's that brand on the black horse? Sixteen?" A redheaded rancher had stopped Quincy and Ella at his gate on the second morning and offered them a drink of fresh milk. While they filled their cups from his pail, he leaned closer to Hike and ran his freckled hand over the outline of the figure branded on the left hip. "Yeah, that's Sixteen all right. Did you buy the horse around here somewhere?"

"No, at St. Paul," answered Quincy.

"Then he's sure traveled some. But he's right back where he started. Sixteen was Joe Sweetman's brand, and this ground we're standing on is part of Joe's old ranch."

Hike was tossing his head restlessly, clinking the bit to indicate it was time to move on. If it made any difference to him to be home again, he didn't show it. But the discovery pleased Ella. It gathered together the happenings and sensations scattered over all the miles behind her and strung them on a cord tying the drafty sale barn in South St. Paul to this ranch above the Yellowstone, shimmering green and gold in the heat of a June day. Hike was no longer a nobody from nowhere. He was a Montana bronco. He had once belong here on the Sweetman spread, and now she knew the origin of the '16' she had traced with puzzled fingers.

Late that afternoon she and Quincy walked their sweating horses up the dusty street of Terry, looking for the postoffice. Since their last mail stop, at Bismarck, they had covered two hundred and fifty miles, and done it in well under the three weeks Quincy had predicted.

The postoffice was closed, but the postmaster interrupted his supper at home to come down and open up. "I been wondering who this Quincy Scott was," he said genially. "Seems like almost every day something's been coming in addressed to you folks. Even got a couple of packages for you."

They stopped at the general store to buy grub and a hand axe to replace "George Washington," lost the night before at Crackerbox Creek. Then they went down to the bank of the Yellowstone to make camp on a strip of steeply-sloping beach. They had lunched that day on three pigeons bagged by Quincy with the small rifle near Fallon. Tonight the entree was fried jackrabbit. They opened their postoffice haul in front of the campfire. Film in one package, a pair of bright new khaki breeches in the other, and letters, letters, letters! Ella's sister Jessie had written urging the travelers not to delay. She wasn't sure how far into August she could stay in Seattle.

Quincy tried on his new pants in the morning. Exerting all his push and pull, he had just forced his legs into them and was testing whether he could sit down to breakfast without splitting the seams when Hike and Hobo jumped an improvised brush barrier and whisked up the slope, heading for the fields and gullies beyond.

"What's wrong with those goldarned ponies?" Quincy started after them on the run.

Ella was laughing as she went to help him tie the horses when he finally led them back. "It must have been 'them yaller pants' that spooked the horses. And I wish you'd seen yourself—they're so tight you ran like a pair of rusty scissors!"

He gave her a pained look. "All right, now we're even, Mrs. Potato Pants." He started undoing buttons. "There's only one way for me to get rid of these instruments of torture. I'm trading them off to you. Your trousers are bigger, and they're men's style anyhow, and they're still in good condition, thanks to the protection of your skirt."

After they had packed up they led the horses down to the ferry. It was much like the craft on which they had crossed at Fallon yesterday, a shallow wooden scow covered with a railed platform and operated by cables. The ferryman was lounging against the side, his battered felt hat tilted low against the early sun.

"Lord, yes, any ranch'll feed you." He stopped picking his teeth long enough to answer Quincy's question about food supplies on the way to the Musselshell valley. "Where you headin' for in particular?"

"Helena. We'd planned originally to keep to the Yellowstone as far as Custer, but we're anxious to reach Seattle while my sister-in-law is still there on vacation. A man here in town told us we'd save time to turn west at Miles City and follow the C. M. and St. P. railroad construction route."

The ferryman tossed his toothpick over the railing and spat after it as it bobbed away on the muddy current. "You'd do even better to strike straight from here to Jordan. Save you maybe fifty, sixty miles. Stay on the road through Cherry Creek valley till you hit the Government Trail. Anybody can tell you how to go from there. Yessir, that's the way I'd travel if I was ridin' horseback to Helena."

It sounded so casual and easy! But on the ride down from Glendive, Ella had looked often to the west, beyond the ranches that lay near the river. What she had seen was desolation. No railway, no telegraph lines, no houses, no roads. Nothing but the rumpled plains. And Jordan? She had never heard of it five minutes ago.

"Are you sure we can get plenty to eat if we do go that way?" she asked earnestly.

"Sure I'm sure," the ferryman snapped with some irritation. "I said the ranches won't turn you away."

She said nothing more, not even to Quincy, until the ferry deposited them and the horses on the west bank. A hundred yards beyond, she reined Hobo to a halt.

"Quincy—"

"Yes, Bunny. I'm puzzled too, as to what's best. But we needn't decide right now whether we'll turn south again to Miles, or north to Jordan. We have to follow Cherry Creek until we reach the Government Trail, and maybe by that time we'll have met somebody with an even better idea!"

"All right. Remember, though, all we've got is one day's supply of grub and eleven dollars."

It was easy but lonesome riding through Cherry Creek valley. Before nightfall they found the Government Trail and turned into its well-worn trace. The Army had used this route to haul supplies to Fort Keogh and other posts in the Yellowstone valley. When one set of ruts had worn or washed out too deep, the wagons had simply started a new set alongside the old, so that wherever the soil was soft the Trail widened out in successive pairs of ruts. In one place Ella counted sixteen grooves.

She and Quincy found a sheep bed half a mile off the Trail. It was empty. Ella stepped inside, curious to see the interior of a sheepherder's wagon. It was roomier than she expected. The wagon bed extended to six feet wide, making space for a bunk across the back. Under the bunk and along the sides were chests and cubbyholes where she discovered a generous stock of food supplies, and the absent herder's extra clothing. A table was hinged to the bed. In the front end, at one side of the door, stood a small kerosene cookstove. With flour and lard from the cupboard, Ella baked a pan of biscuits to add variety to their staple supper. Afterward, she and Quincy had a good sleep in the bunk, where two wool sacks stuffed with straw made a comfortable mattress and the heavy soogan comforter kept them warm.

At breakfast Quincy brought to the table a can of condensed milk he had found in the cupboard.

"It's already been opened. Would it be immoral to help myself to a few drops for my coffee?"

"Not immoral, but is it safe?"

He put his nose to the can. "Smells perfectly all right. Here goes!"

Ella left a note to thank their unknown host. She was able to thank him again in person two hours later when she and Quincy met him and his flock outside the tent which he had pitched at a temporary feeding ground. He said his name was Sam Morton and that they were welcome to such of his supplies as they had used. He rode along with them a short distance, talking over possible routes to Helena.

"I'd advise you to go through Jordan." He pointed to a flat-topped hill in the northwest. By the magic of atmosphere and distance, it rose darkly purple above the yellow-gray-green of the broken plain. "That's Sheep Mountain. I wintered the herd just to the right of it, where you'll see some trees. Strike past that bedding ground, and pick up the trail leading toward Jordan. I can't tell you exactly how far Jordan is from here. Say maybe a hundred miles, counting all the zigs and zags."

Ella was not much given to examining the motives and feelings that went into a decision, once it was taken. But often during the next four days she asked herself why she and Quincy had reined Hobo and Hike off the Government Trail and started for Sheep Mountain, with the makings of one meal in their saddle-bags, two small canteens of water, and directions for only the first half-day's ride. They must have been hopelessly romantic. Saving time was the ostensible reason. But there was more to it than that. The purple mystery of Sheep Mountain called, "I dare you!" The desolate breaks and coulees called, "I dare you!" And

In this "sheep bed" in eastern Montana Quincy and Ella made themselves at home overnight—with grievous consequences.

somewhere, miles and miles beyond the shimmering horizon, a little unknown town called, "I dare you!" And they had taken the dare.

This was June 23, the season of the summer solstice when the sun burned in the sky for more than fifteen hours a day. The High Plains soaked up the heat and glare, radiating them back unsparingly. Humps and hillocks weren't high enough to shade the trail. Along the few watercourses, cottonwoods were held to a miserly growth, and in between there was no shield from the sun except the quickly passing clouds of a thunderstorm. Ella and Quincy had cut across country before, but only for short distances, and never more than half a day's ride from a railroad and a town. There was a difference here. How much, they soon learned.

Steering toward the northeast corner of Sheep Mountain, they reached the wintering grounds of Sam Morton's flock by early afternoon. Quincy almost didn't get there. When the horses stopped at the dugout scoured into the bank, he let go the reins and slumped off into the grass, knees drawn up in agony.

Ella had guessed the cause when he had first begun to feel ill, two hours ago. "Food poisoning, from that can of condensed milk." She had watched him grow whiter and weaker, and encouraged him to hold on until they reached some place with shelter and water, and he had barely succeeded.

Now she jumped off Hobo to half lift, half drag Quincy into the shade of the dugout. He was nauseated, sweating heavily, and near fainting with the violence of abdominal cramps. She fetched the only "medicine" they carried, a small flask of whiskey. He got down a swallow or two. Using a broken cupboard door padded with thatch torn from the sheep shelter nearby, Ella made him as comfortable as she could. Then she unsaddled and hobbled the horses, took the canteen and started for the creek, a quarter of a mile away. It was past lunchtime, but Quincy couldn't even bear to think of food, and she had decided she would skip a meal too, leaving what little they had for both of them to eat tonight and tomorrow. Perhaps it was foolish to think that he would be recovered enough to be eating tomorrow.

But she had to think it to keep at bay the terror that threatened to overwhelm her. She was too distraught for formal praying, but with every step through the buffalo grass and down the pebbly slope, she sent up an anxious petition. "God, O God, please—please."

At the creekside she splashed water on her burning face and arms and filled the canteen. She got to her feet and started back toward the dugout, carrying her head down as she climbed the rise, on the lookout for rattlesnakes as well as gopher holes. At first she didn't see the cattle on the slope above her. Suddenly, startled by a loud snort, she looked up. A bull, enormous, black, and hostile, loomed over her on the bank. Behind him a sizeable herd, a hundred or more, were milling nervously, waiting some signal. She had heard that range cattle rarely attack a rider on horseback. But she was on foot, armed only with a small canteen. And her fear was less of attack than of being crushed to death in a stampede if the animals panicked. She was afraid to run or to scream for help—and how could help come, with Quincy too weak to walk, even if his head was clear enough to interpret her cry?

The bull snorted again, lowered his horns, and shook them threateningly. She took a firmer grip on the canteen strap, determined to lay about her with that makeshift weapon as long as she could keep her feet.

"Eeee-yah!"

A wild long-legged figure came leaping and hallooing from beyond the edge of the draw, waving his hat with one hand and shaking his carbine aloft with the other. "Eeee-yah, get along, eeee-yah!"

The bull hesitated, made a half-step toward Ella, then swung ponderously away from the noisy apparition bearing down on him and broke into a run along the rise, bellowing as he went. The herd swung with him. A few cows on the outer fringe spilled over the slope toward Ella, but she was no longer the focus of their attention, and a couple of wide whirls of the canteen and a warwhoop of her own sent them galloping after the main herd. When the earth stopped shaking, and all that was left of their

A wild long-legged creature came hallooing, "Eeee-yah, get along!"

going was a pillar of dust, Ella scrambled up the slope to find her rescuer collapsed in a dead faint.

A dousing from the canteen revived him enough to stagger back to the dugout and the thatch bed.

"Quincy, how did you know the cattle were there?"

"I heard the tramping. When I saw they were headed toward the creek, I forgot that I was too weak to move. I forgot everything except that if I didn't get out there instantly, I might not have any wife."

He tried for a jaunty smile, but couldn't quite make it before he blacked out again. She sat down on the dirt floor, shifting him so that his head rested in her lap.

"Well, darling," she whispered, "you've still got her, and she's mighty glad of it."

She couldn't be sure whether he heard her or not. A few minutes later he turned on his side and put his arm around her waist. "That sprint . . . must have jounced away the . . . worst of the cramps . . . I'm going to live."

He drifted again, and she continued to hold him, using her hat as a fan to cool his face. The motion stirred the sweat-dampened hair on his forehead and the lighter hairs that glistened on his arms below the rolled shirtsleeves. How strange it had been for her, after growing up with a black-haired brother, and uncles and cousins equally dark, to be joined in flesh to this red-gold man! She still caught herself in moments of surprise.

Surprises were part of marriage, weren't they? She supposed she and Quincy had found no more than the average number in their "little honeymoon," spent on a guest farm in the Catskills after the wedding last September. But she had welcomed the chance for this second, longer honeymoon eight months later. A winter as a wife had made her a better bride.

Not that they weren't still pushing into unknown country. Like the trail west, she could see that marriage led through hidden quicksands, over uncharted hills of delight, and into crinkle-crankle valleys where it was necessary to cross and recross the same obstructive current. There were poisons to avoid, and animal forces that would trample you down if you panicked. She and Quincy had begun their life together as they had begun this journey, with the unexamined conviction that *of course* they would win their way handsomely past all obstacles. But they hadn't taken the full measure of the obstacles nor foreseen their detail. Now that she was well into both adventures, that facile *of course* was being replaced by a workaday accommodation to whatever circumstances were at hand. But the purpose that underlay the innocent self-confidence of the beginnings was as sturdy as ever, and here on the High Plains it was emerging in a resolve, both for the trip and for the marriage: *Whatever it takes from me to make it through to the end, I'll give.*

Quincy could eat no supper that evening, so Ella snacked on pasty rice and tea, and made up the last of the cornmeal into a cake which she set aside for breakfast. Quincy wakened in the morning still sore and feeble, but ready for the corncake—which was nowhere to be found. So no breakfast except coffee, and the mystery of the corncake wasn't solved until Quincy was saddling up and saw the yellow crumbs sticking to Hike's muzzle.

A hundred yards beyond the dugout there was a trail that led eventually to a sheep ranch. A young woman was standing in the yard in front of the tar paper shack. Ella smiled and waved. Here was a chance of getting directions and at least a couple of eggs and some bread.

As she and Quincy turned off the trail, the woman drew back a few steps. She wore a bedraggled red wrapper over a bedraggled gray wrapper. Her uncombed hair hung in strings on either side of her face. Clutching her coverings together at her breast, she held the other hand down and back, fingers spread, as though she were reaching for support. Suddenly she picked up the trailing skirts of her garments and ran toward the shack, paused, then came forward to stand for a moment of intense watching before she broke and ran again. She repeated this several times, until dismay overcame curiosity and she fled inside, slamming the door.

"Poor little soul," murmured Ella. "Ranch crazy." It was a

disease of mind and spirit, she knew, that struck isolated home-steads and ranches where a wife could go for months without anyone to talk to except her man, and be without even that support for long stretches of time when he was away driving cattle or moving sheep to seasonal ranges. Ella's heart went out to this forlorn and frightened woman. Yesterday, at the dugout, after writing up the journal, she had glanced over earlier entries and noted how often the word "deserted" appeared in describing various campsites, beginning with the dilapidated house where she and Quincy had spent the third night from St. Paul. Abandoned cabins, barns, sheds and soddies had dotted all the route. Some of them, of course, had been forsaken because their owners moved on to more prosperous quarters. But many remained as decaying evidence of faded hope and bitter failure. This ranch wife's real self had already taken flight. How long before her shack too would stand empty?

By persistent knocking Quincy persuaded the woman to open the door. When she came out, she had added a blue wrapper on top of the red and gray.

"Good morning," he said gently. "How do we go from here to reach Jordan?"

Her directions were unintelligible. All they gathered from her nervous mumbling was that they would find a ranch about twelve miles along the trail. Next Quincy asked if she would supply some food. This frightened her even more. Her deep-sunk eyes darted wildly as if she were looking everywhere, anywhere, for help.

"Some bacon, perhaps, or a few eggs?" he suggested.

This was too much. The woman whirled and vanished into the shack. They heard the heavy bar dropping into place across the door, then after a moment the stealthy creaking of a rear door. A pack of sheep dogs and mongrels came snarling around the corner of the house. Quincy held them off with slashes of his quirt until Ella had mounted. Then he jumped for the saddle and they got away, with a few nips as souvenirs, but neither directions nor food.

By one o'clock, when they stopped to let the ponies graze,

they had been lost more than three hours. For lunch they shared a tablespoonful of grapenuts scraped from the bottom of the saddlebag, moistened with a few swallows of water that almost emptied the canteen. They were so tired that it seemed wise to rest until the hottest part of the day was past. Quincy still felt weak, and both of them were faint from lack of food.

The trail had divided twice during the morning. Relying on their experiences with Hobo, who always took the wrong turn when he had a free choice, they let him have his head at each split in the trail, and when he started along one branch, they promptly swung over to the other. By compass readings and sun positions, Quincy judged they were traveling the correct general course. It led them through a wasteland rimmed with buttes—magenta buttes, yellow buttes, blue-gray buttes. Grass and rock and sky. As the air grew hotter, the earth became more silent and empty. Larks and sage hens rested quietly out of sight. Even the hawks and scavenger magpies disappeared. Here, on the north-running ridge where the trail had finally brought them, nothing broke the midday quiet except the grasshoppers, clicking away like dozens of tiny typewriters in the grass. Typewriters? Ella smiled at the simile that had sprung to mind, absurd in this primeval setting. From the stony outcropping where she stood, the plains dished to the horizon for forty miles all around, and she could see no road, no fence, no ranch, nor any sign that a human being had ever passed along the green windings of the creek that began at the foot of the ridge.

Yesterday, during the worst hours of Quincy's attack, the loneliness of the land had frightened her. But today she could give a little shrug and switch her attention to helping him construct a patch of shade by spreading a poncho from the two rifles lashed together as a prop.

They started down from the ridge about four o'clock. "This high ground must be the watershed between the Yellowstone and the Missouri," Quincy said. "There should be some sheep ranches along that stream there below us." His guess was right. Following its course they soon picked up a road. After traveling about two hours, they saw a fence, and then a man on horseback who directed them to the Lovigs' ranch, further down Timber Creek. It was well past suppertime when they reached it, but the Norwegian mistress of the log-and-dugout house cooked up a big meal for them and cheerfully served second and third helpings when Quincy told her he had been thirty-six hours without food—he didn't count the half-tablespoonful of grapenuts. Mrs. Lovig put them up overnight in a tent furnished with a brass bedstead, the first proper bed they had slept in for a month. In the morning Mrs. Lovig piled their plates with pancakes and sent her son Ernest to fill the horses' nosebags with oats.

Young Ernest seemed to know the country fairly well, and he gave Quincy careful pointers on finding the Glendive-Jordan furrow and following it west. "You'll see it about fifteen miles from here, Mr. Scott. It's a real furrow. Some fellows dragged a plow behind a wagon clear from Glendive to Jordan to mark the way. That's about a hundred and fifty miles. It's sort of worn out in spots, but if you lose it, just ride in circles till you come across it again."

For all their hospitality and help the Lovigs would accept only thanks, but that was as plentiful as their bounty. The drawback was that Ella and Quincy didn't feel they could take advantage of such generosity by asking for extra food to carry with them. Once again they had to set out in faith.

They found the furrow in the early afternoon, after stopping at the ranch of another hospitable Scandinavian, Ole Hedstrom, to buy milk and a can of tomatoes. Seen close up, the furrow was scarcely distinguishable from other irregularities in the soil. The sharp contours of the plow mark had weathered down. But when Ella pulled the brim of her straw hat low enough to screen out the sun's dazzle and looked directly along the furrow where Quincy was pointing, she could see it running in a steady crease in the pale sageland. It led them for two days before they lost it. By that time they had covered fifty miles more. One night they camped where a richly fertilized stand of grass and piles of whitened bones showed that dozens of sheep had died in a winter blizzard. Camp the second night was made on the edge of a wash so infested with rattlesnakes that Quincy ringed the blankets with cactus lobes for protection. Ranches were still half a day's ride apart, or farther. But Ella and Quincy hooked food at one sheepherder's wagon and were invited to lunch at another. They parted with a dollar for midday dinner at Mc-Kenzie's Road Ranch: "Meels, 4 bitts." The meal was mainly salt mackerel, potatoes and bread pudding. The proprietor didn't want to sell any extra supplies, but Quincy wheedled him out of a can of tomatoes, some sugar and a handful of dried apples, for which the charge was fifty cents.

"Maybe it does seem high, Mr. Scott, but you got to remember there's no railroad through here, and not enough water for gardens. We go out three times a year and haul in everything by wagon."

Between the ranches the chief problem for Quincy and Ella was drinking water. Their canteens were small. To save a little water in them for the next morning meant being thirsty all the time. When they came to one of the dwindling streams, like the Little Dry, the urge was strong to dip up a big cupful. But most of the creeks and pools were so soupy with alkali that even the horses wouldn't put in their noses. And there was Old Mac's comment to enforce discretion: "That alkali stuff, it'll go through ye like an arrow from hell." Safer to go thirsty. Ella was also suffering from the sun. Her fair skin was scorched, and her lower lip painful with a deep crack that had begun a week ago and would not heal.

On Thursday morning they lost the furrow and wasted six miles trying to locate it. That was when Ella began singing a line from one of the spirituals heard in her Kentucky childhood, "Jordan am a hard road to trabbel."

Eventually they came upon the trail again, crossed Big Dry Creek five times, and struck into the final section of the route. There were fresh tracks in the soil. Quincy called attention to one set. "Somebody's been along here today on a pigeon-toed pony."

Ella had her eyes, not on the tracks, but on the horizon. She was the first to see the town, a cluster of wooden buildings along the bank of the Big Dry.

"Look ahead, Quincy. Is that Jordan, or just a mirage?"

It was Jordan, so wind-beaten, sand-scoured and sun-faded that it blended into the colors of the desolation around it.

At five-thirty Quincy and Ella tied the horses to the rack and strolled into Jordan's one store. The town's population, thirteen plus a few nonresident cowhands, came en masse from the saloon across the street to inspect the strangers. An old man, with a breath as fiery as his hair and mustache, wobbled up to Ella, took her hand, and said earnestly, "I'm shprised to shee you fellersh here. Damn town's yoursh!"

It wasn't a very large gift. Jordan was only six years old and consisted mainly of the saloon, the store, three hotels, several stables and a cemetery. Most of the year the place lived up to its reputation as the lonesomest town in the world. But a number of the big cattle drives of eastern Montana ended near here, and when the cowboys came in for the traditional roundup celebration, if anyone was lonesome, it was his own fault. There was one such celebration scheduled for Saturday, the storekeeper told Quincy. "Better stay over for the dance," he urged.

Ella was sorry to miss the party. What fun it would be to tell her Seattle and New York friends that she had skipped around the floor at a cowboy shindig! But it wouldn't do to waste two days waiting for Saturday night. In fact, Quincy seemed impatient to press ahead a few miles further this evening.

Everybody in the store was giving advice on the best route to Helena. Opinion on the distance ranged between two hundred ninety and three hundred eighty miles. Ella listened, and bought food supplies, though not lavishly, for the remains of that eleven dollars had to last to Helena. As at Mandan, her one extravagance was a nickel's worth of candy, this time stale pink peppermints. Quincy filled the canteens and watered the horses, and they were on their way.

But not for long. They were tired, the horses were tired. A few miles beyond town they turned off into the sagebrush, made camp with the fewest possible motions, and lay down on the sand, heads muffled with the halves of Ella's skirts as protection against the mosquitos. It was sweltering hot. Once, just before dusk blurred the landscape, Ella sat up to loosen the wrapping so that she could breathe more comfortably. She stared for a moment back along the way they had come, toward the ridges and mesas, the wide flat channel of the Big Dry, all soft gray now, tinged with the faint lavender and pink cast from a rack of clouds still holding their sunset colors. She couldn't see the town. But she heard rollicking voices and the tinkling of the saloon piano—no, that couldn't be. It was only the high-pitched *zzing* of the mosquitos. But Jordan was there. They had found it, across more than a hundred miles of the unknown. She was thankful, and proud.

JULY: *The first mountains*

To me high mountains are a feeling.

Lord Byron

VIII

It was idle to look so early for the Rockies. The Musselshell River was sixty miles away, and the outpost ranges another seventy miles beyond that. Yet Quincy felt a shiver of expectation every time he crested a rise in the trail, or came out on the edge of a break with a view ahead. All his life he had heard talk about the Rocky Mountains. He had read of the men who climbed their peaks, hunted their game, mined their gold, and ranched their high valleys. They would be different from the eastern mountains he loved. But how different? And would the Rockies in actuality excite him as they did in imagination? At some moment in the next few days he would begin finding the answers to those questions.

But not this hot morning. The only "mountain" on the horizon was Smoky Butte, south of Jordan, and they were leaving it behind as they faced into more sagebrush and rolling plain. They had to ford the Big Dry again. Quincy stripped and waded out to test the crossing. The bottom proved firm, so he piled his clothes on the saddle and led Hike through. As Ella came splashing behind him on Hobo, Quincy said, "I'm going to have a dip before I dress. Do you want a swimming lesson? You've got to learn sometime."

"But not here. Not in this alkali soup."

Quincy had to admit that, as a bath, his dip didn't amount to much, but it put him in a little better condition than Ella to be a luncheon guest at the surprising home of Ethan Brainerd. The evening before, as they were leaving Jordan, a pleasant-spoken man on a buckskin pony had overtaken them and invited them to stop in the morning at his cabin fifteen miles west. When they arrived shortly before noon, Brainerd came out into the yard to greet them. He was a man of medium height and slender build, with a neat, delicate look about him that made the strength of his handshake all the more unexpected. He gestured to the small wiry woman who stood smiling in the screened doorway.

"Mrs. Brainerd has a chicken dinner ready for you. We'd be pleased if you'd stay a few days with us, or at least long enough to attend the roundup dance tomorrow night."

Once again Quincy declined the dance, but he and Ella were glad to linger for a couple of hours after dinner in the coolness of the shaded cabin, enjoying the rarity, in this wilderness, of a home graced with books, music and informed conversation. The rarity, too, of being regarded as normal citizens engaged in a rational enterprise. The Brainerds asked many questions about the trip, but they didn't seem to classify Quincy and Ella as either freaks or pseudo-cowboys. In fact, they agreed that crossing the West on horseback was a sensible way to spend the summer.

"You're having a great opportunity," said Brainerd. "If my wife and I were your age, we might try an expedition like that ourselves. To get out and see the country before it changes completely from the old times."

He couldn't furnish any exact information about the next problem on their route, fording the Musselshell. "It may be possible to swim your horses. That will depend on how high the water is. But there'll be somebody at Mosby who can tell you the best way to cross."

When Quincy and Ella reluctantly took their leave, with earnest thanks for such a refreshing visit, Brainerd went out to the barn with them to get the horses. Quincy noticed an interesting peculiarity about Brainerd's buckskin pony.

"I guess you were riding over east of Jordan yesterday, weren't you, Mr. Brainerd? Near Sand Creek?"

Brainerd's eyebrows shot up. "How the devil did you know that?"

It was a minor bit of plainscraft, but it tickled the small boy in Quincy to be able to point to the buckskin's front hoofs, worn at an angle, and say, "Those feet. For several miles we followed the tracks of a pigeon-toed pony."

The civilized atmosphere of Brainerd's cabin made the wretchedness of the next stopping place and the eager humility of Leah's welcome all the more poignant.

Leah was a sheepdog. Quincy and Ella named her Leah the Forsaken, after the heroine of a play they had once seen. When they turned in at the tumble-down hut, about seven miles beyond Brainerd's ranch, Leah came slowly toward them, a soft whine in her throat, tail down but wagging. Her body was gaunt under its tangled coat of brown and white. As Quincy dismounted, she lifted her muzzle to lick his hand, then led him into the hut. The door was off its hinges, lying in the scuffled dust of the dirt floor. The cookstove was cracked, its pipe drunkenly awry. A rickety table, a bench, and a bare wooden bunk were the only other furnishings. Leah, still whimpering, urged him across the room to show him three little blind lumps of fur under a bench. One lump was black, one brown and white, one brownish gray. Quincy put out his finger and stirred each one gently. They were alive, but not much more.

With his hand on Leah's head, he said, "All right, old girl. We'll see what we can do."

He went to help Ella unsaddle. "I can't figure it out. Somebody's been here within the last couple of weeks, judging by the remnants of a sack of coffee, the empty cans, and the ashes in the stove. And you saw the horse in the pasture back there. But the place is certainly deserted now. So how about the dog? Does she belong to a sheepman passing through, who left her to have her pups? Or does she belong to whoever owns the horse? Or did she get lost? Or was she abandoned here deliberately to get rid of her?"

They shared their supper generously with Leah. Then Quincy brought some straw from the dilapidated barn to replace the half-rotted gunnysacks on which the puppies were lying. He propped up the broken door, leaving an opening so that Leah could slip in and out. She seemed to understand their concern for her. When she wasn't giving her nearly-dry dugs to her babies, she nuzzled close to Quincy or Ella, or stood at a little distance, watching them with sad, intent eyes and a slow wagging of her tail.

Quincy spent a restless night, thinking of the dog. He had told Ella there could be no question of taking her and the puppies along, because of the extra food required and the added weight for the horses to carry—Leah was too weak to keep up on foot. The only question was whether to shoot her in mercy, or leave her as they had found her, knowing that she and the pups would die if no one returned to feed her.

He wakened heavy-hearted and still undecided. But a decision had already been made. Ella was up and busy at the table, mixing cornmeal with water she had fetched from the thread of a creek that ran near the hut.

"We can't shoot her, Quincy. After all, there *is* a chance somebody will feed her—her master, whoever he is, or some other rancher passing by. If I were Leah, I'd want that chance, for myself and my babies. Let's give her half our breakfast, and I'll make up the rest of our cornmeal into bread for her, though I suppose she'll wolf it down in three bites."

"No, she won't," he said after a moment's thought. "Not if we break it into small pieces and hide them in different places around the cabin."

Before they left, Quincy helped Ella tuck bits of the cornbread into crannies that Leah could reach, but only with persistance, so that hopefully she would space out the supply. He was satisfied with Ella's decision. Whatever the final outcome, they were at least giving Leah another day or two of life.

Leah came into the yard to watch them saddle up. She drooped under their farewell stroking, then walked slowly behind the ponies to the gate. There she settled down on her thin haunches, voicing her despair in a low keening whine. In the winning of the West, not everyone was a winner.

The trail to Breed's Crossing on the Musselshell led onward plainly enough, but the country was as wild and lonely as any between Terry and Jordan. The two ranches that Quincy and Ella passed on Saturday and Sunday were low on supplies, waiting for the Fourth of July wagon trip to the railroad to replenish the storeroom. At one, food was flatly refused. At the other, Quincy had to talk fast and slip four bits into the cook's hand to get two cans of vegetables, a little bacon, and the makings for a pan of biscuits. Camp dinner the first night was jackrabbit, eaten raw because there wasn't a stick of sagebrush in sight for a fire, and the cow chips were soaking wet from the afternoon's rain.

The next morning a blast of prairie wind blew Ella's hat away, whirling it off beyond retrieving. Quincy gave her his, knowing that the sun was doing damage to her skin. The crack in her lower lip continued to be painful. She was also suffering from what they had dubbed her "Queen Anne brogans," the badly-fitting shoes bought in Bismarck. By the end of those hours when she and Quincy walked to rest the horses, she was usually limping. She had tried at several stores for a better pair, but boys' shoes were too broad, and women's shoes too flimsy. So she stumbled on, favoring her feet when she could, cracking jokes when she couldn't. "I'll bet that if Pilgrim had had Bunyans like mine he wouldn't have made much Progress."

The horses had come through this chancy week in good shape. Though short on water, they had grazed well on needle grass, blue grama and buffalo grass. Quincy wished his father could see how healthy they looked. In the letter received at Terry, his father had written some wise counsel on the subject. Quincy smiled a little, remembering what he had written in reply: "Your advice about horses and camp, Daddy, is OK where followable, but as you know that is not always. Out here it is difficult to camp as one would like. Firewood has been very very scarce. Water the horses get when there is any, which is often enough but by no means regularly. As for blankets at night, these western horses never see a blanket except in winter, and no oats at all . . . Hike's condition is the admiration of every man we talk with." The horses, in fact, had done better pound for pound than their riders. Weighing in at the Jordan store, Quincy had tipped at a hundred and fifty-three pounds, Ella at a hundred and twenty, a loss of about seven pounds each. "So much less for the horses to carry," Quincy had said cheerfully.

Sunday was the last day of June, and under its dateline in the journal went a note about the lost hat, and the sighting of the only antelope of the summer. Quincy tried one shot at it and gave up, as much in admiration as despair. It looked to him as if the pronghorn had simply outrun the bullet!

The travelers walked more than usual that day, and there was more uphill than downhill to the trail, so they were footsore and weary by evening. They plodded toward one last ridge, looking for a campsite. Quincy was ahead. As he drew nearer, the shadow along the top of the ridge resolved itself into a stretch of pine growth. The trees were scrubby, but definitely pine. He could smell the resinous scent, distinct from sage or grass.

"Hey, Bunny, see here! Real firewood, and boughs for our bed."

They unsaddled and hobbled the horses, then went hand in hand to explore the other side of the woods. A few yards over the crest they came out suddenly on a rocky ledge. The earth dropped abruptly away to a jumble of hills covered with intermittent clumps of small pines and cedars. A solid line of green marked the course of the Musselshell, about twelve miles away. Tomorrow he must find a way to get safely across it. But as his eyes moved on, forebodings were pushed aside by a discovery. Far, far to the west, beyond the river and beyond the headwaters of its tributary streams, a snow-tipped mass glinted rosy gold in the sunset.

"The Rockies!"

At this distance they made only a small thrust into the sky, most of their bulk merging into the horizon. But there they were, the eight-thousand-foot summits of the Snowy Range, eastern sentry of the Montana Rockies.

It was not the "first view of the mountains" that Quincy had dreamed of, a close confrontation with towering walls of granite, but it was awesomely satisfying. The sense of remoteness and mystery was heightened by a thunderstorm which draped the southern quarter of the sky with a purple-black curtain streaked by darts of lightning, while the west glowed in tender shades of pink against pale blue. The storm was too far away for the sounds of its thunder to carry. On the ridge where Quincy and Ella stood, still holding hands, the air was silent except for a moaning wind in the pines. Quincy let it all pour into him, let the colors and shapes possess him, let the space and size and distance stretch him to a new dimension.

Finally he turned to Ella. "You didn't tell me it would be like this."

"How could I? It's something you have to see for yourself."

There was something else he saw for himself—and did not tell her about, at least not until the morning. Gathering wood in a clump of pines some hundred feet from camp, he found a litter of twigs and needles pushed together under some low branches, with a pile of bones in the middle. They were sheep bones. Remnants of fresh meat clinging to them showed that they had been gnawed within the past twenty-four hours.

Wolves, he thought, remembering the wolf tracks he had seen at several places along the trail since leaving Jordan. He put the carbine handy by the side of the bough bed when he and Ella turned in at dark.

They were up at dawn. "Sleep well, honey?" he asked.

"Yes, except that I had a queer sort of nightmare. Not exactly a dream, but an awful sense of uneasiness."

"That's odd, because I had some dream feelings of the same kind. But there was a reason for mine." He told her of the bones in the animal's lair.

She shuddered. "I suppose he came sniffing and snuffling around us in the middle of the night. How about the horses? Are they okay?"

The horses were gone.

That was surprising. Hike and Hobo had been behaving themselves unusually well on this trek across wild country, probably because they were seldom near enough a ranch at night to be tempted to run off and socialize with other horses. But Quincy knew they had worked out a way to synchronize their movements so that even when hobbled to each other, they could cover quite a bit of ground. He asked Ella to scan the country from one small hill along the ridge while he went to climb another. Ella soon signalled that she had spotted Hike and Hobo. Quincy went with her to get them, wading down through the dew-drenched grass of a hollow. As they led the horses back to camp, Quincy saw by their outbound tracks that they had run some of the distance, in spite of the hobbles. Had the wild animal frightened them?

It wasn't until after breaking camp and starting out along the trail that Quincy found the right answer to the gnawed bones, the bad dreams, the running horses. It was pressed plainly in the dew-wet sand beside the trail—the huge paw-print of a grizzly bear.

Ella swung off Hobo to stoop down and take a careful look. "Isn't it lucky that Old Ephraim had dined so well on mutton before we came along!"

The old man at Breed's Crossing operated a skiff ferry and also presided over the Mosby postoffice, which was located in his ranch house. After talking with him and going down to inspect the turbulent yellow waters of the Musselshell, Quincy said to Ella, "We'd better mail an optimistic letter to each of our mothers from here. Then even though they may not hear for two or three weeks that we succeeded in getting across alive, they can assume we did."

The day was oppressively hot, so while the postmaster-rancher finished his noon dinner, Ella and Quincy went around to the shady side of his house to write their cheerful accounts of the past week's march and plans for the week ahead. Ella added to her note, "We may have to swim the horses here, but there's no danger." Quincy indicated his faith in survival by asking his mother to send him at Helena a forty-dollar money order from his bank funds.

From time to time during this trip he had thought about its effect on the parents at opposite ends of the country, and on the mothers in particular. His mother, steady and sensible in a real crisis, was much given to stewing over vague possibilities. It was a good thing she didn't know how many possibilities there were out here! Ella's mother had crossed the West by train several times and was better able to assess the hazards, but he considered her only a normal worrier, as mothers go, so the strain more or less evened out. He wondered what difference it might be making that each day's travel carried him and Bunny farther from one mother and closer to the other. In any case, it would be cruel even to hint about the difficulties to be faced in the next half hour.

The old man—more old in looks than years, Quincy guessed, with his deliberate stride and his seamed, weather-toughened skin—had sold them a fair supply of staples and canned goods from his ranch storeroom, and offered to help them at the river. He came out of the door now, wiping the last of his dinner from his lips with the back of his hand. He took the letters and started to slip them into the pocket of his sweat-stained blue shirt, then walk back inside to toss them into a box on the table. "Might get 'em wet if I take 'em with me. That skiff has been known to splash around some."

On the river bank, Quincy unstrapped the guns and saddle-bags. The old man put them into the skiff, a small craft connected by a sliding pulley to a rope rigged across the stream. "Well, we'd better get this business done with," he said. "I'll show you where to take the horses across." He beckoned Quincy and Ella to follow him southward along the bank.

About a hundred and fifty yards upstream he stopped and pointed to the surging current, opaque with yellow mud.

"Right there. First over that boggy flat, then into the water. There's a narrow ledge of gravel that angles downstream and reaches the west bank just above that bush, opposite where we was standing a few minutes ago. See the bush? If you go beyond that, you'll drop off into deep water. Keep your horses' feet *on* the gravel ledge clear across and you'll be all right. One of my ranch boys rode over this morning, only one to try it since that cloudburst way up the valley sent the river so high. Worst rain in twenty-five years, they say. Of course, my boy was riding

Old miner, old rancher, or old cowhand—if he had lived long in the West, a man bore its mark in his looks and his outlook.

Baldy, which is a lot bigger and heavier than either of your ponies. And both him and Baldy know the ford pretty well."

"Wouldn't it be better just to swim the horses?" Quincy asked.

"Nope. River's too shallow and too swift. It's almost too swift to wade. If they lose their footing off that ledge, or if you let 'em be carried downstream past the bush, God help you. The river will swirl you into the quicksand at the bend. Now you take the ponies, mister, one at a time, and your wife can come with me in the skiff."

"Thank you," said Ella, "but I'm going with my husband."

Her voice wobbled a little, but her decision remained firm as both men tried to dissuade her. She yielded only so far as to agree to ride Hike, who was sure-footed and, since his "conversion" at Glendive Creek, dependable in handling. Hobo? Although the roan had slogged his way faithfully through every situation so far, Quincy couldn't forget that he was wind-broken, that a strain might suddenly produce those gasping struggles for breath. But it was too late to agonize over that. Better to drown going forward than starve going backward. (Now there was a nifty line for the book—if he lived to write it.)

"Don't worry," said the old man, having given them enough and to spare for a month's worrying. "Just keep on the gravel bar and land upstream from the bush. I'll bring your baggage over as soon as you've made it safely." He waited to make sure that they were heading toward the right spot to strike the ledge, then turned and started back for the skiff at his ruminative pace.

"He's not going to waste a trip across in his boat if we *don't* make it." Quincy tried to say it jokingly, but there was no answering chuckle from Ella. Her face had gone a pasty color under her sunburn, and her blistered lips were pinched together.

"All right, kiddo." Quincy lifted his quirt. "Take this boggy stretch at a run. Here goes!" He brought the quirt down sharply on Hobo's rump.

It was at least sixty feet from the solid bank to the water. Plunging stirrup-deep at almost every stride, Hike and Hobo pistoned their way through the oozy sand. They were tired and excited when they reached the water. Quincy gave Hobo no chance to balk but put him directly into the current.

"Keep right in line behind me," he called to Ella.

They had struck the gravel ledge. He took a sight on the opposite bank more than three hundred feet away, and guided Hobo toward a point just upstream from the bush. Quick glances over his shoulder assured him that Ella and Hike were following. The water rose shoulder high on the horses and threatened to bowl them over. Quincy and Ella had to rein them lengthwise to the stream and sidle across. Each step was a small triumph of balance and discipline. Twice Hobo missed his footing, twice he regained it by a lucky lunge. Yard by yard the bush was coming closer. Quincy thought he could already distinguish its individual leaves. But most of his attention was on keeping Hobo on the ledge. The continual rush and whirl of water all around was dizzying. He suddenly looked up and saw that the current was forcing Ella past the landing place.

"Watch out, Bunny! Aim for the bush! Turn Hike's head and let his rump swing."

Quincy maneuvered Hobo slightly upstream, breaking some of the strength of the current so that Ella could stop Hike's drift. For a few nightmare seconds the two horses teetered at the far edge of the gravel bar, holding their own by a sheer margin. Then, under the cautious urging of their riders, they leaned into the surge and slowly pushed back to sounder footing. The water began to shallow. Three minutes later Hike and Hobo were flailing their way across another strip of ooze and up the crumbling bank to safety.

Hobo was trembling, and breathing gustily. So was Quincy. He slid from the saddle and flung one arm over Hobo's neck.

"Thank God for you, you homely old cuss. You did nobly!"

Then he went over to help Ella shower pats and praises on Hike.

"You're all right, Bunny?"

"Yes, I am now. A little shaky, but all right. Really I am!"

He had his arms around her, his face close to hers. "Tell me, why did you insist on fording the river? Didn't you know it was dangerous?"

There was no answer for a moment. Then Ella said, her voice muffled against his shoulder, "Yes, I knew. I was sure you would . . . drown. That's why I had to go with you."

"Bunny, my Bunny! Hey, you're crying."

"So are you, you big galoot."

She dried her eyes on his shirtsleeve, then twisted in his arms to point to the muddy strip below the bank. "Can you retrieve the cans of peas and tomatoes that flipped out of my poncho roll?"

Quincy brought back the precious cans just as the old man pulled in at the skiff landing—he hadn't waited after all.

"Thought you two was goners, there about the end," he said, handing up the saddlebags and guns. "Another couple of feet further downstream and you would of been. But, God damn, you got plenty of luck and pluck. May they both last!"

IX

The Snowies were invisible from the bottom of the Musselshell valley, but they loomed in sight again as Quincy and Ella mounted the succession of benches beyond. The upward-sloping plain, whose floor was the bench tops, was deeply intersected by creeks—the Box Elder, the Flat Willow, and dozens of smaller tributaries. This meant many hours spent easing down into washes and scrambling out again. Noontides burned hot, and nights in camp were plagued with swarms of fiercely persistent mosquitoes. But by comparison with the eastern barrens, this new country was to Ella sudden paradise, where streams ran clear and sweet, trees grew tall along their borders, and the cool blueness of the mountains reappeared westward at the end of every ascent. For two days she and Quincy steered directly for the Snowies, and for two days more they circled to the left around their flanks.

Best of all were the ranches with ample food and an urgent welcome, the welcome Ella had taken for granted they would find everywhere west of St. Paul.

At the Lewis spread on the southern skirts of the Snowies, Ella had time to write her family in Seattle, where by now Jessie should have joined her mother and Riley. After a purposely low-key description of fording the Musselshell, Ella continued: "We stopped one noon at a fine ranch on Flat Willow Creek and were invited to lunch. Then after lunch a little judicious maneuvering resulted in an invitation to rest our horses (which are very tired) overnight, and we did. The owner was a bachelor with a 'lady' housekeeper and about 12 hired men, and they set what seemed to us a luxurious table with milk, fruit and veg-

etables galore. We had a cool white bed in the dainty spare
room, and I got a bath and a shampoo . . .

"Yesterday, July 4, we came to Mr. Asbridge's ranch just at
lunch time—queer coincidence—and when he asked us to join
them at dinner—oh well you know what we did. There was a big
dish of roast chicken and fixin's and we left the dish full of
bones. After lunch a heavy thunderstorm came up, continuing all
afternoon and they made us unsaddle again and stay all night.
There were three nice children, their teacher, the housekeeper
and wads of hired men as usual. On these ranches there are
often 3 or 4 dwelling houses for the family and help, a bunk
house for the men, numbers of barns, sheep sheds, shearing pens
(mostly sheep ranches through here) and one man's place will
look like a small city. All afternoon they fed us on oranges,
candy and peanuts, and at night we had a few fireworks mixed
with some of the finer kind from the thunder clouds over the
mountains . . . The air is very clear and rare, the roads—good
roads by the way—wind among the pine-groves and along the
hillsides in a picturesque way . . .

"Everybody is living up to Western traditions of hospitality
and keeping us well fed. We are finding more gardens as water
becomes plentiful and less canned stuff. But there are the same
confusing directions. Every man tells us to take a different road
and no two agree as to distances. A man told us it was 70 miles
to Martinsdale, 39 miles further on in the right direction we were
told it was 105, 17 miles further we learn it is 65. And we ourselves haven't the slightest idea which to believe.

"If the mosquitoes leave enough fragments of us to hold the
lines and keep our feet in the stirrups we'll be in Helena in
about six days."

It took ten, even with the distance saved during the first week
by leaving the road beyond Swimming Woman Creek and aiming forty miles straight across country to Martinsdale and the
notch between the Little Belt range and the Crazy Mountains.
Approaching the town on the morning of July 9, they came upon
a deserted hotel. The ground floor had been used as a sheep pen,
but Ella found upstairs a sunny room with a clean dry floor.

"We haven't had a full rest day for four weeks, Quincy. Let's take today off. If we cart our stuff upstairs, I can have a nap while you take the horses into Martinsdale for shoeing."

"Well, I guess we can afford the time. I know it's a good idea to give the horses a breather before we begin the climb over the Rockies. Hobo's come through heat and drought and quicksand without 'roaring,' but we don't know yet how he'll stand the steady uphill pull to high altitudes. So, a holiday for all of us!"

He carried the equipment up the rickety stairs. After he had helped Ella spread her blankets on the floor, he stopped at the window for a long look at the mountains. Below a crest of snow, dark pines caped their shoulders, and below the cape, ample grassy skirts fell in a broad sweep that blended with the valley.

"They fascinate me, these Montana mountains. See how they rise directly out of the plain, with no clutter of foothills. It seems as if I could walk across a few miles and climb right to the top. I tell you, Bunny, I think I've found *my* West. I could give my heart to this country."

After he had gone off to town with the horses, Ella took her own long look, southward now, to the Crazies towering steeply skyward. Mad Mountains, the Indians called them. A rancher had told her it was because of the weird shrieking winds that blew through the canyons. Mad or Crazy, either name fit. With its highest peaks at eleven thousand feet, the range was a tortured mass reaching granite claws to scratch the sky. Ella was glad she and Quincy would make their first attack on the Rockies over the softer shapes of the Big Belt range.

Ella leaned the loose door of the room in approximately its proper place and sat down on the blankets to do some mending. Growing drowsy, she laid the mending aside and stretched out to sleep.

She was wakened by a boom of thunder and the blow of a heavy weight falling across her body. The room was murky black, and it took her a moment of frantic feeling about to determine that the door had blown down on her. All through the old hotel beams were groaning, frames rattling, strips of tattered wallpaper drumming in the wind. Ella pushed the door aside and scrambled to her feet. Could it be night already? What was happening? And Quincy—where was he? She got to the window just as a brilliant zig-zag of lightning crackled across the valley. By its green glare she saw the treetops bent nearly level before the wind, and out of the frightening blackness that covered the valley a white wall rushing upon her. The cloud-burst hit the building with a roar that deepened as hail followed the rain. Ella ran from room to room calling wildly for Quincy. Where *was* he? Out somewhere unprotected in that fusilade of stones?

As suddenly as it had come, the storm ended. The sun burst from behind the departing cloud, revealing hail piled a foot deep in the corner of the dilapidated porch. The mountains were sheeted with white. Ella's watch had stopped, but she judged from the sun's position that it was midafternoon—and still no Quincy.

Half an hour later she saw a speck coming slowly along the road from town, soon recognizable as Quincy riding one horse and leading the other. She ran downstairs and threw her arms around him when he dismounted in front of the hotel. He was a wet armful, drenched and shivering. He grinned wanly, took off the new hat bought in Martinsdale, and showed her a few tender swellings on his head. "Got those before I could rush myself and the horses into the blacksmith's barn. But there's no real damage to either us or the food supplies, unless—"

He handed Ella the soggy package, in which she found the only permanent casualty of the storm. The sweet chocolate, which Quincy had brought her as a special treat, was so thoroughly melted into the flour that the whole brown sticky mess had to be thrown out.

Over their delayed lunch of beans and biscuits Ella said, "You were saying that this part of Montana was your West, that you could give your heart to it. Do you still feel that way?"

Quincy wiped up the last of the beans with the final biscuit. "You bet. To have a rip-snorting show like this storm every now and then would keep things interesting."

"You couldn't make a living as a political cartoonist this far

Quincy exaggerated the slope but not the sensation of the climb up the Rockies.

from New York. What would you do—raise horses? Or sheep?"
"I'm thinking Montana would be a great place to raise our kids."

> *Up the mountain you climb and you climb,*
> *For you've heard that the View is sublime.*
> *But you find it's a sell,*
> *You must hang on like hell,*
> *So your back's to the View all the time!*

The limerick was a joint effort, composed on the wagon road that labored up the eastern front of the Big Belts toward Duck Creek Pass. Ella and Quincy tinkered with the lines, debating about spelling "sublimb" and "timb" to coordinate with "climb." And should they find a coy substitute for "hell" in deference to public sensibilities?

"Oh, the whole thing's silly anyhow," laughed Ella. "Let's stop and turn around long enough to really look at what we're versifying about."

White Sulphur Springs was behind them, and the headwaters of the Musselshell. She and Quincy had been doing part of the ascent on foot, leading the horses upward through bitterbrush and ponderosa pine. Now, from the shoulders of the Big Belts, the outlook widened to a semicircle that encompassed the beginnings of the Smith River and the Little Belt range, the Castle Mountains and the Crazies. Ella could see the crisscrossing lines of fences in a valley a thousand feet below her, and the angular dots of ranch buildings. All else was wilderness, horizon upon horizon.

The day had begun hot and clear, as on that deceptively serene morning in Martinsdale, and again the heat was creating forces for mile-high melodrama. But this time Ella had the sense of being caught right up into the making of the storm. Toward noon there was a visible thickening of the air. Distant mountains took on denser tones of blue. The few gauzy clouds began mingling, multiplying, changing from strands to clusters to massive pillars, darker and deeper with each change. Ella felt on her skin the prickling build-up of the electrical charge.

Quincy said, "Look at this," and got sparks by rubbing his hand through his hair.

Still short of the summit they came to an exposed knob fringed with young lodgepole pines and dominated by the skeleton of an ancestor pine that thrust one bleached finger high above the clearing.

"Hadn't we better get under shelter?" asked Ella. "Those clouds aren't going to let us off with a light sprinkle."

They reined the horses toward the trees, dismounting just as the uplifted finger of the dead pine beckoned the first lightning bolt. The flash leaped down the tree, shattering limbs and trunk. The shock threw Ella and Quincy and Hobo to the ground. Hike was flung against one of the small trees. Quincy got the party back to its feet, dazed and bruised, noses stinging with ozone and the smell of scorched wood. Before they could shake the thunder out of their ears, two smaller thunders roared down upon them—the pounding of hail and a cannonade of hoofs. In a lash of ice pellets a band of wild horses burst out of the woods and galloped past, nostrils wide and manes whipping in the wind.

"Golly! Beautiful!" It was all the horse-lover had time to say, for Hike made a lunge to join the runners and Quincy had to dig in his heels and pull on the reins with all his strength. The wild horses, led by their storm-wise stallion, stopped in the center of the clearing, bunched tightly, rumps to the wind. They got the full brunt of the hail, but they were safely distant from the trees.

"We'll have to get Hike out of here," Quincy called. "He's so excited I can scarcely hold him. If he joins those cayuses we'll never catch him again."

Lightning was still crackling along the top of the range, with a constant bombardment of thunder. Quincy jerked the protesting Hike toward the trail, and with Ella and Hobo behind him, faced into the storm. Farther along they took refuge in the opening of an abandoned mine until the hail and following downpour were over. When they crept out, the storm was sailing away eastward, its upper clouds jabbed by forked lightning, its lower edges dissolving in curtains of silver rain.

The wind behind the storm blew cold. Ella's teeth were chattering as she and Quincy took up the march toward Duck Creek Pass.

"Want to stop and dig out your woolen pullover?"

"N-no. Too much t-trouble."

Before they reached the top she wished she had taken Quincy's suggestion, for in the last two hundred feet they were in snow. Last winter's snow, in patches mottling the shaded side of the canyon, then, further up, in drifts rising above their heads. They stopped at the summit to let the horses blow, as they had periodically throughout this climb to forty-six hundred feet altitude. Their care not to push too fast had paid off. Even Hobo showed no signs of abnormal distress.

The ridge here at the top was clear of trees and snowdrifts, giving a view westward over a great valley.

"What's that down there, about half way across?" asked Ella.

"That's our old friend, the Missouri River, but a lot more docile now, I'll bet, than when we bumped over it in the transfer car at Bismarck."

As they rested, the clouds glooming over the valley began to tear apart. The sun poured through in columns of hazy gold, touching the pale green of sagebrush and prickly pear on the valley's floor, and lighting up the Elkhorn range and the main spine of the Rockies beyond. Seen from the elevation of the pass, with almost no foreshortening, the mountains opposite attained a stunning effect of height. Blue-black and snow-crested, they walled the horizon solidly from north to south. Between the columns of sunshine the clouds hung in dark immensities. Each mass harbored a separate thunderstorm even while the upper surfaces gleamed white against the clear blue sky above.

"The heavens declare the glory of God, and the firmament showeth his handywork." Quincy gestured in a broad arc. "That. That out there. It gives me more insight into what the Bible means about God's glory than all the Sunday school lessons I ever sat through."

Ella nodded quietly. There was no need to add anything. This had been a day of beauty and danger, of slow endeavor and sudden reward, climaxed by this moment's splendor of earth and

sky. She wanted to concentrate on the exaltation and awesomeness of seeing it from this high place. In a few instants the
golden dazzle was gone. Clouds shut out the sun and she was
quick to swing into the saddle when Quincy said, "It's late. We'd
better start down so we can make camp well below the snow
line."

In the crisp sparkling morning, as they rode singing through
the huckleberry and kinnikinnick, a voice suddenly called, "Hi,
there, boys! Where you going?"

A tall, black-bearded man came jauntily out of the woods,
balancing a pick and drill on his shoulder. Looking more closely
at Ella, he doffed his knitted wool cap and apologized. He was
Charlie Wilmer, he said, a miner who lived in one of the shacks
at an abandoned gold diggings "just down the gulch a ways."

"I been prospecting around the West for most of my forty
years," he said cheerfully. "Never made much money, but I've
had me a damn good time. Still, it's a lonesome life and I'd be
pleased with a bit of company. I've got flour for biscuits, and we
can try our luck for a mess of trout. How about it?"

His eagerness and his open, frolicsome manner were irresist-
ible. The three of them spent the afternoon swooping after grasshoppers for bait (Let's see who can catch ten the quickest!) and
fishing in the icy waters of Duck Creek. It was pure play, and
Ella enjoyed both her part of the fun and the high spirits of the
men. Quincy was elated to be the one who pulled out the only
two trout that were caught. He also shot a marmot and insisted
on converting the "whistler" into a stew to accompany the fried
fish and hot biscuits. The men forked down the stew, Charlie out
of politeness and Quincy because he was responsible. But Ella,
after a few reluctant samplings, said that her only advice about
eating whistler was, "Don't."

Charlie knew many stories about Montana in the days of the
gold strikes around Virginia City and the hell-roaring times when
Helena was Last Chance Gulch. He was also liberal with nuggets
of miscellaneous information. The Big and Little Belt Mountains,
he said, came by their name because of a wide bank of limestone

that girdled part of the larger range. The ferry crossing the Missouri River operated a mile and a half below a dam which had been built in 1898. In the next canyon northward from Duck Creek there had once been a mining camp, Diamond City, with a population of ten thousand. Now it belonged to the bluejays and squirrels, the marmots and porcupines.

"But Helena was never deserted, you know, Mrs. Scott. It's the state capital now and they're pretty fancy over there. On your way out of town you'll see the famous Broadwater Hotel, put up for people who want to come and paddle in the mineral hot spring. I doubt if the clerk would let you roughnecks register." Charlie grinned at her, adding, "But *I* got no objections. You're welcome to the bunk in my back room."

While Quincy and Ella were spreading their blankets on the bunk, the door opened a crack and Charlie tossed in a large white fluttering object. "Here's a nightshirt, Mrs. Scott," he said bashfully, "if you know how to use one."

It took less than an hour the next morning to follow the creek to the mouth of the canyon. Even under a cloudy sky the contrast in shapes and colors caught Ella's attention, and she pointed out to Quincy the pyramidal hill of red soil and rock that guarded one side, and on the other, the white poplar whose leaves were stirred in the wind to a constant shimmer of green and silver. Yellow flowers of the sage blossomed in an illusion of sunlight across the open ground sloping toward the Missouri.

They covered twenty-eight miles that day. The weather stayed cold and wet, and there was nothing to do but ride northward, up and down, up and down, over the rippling apron of moraine that spread from the Big Belts to the river. Scrubby pines and junipers grew in the folds of gravelly soil, but the penetrating herbal smell of wet sagebrush overlay every other scent. They spent the night in a barn where the rancher charged seventy-five cents for horse feed and a roof for themselves.

Quincy ruefully fingered his remaining change, the last of the eleven dollars with which they had started out from Terry. "We may have to work our passage on the boat tomorrow!"

It didn't quite come to that. After they arrived at Canyon

Ferry, they bought soda crackers for breakfast, paid the crossing toll, and had thirty-five cents left.

The ferry ride took only a few minutes, once they and the horses were aboard.

"Our second intersection with the trail of Lewis and Clark," Quincy reminded Ella as they steadied the horses on the small open deck of the scow. "They came along here, up the river through the Gates of the Mountains—"

"What a lovely poetic name!"

"It's a narrow, dangerous passage, closed in by high rock walls."

"But still a lovely name." Ella turned it over in her mind. Gates of the Mountains . . . She could understand how Meriwether Lewis and William Clark and their plains-weary men had felt when they got their boats through and saw, close at hand, the mountains they had been aiming for. A gate protects—and promises. Explorers weren't required to be poets, but by chance or by choice, that rock chasm had been christened with a name that Byron couldn't have bettered.

What would Byron have said about the Missouri, Ella wondered. He should have had a chance at it six weeks ago, at Bismarck. There was no drama today. The spring floods were past, and the dam upstream had tamed what unruliness remained.

On the other side Quincy and Ella had a climb up the bluffs and a fifteen-mile ride to approach Helena. Long before they arrived they could see the cupola and copper dome of Montana's capitol lording it above the rooflines of the city, backed by the solid bastion of the mountains whose measure they had taken from Duck Creek Pass three days ago.

Forty dollars was waiting for them at the postoffice, along with letters from the families in New York and Seattle. Ella felt a great relief as she watched Quincy cash the postal order and fold the bills into his purse. Being homeless and hungry wasn't bad, but being broke at the same time was scary. Leaving the horses switching flies at a tie rail, they found a store where they could buy new army shirts. Their original dark blue shirts were unrecognizable, sun-bleached and rain-washed to splotches of green-

ish brown and pinkish mauve, and Quincy's was minus most of
one sleeve. They paid two bits apiece for straw hats. Ella tried
on shoes. The best she could do was a pair of boys' clodhoppers.
They felt dreadfully clumsy, but more comfortable than the
"Queen Anne brogans" she had endured since Bismarck. She also
bought bandannas to replace the rags into which their old
neckerchiefs had deteriorated.

After laying in a fresh supply of food, they debated whether
they should write home for another money order to reach them
in eastern Washington.

"We've put quite a hole in our forty dollars already, Quincy.
Shouldn't we ask for at least ten or fifteen more?"

"We won't need it. The thirty dollars we got in Dickinson
lasted all this way, over a month. What's left of our forty certainly should see us to Seattle."

"Yes, but suppose we run into some kind of emergency and it
doesn't see us through." Ella paused while she finished tying the
last parcel to Hobo's saddle. "What would you have done if the
postal order hadn't been waiting here? If we'd been stuck with
no money at all?"

"Well—" Quincy looked at her solemnly over Hike's back. "I'd
have robbed the bank. Or turned somersaults on the Capitol lawn
and passed the hat—my nice new straw hat. Or I'd have hired a
hall on tick and charged admission for a series of political chalk-
talks. You can bet I'd have thought of something." He was
smiling now, a sweet smile that invited her to take his nonsense
just seriously enough to quiet her anxieties, to believe in him if
not in what he was saying.

She did believe in him. How many times this summer his
ingenuity, his persuasiveness, his steady will in the face of danger
had brought them through! The one time when she felt the
whole burden of survival on her shoulders, he had leaped from
his sickbed to run to her rescue. Yes, she believed in him, and she
smiled over the saddle and said, "It's not that I care for millions,
you understand. It's just that I prefer to be fixed so that if I lose
a nickel down a crack, I don't have to hunt for it with a hairpin."

"I know." His face went sober again, really sober. "You don't feel that any more strongly than I do. But our bank account is getting anemic, and we still have to pay our railroad fare east, so I don't want to draw down any further than we absolutely have to."

She understood, and didn't press the point. If by ill chance they did run out of cash between here and Seattle, he would think of something. What that something would be, she found out at Wenatchee.

But today Helena was treating them kindly. Clerks in the stores had been accommodating, passers-by nodded friendly greetings. At the grocery, the owner's son had drawn a careful map showing the route over the Divide. Ella liked the look of Helena's main street, where neat brick and stone buildings had replaced the false-fronts destroyed when fire ravaged Last Chance Gulch. Even more she enjoyed the houses of the mining aristocracy, handsome Victorian houses that she and Quincy passed as they rode northward through the town.

Two miles beyond Helena stood the Broadwater Hotel, imposingly ornate in its Byzantine style, with towers and arches and enough rooms, it looked, to accommodate a regiment of the well-heeled.

"Charlie was right," murmured Ella as they came abreast. "Even with our new shirts and clean bandannas, I doubt if we'd be allowed in."

They did better—free lodging with the young engineer who was camping out in the ruins of a hotel a mile farther along. He had charge of landscaping the Broadwater grounds. Like Old Mac and Charlie Wilmer, he was a raconteur and gratified to have an audience.

"Where did you come by all those yarns?" Quincy asked at the end of the evening.

The engineer's healthy, homely, sunburned face crinkled with laughter. "I was marooned one winter with only *Hostetter's Almanac* and a Bible for company, and when they dug me out in the spring I could quote the *Almanac* by heart."

"How about the Bible?" said Ella.

"Oh, that too. It comes in mighty handy in an argument."

"This is written astraddle of North America. Eastward is the Atlantic and westward the Pacific and each is downhill form here."

Sitting back to back in a green swale on top of the continent, Quincy and Ella were using their noon rest to answer the family letters. The ascent to McDonald Pass had been relatively easy. Part way up they had seen a jagged ridge above the canyon's north wall, a dragon crest of fierce high rocks that looked like the backbone of a continent ought to look. But their route passed well beneath the ridge, and when they came out of the forest at the head of the canyon, the road ran before them on such a gradual rise that it was hard to tell where the change from uphill to downhill marked the watershed.

Though Quincy's eyes couldn't distinguish the exact summit, gravity could. Day and night, season by season, each raindrop and trickle of melting snow was shunted in its ordained direction, toward the Columbia Basin or the Mississippi. For this was the Great Divide, sixty-three hundred feet above sea level, and because the pass was open land for a mile or more in all directions, the view swept an infinity of mountains. Mountains to the south, thickly covered with larch and pine. Mountains to the west and north, part forest, part grassy slopes. Seen through the V of the canyon, the flat valley Quincy and Ella had crossed yesterday rolled eastward, with the sparkling of snow on the Big Belts beyond.

Colors today were green near at hand, blue at a distance, shifting in depth as the cloud shadows sailed over. Astraddle of North America, Quincy brought his eyes back to the writing pad balanced on his knee, and went on with his letter to his parents.

"We have 770 miles or so to go, maybe less, as the trail is sometimes shorter than the Ry . . . Don't worry about us at all . . . We have enough in pocket to see us to Seattle, and we are making 25, sometimes 30, miles a day, the horses having had less than half a dozen feeds of oats for 500-odd miles. That tawney-black Hike horse is wonderful!"

Quincy glanced up to admire, with some personal pride, Hike's sleek and healthy appearance. As if aware of the admiration, Hike raised his head from the grass and looked around at Quincy, meanwhile champing away on the stems that stuck out like emerald whiskers on each side of his black muzzle. If there's one smart thing I did this summer, Quincy thought, it was buying that bronco. He's been well worth his price.

That reminded Quincy to add one practical request near the end of his letter: "Please let us know what is our bank balance."

Ella was taking longer over her answer to Seattle. Mother Allen, having shrewdly read between the lines of the account of trail life in eastern Montana, was now urging that the journey be finished safely by train. For himself, Quincy wouldn't even entertain the thought. Such an ignominious conclusion to their much-advertised exploit! Ella, he hoped, fully shared his feeling. Last night, and again this morning, when he had offered to quit if she thought they should, she had protested that she was as able and eager as he to complete what they had undertaken to do. She certainly looked it, this slim, brown, dependable western girl of his. But how to convey the assurance to an anxious parent, and make it clear that the choice to continue on horseback was a joint decision, not forced by his will? With a new husband's sensitivity to the opinion of his mother-in-law, he pivoted around and obtained permission to rest his chin on Ella's shoulder and read as her pencil moved over the page:

"You mustn't worry about our starving. The hardest part, as far as that went, is over—the part from Terry across Montana to Jordan and the Musselshell . . . As for our being tired and wanting to quit—well, we're mighty anxious to get to Seattle and see you . . . but since we got into the mountains we've been enjoying ourselves more and more and we have almost forgotten

Good campsites were easy to find between the Continental Divide and Missoula. McClellan saddle left of tent, saddlebags on right.

what it is to be tired. At the end of the day's march we feel like playing tag. Besides all the fun, we've a sort of pride about sticking it out . . . Of course we mustn't carry this to an extreme but we want to see it through if possible."

He was satisfied. Mother Allen was a level-headed woman, used to taking risks and doing without. She would understand and respect the decision.

Riding down beyond the Divide, Quincy and Ella struck the Northern Pacific line at Elliston and followed it as far as the mountain prairies where Avon's narrow white clapboard church and log houses clustered near the station. On the counsel of the storekeeper, they turned northwest from the railroad here to pick up the Mullan Road.

"That'll take ye the easiest way," said the storekeeper, whose snowy beard grew almost to his belt. "Down Nevada Creek, then along the Big Blackfoot River, which runs down to Hell Gate, just afore ye hit Missoula. They's ranches every few miles, and you can buy grub at Ovando and Potomac. Ye come over McDonald summit? They say that road up there was built in 1870, operated by a fellow named Alexander McDonald—he collected a toll from everybody using it. But the Military Road was started in 1859. Cap'n John Mullan, he was in charge, and he pushed that road clear from Fort Benton to Walla Walla. Finished it in '63, considerable before you was born, young feller."

One long picnic. That's what Quincy called the week spent in progress to Missoula. Pleasant weather, a downhill road through forested valleys and across meadows fragrant with wild roses. Fresh game, garden produce from amiable ranchers, and a Sunday rest in an empty log cabin. Now that they were free from immediate anxieties and regaining vigor after the period of scant rations, Quincy and Ella felt like a frolic. Their surplus energy overflowed into word games, verses, songs and light-hearted tomfoolery as they traveled along. When original inspiration temporarily ran dry, he would ask her to spiel off one of the dozens of poems she knew by heart. One day she chose Shelley's *The Cloud*. He listened for what he called the "moon stanza":

> *That orbed maiden with white fire laden,*
> *Whom mortals call the Moon,*
> *Glides glimmering o'er my fleece-like floor*
> *By the midnight breezes strewn;*
> *And wherever the beat of her unseen feet . . ."*

At that point a tremor shook him, as if those unseen feet were breaking through the cloud-roof of his soul to flood it with white fire. Slightly embarrassed by his feelings, he came down to earth by calling for "Oxydoner Victory," and Ella gave him, rapid fire and all in one breath, her favorite patent medicine ad: "The Oxydoner Victory, when applied by buckling the contact disc upon the skin of either ankle and placing the vocer in either cold air or water, generates in the whole human body a positive amount of heat and an affinity for negative gases, the most negative of which is oxygen."

He tried to say it as fast as she had, tangled his tongue halfway through and gave up in rueful admiration.

An amateur evening climaxed the restful Sunday. This day began with the howling of a wolf near the log cabin refuge to give a wild flavor to the setting. They took sun baths, and naps, and feasted on roast venison, courtesy of Quincy's good aim the day before. As the sun went down with coral-pink banners flaming in the western sky, Quincy handed Ella the frying pan and said, "You be mistress of ceremonies—here's your gavel. You can introduce me as the first act. Let's hope the pines and firs, and whatever critters they harbor, will make an appreciative audience."

It was Quincy's idea to make a game of it. Taking turns, each invented a stunt for the other to perform, the trick being to think up something ludicrous and implausible. Songs, jokes, dances, impromptu monologues, spoofs of operas and melodramas—the rollicking nonsense went on for an hour. Finally Ella banged the frying pan on a stump and said, "The concluding number on our program will be a cantata entitled 'Spring in Autumn, or Grandma, do the Angels Wear Daisy Chains Like Me?' It will be sung by six little girls."

By this time Quincy had laughed so much that he couldn't sing like himself, let alone imitate six little girls, so they rang down the curtain and went to bed.

Next morning he woke full of high-spirited ambition.

"Bunny, for one day we're going to put all our gear on Hobo, and give Hike nothing but you to carry. That'll make an easier stretch of travel for both ponies. I'll jog it on foot."

He kept his resolve, though he was footsore and far more tired than Ella by the time they made late camp just east of Bonner. But there had been one moment that put a smile on the weary day. West of the little lumbering settlement of Potomac they came upon a piece of road that curved around an open field and for a half mile was in sight of a group of men lounging on the porch of a hotel.

"Let's give 'em a shock." Quincy broke into a run and hit top speed as he zipped past the startled onlookers. Ella rode about fifty yards behind, leading Hobo. As she came abreast of the porch, one of the men jerked his thumb toward Quincy and yelled, "Is he running against time?"

"Yes!" Ella shouted back.

"Where to?"

"He's setting a foot record from St. Paul to Seattle."

"Gee whiz, Seee-yattle?"

In Bonner the next morning Quincy and Ella did something they wished they had done weeks earlier. They got rid of the saddlebags. Although the leather pouches looked very neat and military, they were a nuisance because of their weight and their continual bumping against the horses' sides at any pace faster than a walk. After rolling all the necessary equipment in the two pup tent halves, Quincy paid two dollars to express the saddlebags in care of Mother Allen, along with the .45 Colt revolver and a few other items. This reduced the pack load on the horses to fifty pounds apiece, including the McClellan saddles. With three more mountain passes to cross, the saving might be crucial.

Beyond the lumber mills and company houses of Bonner lay Hell Gate, where the Clark Fork River squeezed between the flanks of Missoula's mountain guardians, Sentinel and Jumbo. Missoula, a clean bright little city, reigned over a stretch of farms and ranches girdled by the misty blue ranges of the Bitterroots. The river, broadening around graveled, brushy islands, divided Missoula between the business side, and the campus side where the state university lay at the foot of Mt. Sentinel. Residence blocks on both sides were bowered in the shade of maples, cut leaf birches, cottonwoods and fruit trees. Streetcars *ding-dinged* along Higgins Avenue. Quincy saw moccasined Indians sitting on the curbing or leaning against the store windows. The men wore black tall-crowned felt hats, beneath which their blacker hair fell in heavy braids, tucked under their coat collars. The somberness was offset by colored shirts and silk neckerchiefs— orange, cerise, green, cerulean blue. Some of the men had a blanket draped across their shoulders. The women, the younger ones with children around them, kept at a little distance from the men. Quincy noticed two very old women in creamy doeskin shifts and leggings. The rest of the women were dressed in long dark cotton skirts. Bead and bone necklaces brightened their dark blouses. Many had silk kerchiefs tied around their heads.

A generation ago the Flathead Indians had come down to this valley to dig camas roots and fight off marauding Blackfeet. Now

"Is he running against time?"

it was a place to spend a little money and a lot of time on a hot sleepy July afternoon. There was no excitement on the streets today, but even so, Quincy supposed, it was a change from the dead-end monotony of the reservation. He longed to talk to these people, urged on by curiosity and respect. But when he approached a handsome middle-aged Indian, the man met his smile with a glance of such unfathomable reserve and dignity that Quincy merely nodded and passed on by, abashed at his own presumption.

After a few errands—it was Quincy who needed shoes now— he and Ella spent twenty cents in a refreshment parlor, grateful for the icy tingle of ice cream soda in their throats and the coolness of the marble-topped table against their sweating forearms.

They camped nine miles west of town and turned in early, to swat mosquitoes and mull over a problem that had to be settled at breakfast time: whether to continue on Captain Mullan's road over the Coeur d'Alene mountains to Spokane, or to swing northward through the Flathead reservation and cross Idaho near the top of the panhandle, where the grade was easy. The advice in Missoula had favored the long detour, and it was reinforced by a farmer they met outside of town, who warned them, "Stay offa them goddam mountains. Your horses'll be belly deep in snow all the way."

XI The horses were blowing, snorting dust from their nostrils and heaving great windy sighs. Ella loosened Hobo's girth and sank down on the pine needles with a windy sigh of her own. She tilted her head to look at the lettering carved into the board nailed against the tree above her.

This is the domedest
hill I ever saw
but thank the Lord
I am on top.

With a stub of pencil Quincy was copying the words into his pocket notebook. "First time I ever saw 'damnedest' spelled that way," he laughed. "But the meaning is clear. And there's another sign over there."

He pointed to a smaller piece of board where someone had pencilled the outline of a bicycle and the resolve, "Portland or Bust."

"A *bicycle?*" Ella was incredulous. "Well, if a fellow made it this far with a bike, I'll bet he got to Portland without busting. Whooh, what a hill! Thank the Lord *we* are on top." She lay back full length on the ground, snatching a few moments' relief for her aching feet and throbbing legs. She and Quincy had done much of the nine-mile grade walking.

The short steep route had won. She had said, that morning just west of Missoula, "Hills won't scare us, not after the climbing we've done already, and as for being belly deep in snow, the Coeur d'Alene summit can't be as high as McDonald, and we're later in the season. That farmer must have been talking through his hat." So here they were, four days into the mountains, striking for Kellogg by way of the Mullan Road and Lookout Pass. There were no snowbanks, but hills aplenty. Captain Mullan's engineers had never flinched from a steep grade. Ella tried to imagine what straining muscles and blistering profanity had been required to move a freight wagon over this trail before the N. P. put its line through—and there were enough wrecked railroad cars lying at the bottoms of the canyons to show that the Coeur d'Alenes had exacted their toll there too. She turned her mind to pleasanter scenes of the last four days.

There was Frenchtown, a patch of rural Quebec stitched into the western quiltwork of the Missoula valley, where Quincy had used his schoolroom French on the friendly housewives to garner a fair supply of *oeufs, pommes de terre* and *lait.* But at the last house, when he said, *"Donnez-moi de l'eau, s'il vous plait,"* the buxom blue-eyed woman burst out laughing. "The poomp's in the back, laddie."

There was the canyon of the Clark Fork, walled partly by cliffs of yellow, brown or mauve-pink rock, partly by bare-bosomed hills. But always above these lower bastions towered the true heights, darkly mantled with larch, fir and pine. The river ran steady and deep, driving toward its far union with the Columbia. In the afternoons, when the sun was halfway down and the wind blew gently upstream, the green waters were patterned in thousands of tiny arcs rimmed with gold. Larger waves, lifting at a different angle, reflected the sun in round, blinding flashes of silver. Gold, silver, greenbacks—we're rich, Ella had thought, even with a slim purse.

There was the road, twisting up the hills, dipping down when the canyon widened. And there were the towns—the log buildings of Superior, put up in the '70s and '80s, lorded over by a "luxury hotel" for miners, fronted with a two-story veranda. And St. Regis, a sawmill town, where the Clark Fork turned to run

What goes up must get down.

northward around the mountains. She and Quincy had taken the horses across on a ferry this morning and lunched in the dooryard of an empty house, stewing Juneberries picked along the riverbank . . .

"Hey, Bunny, wake up. Time to get going."

Ella jumped to her feet. "I wasn't asleep!" she protested. But another lazy minute or two and she would have been.

Down on the other side of the "domedest hill" they found the choicest campsite yet, a grade carpeted with lush grass and ringed with tall timber. There were springy fir boughs for a bed, lots of dry wood for the fire, and a stream full of sweet cold water and trout.

"Welcome to Nature's guestchamber!" Quincy had a twinkle in his eyes as he added, "I think this has everything to please both the horses and my wife."

There was only one drawback—mountain lions.

Just after dark, as Quincy and Ella were snuggled beside the campfire, an eerie scream echoed and re-echoed from the sides of the narrow canyon. A few minutes later Ella heard a twig crack and saw two bright dots shining from the edge of the forest. She clutched Quincy's arm and pointed, afraid to speak aloud. He snatched up the carbine, leaped the fire and took aim. Then, as suddenly, he lowered his gun.

"Whew, that was a near thing! I almost pulled the trigger on our best horse."

"No mountain lion?"

"Nary a one. The eyes are two daisies reflecting the campfire. See? And it was Hike who snapped the twig. He was right beyond the daisies."

Ella was only slightly reassured. "But that screeching up the hillside, that's a mountain lion. Shouldn't we put up the tent for protection?"

"It wouldn't help much, if Mr. Lion seriously wanted our drumsticks. A better idea would be to keep the fire going all night."

There was no way of proving whether any prowling beasts

kept their distance because of the blaze. But if Quincy and Ella slept uneasy, they also slept uneaten, disturbed only by the irritating *plong-plong, plong-plong* of the cowbell hanging from Hobo's neck as the horses stood head to head, tooth-scratching each other's mosquito bites.

Ella, waking for a few minutes in the middle of the night and seeing how feebly the flickering embers held the darkness at bay, asked herself why a wife has to be brave just because her husband wouldn't let himself be anything else. Then she inched herself a little closer to the comforting solidity of his broad back and went to sleep again.

JOURNAL ENTRIES

      SUNDAY, JULY 28. *Bought grub at De Borgia . . . Nooned by St. Regis river . . . Passed lumber and mining towns of Saltese and Taft . . . streets full of Sunday loafers. Late finding camping place.*

      MONDAY, JULY 29 . . . *Crossed St. Regis river 36 times in 9 miles—bad rocky road—long climb to summit. Nooned half mile from top in deep woods . . . Heavy rain came up. Sat on saddles and blankets under trees till 4:30. Sudden drop from lookout to valley around Mullan. Mines all over mountainsides. River (South fork of the Coeur d'Alene) ruined with lead poison from concentrators.*

They had finally climbed out of Montana, crossing the line at an elevation of forty-seven hundred feet. Ella twisted in the saddle for a farewell glance. Her eyes saw only the road and the forest that swallowed it up. Yet in her mind she was looking back across canyons and peaks, broad valleys and high plains, looking back to the face of a ranch wife crazed with loneliness, to Leah the Forsaken, to the good talk at the Brainerds' shady cabin, to the openhanded sheepmen and ranchers, and frolicsome Charlie Wilmer, to terror, exhaustion, awe and delight. Montana had

treated them rough, and royally. It seemed more like six life-
times than six weeks since she and Quincy had faced the state at
its eastern border. Now it was goodbye, for awhile. She had a
premonition that from this time she would always be a little
homesick for the "land of the shining mountains."

She reached out to lay her hand on Hobo's neck. "And you,
you lazy, wind-broken strawberry roan, we must have done right
by you, because you got us through Montana."

She gave him the signal and rode with Quincy over the lip of
Lookout Pass and down the six miles of road that dropped them
to the narrow valley fifteen hundred feet below.

It was easy to see that silver and lead were big business here.
The towns mingled frontier brashness with unexpected amenities.
Ella decided that Mullan could be described as a "festive crude
mining town," yet a few miles further, in Wallace, she and
Quincy bought food in a grocery store which was far and away
the finest they had found since leaving St. Paul. But they were
heartsick at the devastation of the canyon. Fumes from the ore
processing had killed off acres of forest growth, leaving expanses
of steep mountainside barren except for skeleton trees. The river
ran sullen and opaque and dirty gray. All the roistering vitality of
the towns couldn't counterbalance the deadening effect.

"Don't the people see what's happening," cried Ella, "or have
they become so used to it they don't care?"

She repeatedly warned Quincy about the polluted drinking
water. But on the second day, after marching across a shadeless
stretch east of Kellogg, he was so thirsty that he risked a few
mouthfuls from a side stream that looked clear, and paid for it
with several hours of misery and no appetite for supper.

"You can say 'I told you so,' " he murmured weakly as he lay
by the campfire watching Ella finishing her coffee.

She sighed and smiled faintly. "They claim experience is the
best teacher, but you'll live longer, dear, if you don't always
insist on being the one to have the experience."

He groaned. "But I do learn, don't I? Have I taken so much
as one drop of dubious condensed milk since we left Mr.

The only practical way to ride after drinking from a lead-polluted stream.

Morton's sheepwagon? Will I ever again imbibe from the south branch of the Coeur d'Alene River or any tributaries thereof? Not on your sweet life, being anxious to preserve my own. All of which proves—"

"All of which proves you must be getting better. I'll stop worrying."

Beyond Kellogg Idaho's mountain beauty reasserted itself. From the little hill at Cataldo, where at Ella's suggestion they stopped on Thursday morning to see the Indian mission church, the view encompassed dark green mountains, light green meadows, and silver and blue reflections from the sedgy marsh-land that stretched from the bottom of the hill to the last, low ridge of the Rockies. At the moment Quincy was more interested in the church than in the view, he said. The white, high-roofed two-story building, forty by ninety feet in dimension, had been put up nearly sixty years before by Father Anthony Ravalli, helped by a lay brother and a band of unskilled Indians with the only tools at their disposal—a broad axe, an augur, ropes, pulleys, and a penknife.

Though the church, like the rectory and orchard adjoining, showed the effect of age and insufficient care, time had not diminished its dignity and handsome lines. Quincy dismounted to run his hand admiringly over the curve of one of the six round pillars that supported the roof over the entry, and then backed away far enough to get a look at the "sunburst" carving on the facade above. "Golly! With a broad axe and a penknife! And all the timbers put together with wooden pegs. I guess, Bunny, our new century has forgotten what patience is."

The old apple trees behind the church would have provided shade for a picnic lunch, but it was not yet mid-morning, so they rode down the hill, skirted the marsh and started up Fourth of July Canyon, grateful on this blazing day for moist coolness under the canopies of fir and cedar.

On July 4, 1861, Captain John Mullan and his men flew the American flag from a tall white pine in this Idaho canyon, com-memorating the event by carving the date and the initials "M. R." (for Military Road) on the tree. The roadmakers had cause to celebrate. They had completed building the hardest two-thirds of the route between Fort Benton and Walla Walla. On this August 1, 1907, Quincy and Ella had four-fifths of their distance and scheduled time behind them. They hadn't intended to celebrate, but the opportunity was thrust on them.

They stopped along Cedar Creek to cook lunch and take their customary rest. Ella was dishing up the boiled potatoes when a drawling voice floated toward her from across the creek.

"Howdy, folks. My name's Claypool. Maw says whyn't you come over 'n' eat with us. We got plenty. Pt!"

Out from under the low cedar boughs poked a heap of straw-stack hair. The face below was decorated with a drooping mustache, the mustache was decorated with tobacco juice. The body that followed the face was long and loosely strung together. If Claypool had stood upright, he would have topped six feet, but it was too much trouble.

Quincy explained that he and Ella had their own food ready. "But we'll be glad to come over after awhile."

"Well, I wisht you would. Pt!" Mr. Claypool used spurts of 'baccy juice as punctuation marks. "I got a kinda cross gang, but if you kin stand that, you'll git along all right. My boy Elmer, he plays the mouth organ. And Lizzie, she kin sing for us, and we'll have a hot time. Pt."

The Claypools were "movers," traveling with two covered wagons and ten horses. Originally from the United States, they had been living in Alberta and were now on their way to Baker, Oregon. The party included Paw and Maw, Elmer and his grown-up sisters, Lizzie and Rhoda, three younger children, and a girl called Nette who, Paw said, had "took up" with them at the last ranch. She had brought along her little one-eyed brother "to make things look good." But Paw wasn't fooled. "What she's after, a chap'ron would only get in the way. She's after my Elmer. You'll see."

When Ella and Quincy crossed the creek later in the afternoon they found the movers, their wagons and their horses spread out over both sides of the trail. Maw Claypool was asleep, with her fat body propped against a pine tree and her stumpy legs stuck out in a wide angle in front of her. The soles of her shoes were loose and hung like flaps from the instep. She waked up as the rest of the family gathered around to meet the strangers.

Elmer pointed to her shoes. "Hey, Maw, I see you need half-solin' again."

Maw's pudgy, snub-nosed face split in a wide smile. She wiggled her bare pink toes, highly visible where the soles bent away from her shoes. Elmer, Paw and all the rest of the family went into gales of laughter, and Maw wiggled her toes again. Ella saw that this was a routine of long standing.

Paw wiped his eyes. "She's so damn skeered to stay in the wagon when it begins to shake on the rough places in the trail that she's all the time gittin' out to walk. If she hefted like a human bein', a pair of shoes might last her something decent. But built like she is, she busts them out first thing. It's buy a pair at every store we pass."

"Well, the reason I'm skeered is that they dumped me out oncet."

"Haw-haw! Hi-ee!" shouted the chorus.

"Yep," said Paw. "She was sleepin' that time too—pt!—in the back of the wagon. We come to a bad sidehill place an' off she went like a sack of wheat. Rolled down till she hit spang into a bunch of trees. Wasn't no good place to stop the wagon there so I druv on to where it was more level, an' she had to come hikin' after us. Gee mighty, did I ketch it!"

When the laughter slacked off, Maw bade everybody sit down on the stumps and fallen logs. She looked intently at Quincy. "Scott, your name is? I had me a ol' man by that name oncet. He was before this one." She flipped a thumb toward Paw. "I do believe you must be a relation to him. He had a no 'count brother that run away from home and they never heard from him after. I bet that brother was your dad, hey? You look like my first ol' man too, only he—"

"Aw, shet up!" Paw spat with more than usual vehemence. "These folks don't want to be hearin' about *that* feller."

"Hee-hee!" snickered Rhoda, fluffing her red calico skirt over

her knees. "Paw never likes to have that first feller brought up."
"Sure don't," said Elmer. "When he married Maw he made her
turn his picture agin the wall. Hey, Paw? Hoo-hoo!"
Paw appealed to Ella. "Said they was a cross gang, didn't I?
Jist a pack of fools. You don't want to hear sech nonsense. Pt.
What you want is to hear Lizzie sing. Come on, Lizzie."
Lizzie grinned shyly and hung back. She was tall and strawy-
haired like the rest of the Claypools, but slim and with a coltish
grace. Ella noticed that when she wasn't looking self-conscious,
or laughing with her mouth open too wide, she had the kind of
fleeting prettiness that sometimes comes to a plain girl between
childhood and womanhood. After the proper amount of coaxing
Lizzie seated herself on the ground, tailor-fashion, fixed her eyes
on the top of a dead hemlock tree, and swayed back and forth.
Then suddenly she began to sing. Her voice was penetrating, and
she paid out each vowel as though she were afraid to let go and
catch the next one. All her ballads were mournfully sentimental—
"When the Leaves Come Drifting Down," "You'll Always be the
Same Sweet Girl to Me," "Red River Valley."

"Consider awhi-ile ere you lee-eeve meee,
And consider awhi-ile whaatcha doo-oo . . ."

Paw looked on proudly, calling for encores.
"Did you ever take lessons, Lizzie?" Ella asked.
"Oh, no. They wasn't any other great singers around where
we was. I jist learned them pieces outen the book. Them is all
book songs."
"Don't suppose *you* folks sing?" asked Paw.
"My husband and I can do a duet."
With heads close together and faces solemn, Ella and Quincy
sang, *andante tenderissimo,* a ditty they had made up last week
as they plugged along up the St. Regis River.

"*Tro mama, tro mama,*
Te fassen e geiss,
How kindly mine fa ta te
Tal-li fi flu.

Lizzie fixed her eye on the top of a dead hemlock and began to sing.

My aunty so ziemlich,
A trolley ka rat,
So sudden a fannica,
Where am I at?
A-a-a-men!

"My, aint' that grand!" cried Maw. "It jist about started me a-weepin'. What is it, a anthem?"

"You might call it that," said Quincy, with a wink at Ella. "I don't know what it means, but it's fine, isn't it?"

"You bet. I jist love that holy music. Now, Elmer, git your mouth organ."

"I could play better iffen I wasn't so thirsty," hinted Elmer.

Lizzie and Rhoda put together a concoction of vinegar, lemon extract, sugar and a kettleful of creek water. Ella drank only a little, wondering if they called it a soft drink because it produced such a fuzzy feeling. Elmer downed several mugs of it, urged on by Nette, who kept sending her little brother to the kettle for refills. Watching Nette's adoring face, Ella whispered to Quincy, "Paw's right. That girl's out to get Elmer, and he's as good as gone right now."

After Elmer's stint on the mouth organ, he and Quincy made a giant see saw, using the telephone poles left lying along the road by a line crew. They shifted one pole crosswise of the pile and summoned the girls and children to take turns riding sky-high, giggling and shrieking in delicious terror.

The afternoon came to a wild climax. Quincy and Ella, intending to spend the night further up the canyon, had mounted Hobo and Hike and were splashing across the creek to say goodbye to the Claypools when a herd of bulls came pounding up the trail, driven by three men on horseback. Which was more surprised, the bulls or the camping party, is irrelevant. The result was fright and confusion all around. The animals spilled into the woods on both sides. Two of the riders chased after the bulls that went bellowing one way, Quincy spurred to help the other man drive out the creatures that plunged into camp.

Whooping and hollering in the best cowboy tradition, Ella joined in. After a little vigorous bucking in the first moment of excitement, Hike seemed to know what to do better that she did, remembering, perhaps, from his days in Joe Sweetman's roundup string. She let him go chasing the bulls over fallen logs and dodging around the wagons until the last of them was on the way up the trail.

The Claypools were loud in their gratitude. "Gee mighty, young feller, you an' your wife is regular cowpunchers!" said Paw heartily.

Rhoda sidled up to Ella. "Me wearin' a red skirt, I thought one of them bulls was goin' to horn me. But you kep' him off. You sure do handle that horse good."

Ella accepted the praise modestly, glad that no one had noticed Hike nearly bucking her off. She and Quincy said their goodbyes and rode away. Paw shouted after them, "Come and see us if you ever get to Baker. Pt!"

By the end of the next long hot day they had passed Fourth of July summit and looped down the west side of the ridge to pitch their tent on the stony beach of Lake Coeur d'Alene. Vivid blue in color, with a deeply indented, forested shoreline, the lake covered thirty-five miles north and south and in some places was a quarter of that in width. Altogether a beautifully refreshing sight to a couple of dusty travelers who hadn't seen a lake since leaving Minnesota.

For the first time this season they were not camping alone. Scattered along the beach stood the tents of the summer people from Spokane. The wind was blowing off the lake, rolling up an evening thunderstorm. It was a warm wind, and as soon as darkness fell, Quincy and Ella peeled off their clothes and waded into the lake. There was a sensuous pleasure in paddling naked through the water, as warm to the skin as the breeze, while overhead, unseen in the blackness that enveloped sky and lake, the storm drew steadily closer. Ella soaped and rinsed and splashed, prolonging the delicious feeling. Then, as she and Quincy returned to the shallow water, ready to wade out, a bolt of lightning sprang from cloud to cloud, lighting up the shore with an instant's brilliance.

"Run!" cried Quincy, catching her hand and pulling her toward the tent. He was laughing as they dived into its shelter. "Now don't worry. If any of the other campers saw us, they won't believe their eyes."

Just to be on the safe side, however, they were packed and on the way Saturday morning before the other tenters began poking frowzy heads out from between the flaps.

A streetcar line ran to Spokane from the town of Coeur d'Alene at the foot of the lake. While Ella continued on the road with the horses, Quincy went to the city by trolley for mail, as the postoffice would be closed tomorrow when they arrived in Spokane on horseback. The morning was fresh after the rain that had come with the thunderstorm. Ella pressed Hike to a brisk walk, forcing Hobo reluctantly to keep pace at the end of the lead rope. Ahead of her the Rockies dwindled away. On the last hills, pines began taking over from firs, then brown grass and red rock began taking over from pines. It was as though the army of trees which had marched in close order all down the western slopes of the ranges faltered and broke ranks at the sight of the hot dry land ahead. Soon there would be nothing but grass and rock and plain.

Already Ella's thoughts were overleaping the border into her home state and hurrying on to those other mountains still to cross, the Cascades. On their far side her family waited. She was so anxious for news that when Quincy appeared, walking back from Spokane to meet her, she called out, "Letters? Did we get any letters from Seattle?"

He tramped toward her in the dust and handed her an envelope. "Wallace is gone—he's going to try his hand at real estate back East. But he did stay long enough to set a date with Jessie for their wedding, at Christmas time. Jessie has to leave Seattle on August 27, because of her school schedule. She wants to know how long a visit she'll have with you before she goes."

Ella raced through the note from her sister. "Why, that's just twenty-four days from now!" She couldn't keep the dismay out of her voice. "I expected to have at least a week with her. But you've been saying there's about three hundred and fifty miles beyond Spokane, and we'll need at least one day for rest, so that means—oh, Quincy, we can't do it, can we? Over the Cascades?"

AUGUST: *The last mountains*

XII

Three months from St. Paul to Spokane—and less than three weeks now to reach Seattle.

Hike began, as he had in May, with a bucking exhibition. He humped and jolted and curvetted along Sprague avenue, giving Spokane's Sunday church-goers something to think about besides the sermon. Quincy was proud of the ease with which Ella stayed in the saddle, even when Hike added a few extra flourishes in passing near the falls where the Spokane River thundered into its seventy-foot gorge.

Those horsey hijinks weren't the only similarity between the two sections of the trip. The last part was to be in many ways a reprise of the first. Like Minneapolis and St. Paul, Spokane was queen of a lumber and grain empire, and once again Quincy and Ella were setting out from such a city to ride across wide-horizoned farmlands, into the sagebrush country, and on toward a river and a chain of snow-peaked mountains where they might have to gamble their lives without knowing the odds. Again they were dependent on ranchers for part of their food, and occasional shelter in barn or haystack. They lost their way for several hours in a stretch of wild country. Meadowlarks piped to them, and the same ceaseless wind blew its williwaws over miles of grain, set the windmills spinning, and whispered through the prairie grass. The weather copied the earlier pattern, chill and wet for the first days, then clear and warm. And money behaved as it had before, shrinking from little to less and less. Finally it stranded Quincy and Ella on the east bank of the Columbia River, where sixty cents was not enough to ferry the horses across. But along with the duplications, every day had its new elements.

Temple of the wheat farmer's faith, the grain elevator loomed on the skyline of prairie towns from the Mississippi to the Columbia River.

For instance, the soldiers, and the old Indian. Quincy and Ella rode in company with the soldiers for a mile or two through the western edges of Spokane. The men were driving a wagonload of meat to Fort Wright. The spit-and-polish corporal, who seemed to feel that the honor of the United States Army was impugned by the tattered condition of Quincy's service breeches, persisted in offering to take him to the fort for an outfit of new khakis. Quincy just as persistently refused. "Thanks, but I don't want to arrive in Seattle looking as if I'd just started out!"

The Indian showed up later, slipping quietly through the pines into the ravine where Quincy was kindling a fire for lunch. He was an old man, his bronzed face furrowed with a thousand wrinkles, his bent figure leaning on a staff. He took it for granted that he might share the skimpy meal, and lay down on the bank to sleep until Ella finished the cooking. Quincy inspected the inert Indian, from the cloth headband, as grimy as the mismatched coat and pants, to the elkskin moccasins thonged at the ankle. He was searching for a clue . . . to what? To the broken remnants of a world that had once belonged to a proud Spokane or Kootenai brave? Whether this old man had been a stalwart warrior or the camp rascal, he had been of that world, and Quincy was ready with a string of questions. But the old man woke up to eat, not to talk. He made only three statements: "No got squaw. No like squaw. Squaw no good." Then he washed his own dishes, picked up his stick, and limped away over the far edge of the ravine.

The changing season was a new element too. Quincy and Ella had left St. Paul on the fringe of a backward spring. Now they were in the deep core of summer. Heads of grain hung plump and heavy in the wheatlands stretching to Davenport and Wilbur and beyond. In some of the fields threshing crews were already at work feeding the bundled wheat to machines powered by steam tractors. Overhead, the wind snatched away long golden plumes of chaff. With all this bounty, grain for Hike and Hobo was no problem. Quincy had only to dismount in some concealed dip in the road, crawl through the fence and cut a supply of wheat heads, improvising a sack from Ella's riding skirt. A few days on this rich wheat diet and even awkward old Hobo blossomed out. He began to hold up his head and prick his ears forward. Once Quincy caught him trying to arch his neck!

The ranch houses, each with its windmill nearby, stood on the crest of a rise, or in a hollow, protected by windbreaks of poplars, locusts, fir or pine. Between the planted fields lay rough areas of sagebrush, and occasionally a pond or marsh. The ranch folk along the way were hospitable, willing to sell or give from their now-bountiful food supplies, and to offer a sleeping place in barn or haystack. The only time Quincy and Ella asked for refuge in a house was the one time Washington rebuffed them. On the wettest day, when Ella was half-sick, a sullen housewife gave them permission only to shelter in a leaky shed "if you don't bother nothin'." After a couple of chilly hours with a pig and the chickens, Quincy said, "Bunny, I don't care what it costs, I'm going to get you into a clean, warm, dry place." They hit out for nearby Creston, put the horses in a livery stable, ate a good noon dinner at the City Restaurant, and crawled into bed at a lodging house for sixteen hours sleep.

The next morning initiated the fine weather. The sky was a deeper blue by contrast with the white clouds sailing the horizon. In the shifting light and shadow, the billows of ripe wheat changed color through all the tones from pale gold to rosy umber. Travel was pleasant and easy again, and Quincy renewed his hope of giving Ella her full week in Seattle before Jessie left. At the moment he was worrying more about money than time. When he blithely claimed that their Helena check would see them through, he hadn't counted on paying two dollars to express the saddlebags, nor another two bucks for the stay in Creston. Funds would soon be down to small change, and he had learned before leaving Creston that he couldn't wire home for cash—the telegraphers were on strike. He had told Ella that if they got stuck, he would think of something. Well, he would. He'd have to.

Since the fewer the days on the road, the less expenditures, he set a steady pace for the sake of both time and money. They passed through Wilbur and Govan and Almira that first clear

The ranch wife conceded that Quincy and Ella might take shelter in the pig shed, "if you don't bother nothin'."

day, and Hartline the next, still westward on the hot August road, wading through dust that surged and splashed around them like brown sea foam. Even with bandannas tied over their noses and mouths, they sucked in the dust with every breath.

At Coulee they crossed the ancient river bed below the Dry Falls of the Columbia. Quincy was jolted by the extent of the sage-covered flat that had once been the bottom of a stream tumbling over cliffs wide enough and high enough to create a hundred Niagaras. He hoped the Columbia had shrunk considerably since it carved this trough! From here on the change in the country accelerated. There were still grainfields, but interrupted more and more often by hills and washes. One of the deeper canyons, Ella said, was just right for a Frederick Remington painting. She pointed to the rimrock. "Can't you just see a small band of hostiles lurking up there, waiting to pick off the troopers as the cavalry comes dashing along?"

She and Quincy nooned on August 12 beside a small spring at the mouth of Moses Coulee, another abandoned channel of the river. The bluffs rose vertically on either side in well-marked layers of rock. Near the top they were splashed with stains that could be lichen, Quincy hazarded, but looked as if a prankster had kicked over a row of paint buckets all along the edge of the rock. It was lonesome country, not as deserted as the High Plains, but with the same feel of remoteness. Quincy could picture the Zopstrachs here, all thirteen of them, fighting for a toehold in the soil. Morton and his sheep wagon would look at home in this coulee. Medora and Jordan belonged here too, hot dusty meccas for hot thirsty cowboys. It was a land still bearing the stamp of the Old West.

But not for long. Already Quincy and Ella had glimpsed the Cascade range, beyond whose steep ridges and glaciered crags Seattle waited. The country from the Columbia to Puget Sound was New West. They had earlier sensed the mood of brisk enterprise at Fargo and Spokane, at some of the ranches and smaller towns in between. From here on it would dominate. The creaking of winches would be louder than the creaking of saddle leather, and the smell of blasting powder stronger than the scent of sage.

"How much?" Ella's eyes were on him anxiously as he counted the coins in his hand.

"Sixty cents. Not enough to get us and the horses across the river even if the ferry were running." Quincy thrust the change back into his pocket with one hand and grabbed at his straw hat with the other. The wind was blowing hard, swirling gritty gusts of sand around the foot of the ferry-cable tower on the east beach of the Columbia. Quincy could see the scow itself, drawn up on the opposite shore, and the men crawling around over it. He could see the flash of their hammers in the bright morning air. The ferry was laid up for repairs, and nobody over on this side had been able to tell him for how long. The crossing wasn't going to be any ten-cent ride, either. Viewed from the heights of the Badger Hills earlier in the day, the Columbia hadn't appeared to present any problem. But now that he was confronting it on its own level, with the roar of its current and the size of its waves increased by the wind, the Columbia was formidable.

"Here's what we'll have to do, Bunny. Let's ask if we can put up the horses at that little ranch back there. Then we'll get ourselves rowed over to Wenatchee in a skiff, and I'll see how much Quincy-boy's honest face is worth at one of the city's financial institutions."

"Do you really think they'll cash your check? They don't know you from Adam."

"Adam didn't have money in a New York bank. I do. Trust a cashier to appreciate that fine distinction." He leaned over and planted a kiss on her sunburned lips. She had been so understanding the past ten days, agreeing that they mustn't exhaust the horses while the mountains were still ahead, accepting his assurance that she'd arrive home in time for a good visit with Jessie. But that was all the more reason for his own impatience and anxiety now.

Olsen, the rancher, was willing to take in Hike and Hobo.

Quincy and Ella walked back to wait on the beach until the ferryman should see them and send over a skiff. Presently a small boat put out. Both the ferryman and the single passenger were rowing, but so strong was the current and so relentless the northwest wind that the boat came ashore half a mile below the landing. Quincy went down and helped the ferryman, Jim Bolton, to tow it back upstream. Bolton, an ex-cowboy with the frame of a moose and the neck of an ox, agreed to make the round trip for twenty-five cents if Quincy would take one pair of oars. "And you needn't pay till you come back."

With Bolton at the bow oar, Quincy at stroke, and Ella in the stern, they pushed off. As the boat banged into the third wave, Bolton shouted, "You're the first passenger I've had in this skiff what knows the difference between a oar and a hoe handle. I'll need all you've got, too, with both the wind and current to fight. This is one of the days I wonder why I ever give up cow-punchin'."

It was a battle all the way across. Even to recover stroke, with the oars out of water, was heavy going against the gale. There were moments, as the boat tilted over a larger wave, when Ella's face had that white, pinched look with which she had followed Quincy into the Musselshell. The Columbia was not banked with quicksand like that stream, not brown and brawling like the Little Missouri, not as wide as the flooding Missouri at Bismarck. But it was enormously strong, and not far below the route of crossing its cold green waters broke into foam and fury at the rapids. Bolton didn't need to urge Quincy to row hard.

They were both winded by the time the skiff touched gravel on the west side. "When I'm on a bad horse, I'm all right," said the ferryman as he began to recover his breath. "I know I can ride him. But when I go on that there river, I don't wear no spurs over it. I never know for sure whether I'm due to come off of it, or out of it, or stay in it for good."

In town Quincy walked Ella into the first bank they came to and asked for the cashier. He was out. The assistant took his time looking them over through his pince nez glasses. They were a ragged pair. Shoes cracked and dusty. Leggings flapping loose where the instep straps had worn through. Quincy's pants stiff with grime and worn to shreds at the knees. Ella's skirt stained and rumpled. Flannel shirts, new at Helena, now almost as disreputable as the original ones discarded there.

The blank check which Quincy took from his wallet was in sad shape too, creased and grubby. Along with it he drew out his identification—newspaper clippings with photographs of the travelers and descriptions of the journey intended. He also had a letter of introduction from his father to James J. Hill, president of the Great Northern Railway.

Faced with this evidence, the assistant cashier agreed that Quincy was telling the truth as to who he was.

"My check for fifteen dollars is perfectly good. Do you believe that too?"

"Why, it isn't a question of that, Mr. Scott."

"As a matter of politeness, no. But as a matter of fact, that *is* the question, isn't it?"

"We-el, yes."

"So, is the check good?"

"Why, certainly. Yes, it's good, of course."

"Will you cash it?"

"Why, er, no, sir."

"That is a wonderfully fine line you are drawing. Are there any other banks in town?"

"Right across the street."

At the second bank the details of the conversation were slightly different, but the result was the same.

There was one more bank. Quincy approached its cashier in do-or-die desperation. He hardly dared breathe while the slight, gray-haired man calmly read through the newspaper stories and the letter to Hill.

"Mr. Scott, I'm satisfied as to your identity. But there's nothing here to show what balance you have in your New York account."

Quincy gestured to himself and Ella. "Sir, do we look as if we had any money *outside* of the bank?"

"Why, eh, one might say, no."

"Well, then, if it isn't outside of the bank, it must be inside, mustn't it?"

There it was, the "something" Quincy had promised to think of. Unpremeditated, risky, conceived on the spot out of extremity. But born also out of an intuitive appraisal of the man he was dealing with, born out of nerve to rely on the ridiculous to make the point. It worked.

The flicker of a smile chased across the cashier's face. "Write out your check, Mr. Scott."

A hour later, refreshed by lunch at the Chewawa Cafe and their arms loaded with steak, a big watermelon and other supplies, Quincy and Ella walked haughtily down the street, hoping that the cashiers of the first two banks were looking out the window! As for the cashier at the third bank, well, he was a benefactor whose sense of humor and discernment Quincy was ready to praise for all time.

With the wind at their backs, the return to the east shore was fairly easy. Before they could start, however, both of them had to help Jim Bolton and his partner tow the skiff nearly a mile upstream. The two men trudged along the stony bank hauling on the forty-foot towline. Ella stood in the boat to pole with one of the oars, and Quincy had been instructed to walk along and push against the gunwale with the other oar to keep the boat from being washed against the rocks. The oar kept slipping off, so after a few minutes he waded in waist deep and pushed the skiff with his hands. The current flowed strong and ice-cold. Quincy's worn shoes were little protection as he struggled over the slippery underwater boulders. Near the end of the ordeal he lunged suddenly to catch his balance and jammed his instep between two rocks. He hardly felt the pain, so numb were his feet by this time, and he stumbled on to the end of the tow. The sun warmed him up and the wind dried him out during the return passage across the river. Nerves in his foot came to life and so did the pain. He went limping the rest of that day, favoring that foot in the hope that the injury would heal so that he could do his share of walking over the last mountains.

Otherwise he was feeling well pleased with himself that evening. He'd gone into the dens of Wenatchee's financial lions, tweaked their beards, and come away with fifteen dollars. He had the promise of the ferryman that the scow would be running tomorrow. He had six days to do the hundred and sixty miles to Seattle. And he had, right in front of him now, a steak dinner to be topped off with all the ripe watermelon he could hold.

The fire was blazing on the lee side of the log where he sat with Ella. Though the wind had moderated, it was still strong enough to drive hissing streamers of sand along the beach, and in the back draft created by the log and their bodies, it whipped the sparks crazily this way and that.

Suddenly Ella leaped up shrieking, "My skirt's on fire!"

Quincy had been a husband long enough to interpret the sequence of horrified expressions that raced across her face before she ran toward the river: *It's the only skirt I have. There's no way here to make another. I can't ride through Seattle in pants— all my friends would see me!* But he hadn't been a husband long enough to know he shouldn't so much as crack a smile. In his high spirits, Ella appeared to him not only delightfully dear, but wildly comic, and all the while he was pulling her back from the river (even the edge of the Columbia was no place for anyone who couldn't swim) and jerking off her skirt, he was laughing. He doused the skirt in the water, held it out for inspection, and laughed all the louder. The back breadth had been burned away until the skirt halves wouldn't lap. Scattered over the rest of the fabric were holes of assorted sizes, their charred outlines perfectly round.

He glanced up to share his hilarity with Ella, and abruptly stopped laughing. "You don't think it's funny?"

His surprise made her even more indignant and he hastened to show contrition. "Darling, I'm sorry. I suppose the condition of her skirt is a matter of great importance to a woman, particularly when she's about to make her re-entry into civilization. But can't you patch it so it will be presentable? You saved some pieces from my first pair of 'yaller pants,' and I'll bet the rancher's wife can scare up a few scraps of similar color."

After a fair night's rest in the Olsens' haymow, Ella went at the patching with her bits of khaki and some larger sections cut from a pair of old brown overalls contributed by Mrs. Olsen. The job took all day, while she and Quincy waited for the ferry. He noticed that as each patch was completed, Ella's bleak mood lightened a little more. Late in the afternoon, when she buttoned the skirt over her army breeches and pirouetted for his judgment, he knew he was restored to her good graces.

"That looks okay, Bunny. Very neat. You are without doubt the champion patcher of the Columbia Valley, or at least of the east side."

It was past sunset when the ferry put in at the landing. They led their horses aboard, along with the other passengers, teams and wagons assembled at the landing for several hours. Kept on course by the cable strung between the towers on each bank, the scow made a smooth crossing. The river reflected the still-glowing sky, breaking up its hues of crimson and saffron into strokes of color that shifted with the rolling current. The city, its orchard highlands, and the hills above were hazed with dusk. When the ferry landed, Ella suggested that they make up some of the two days' delay by covering part of the distance to Cashmere before they pitched camp.

The ride westward along the Wenatchee River that evening had a dreamlike quality. The air was warm, and heavy with the sweetness of ripening apples. Beams from the low-hanging moon silvered the drowsy valley and danced in sparkles across the stream. Quincy moved Hike up beside Hobo. Reaching for Ella's hand, he quoted softly, "That orbed maiden with white fire laden whom mortals call the Moon . . ."

She took up the words and chanted with him. Her hat was tossed back on its thong so that the light shone full on her face, and he saw the smile with which she turned to him at the end of the stanza. He stopped the horses and collected a kiss. The marvel of love brimmed over into awesome joy, pouring through him in a double flow of thought and feeling. Last year he had fallen for a girl, practically on sight, attracted by a quick mind, a pert, friendly face, and a gently-contoured body that moved with challenging independence. When he proposed to Ella in Central Park, he was sure he was choosing the right girl. But this long honeymoon adventure, with its chisel blows of hardship, monotony and crisis, had slowly been revealing that he had chosen far better than he knew. Surely it was the providence of God that had set her by his side, laughing, dreaming, risking, forgiving, enduring, balancing his moods and impulses with her quiet competence, her direct and uncomplicated way of dealing with people and situations. Sometimes she mystified him with a whim or a contradiction of her usual responses. Sometimes she humbled him by the depth of her trust. Had any man the right to be as happy as he was this night?

As they rode on, hand in hand, a sober pensiveness like the river mist that was beginning to gather and mingle with the moonlight gradually suffused Quincy's joy. The summer's journey was closing. "Expect us in five days," Ella had written to her mother from Wenatchee. Once on the other side of these mountains there would be no escape from family and friends, from city living and professional labors. He was eager for all of it, hurrying toward it, determined that nothing should stop him short of it. But Seattle would do more than terminate a two thousand mile trip. It would end a unique segment of his life. Because it had been a summer of testing and discovery, a summer of extraordinary liberty, where every day he and Bunny had made their own choices and were judged only by each other and the results, they were not the same boy and girl who had ridden forth into a May snowstorm. There could never again be a summer like this one, and the knowledge that it was nearly over filled him with a sweet aching sadness.

But when he raised his eyes to the Cascades' rough silhouette against the pallid sky, a stir of anticipation quickened his blood. There were strange mountains still to be crossed, and the last few days of the journey might be the most demanding of all.

XIII

JOURNAL ENTRIES

FRIDAY, AUGUST 16. *Woke 3:45 . . .
Packed and skipped in 20 minutes . . .
Through Cashmere up Peshashtin Creek . . . afternoon up
mountains toward Blewett—dark steep cliffs—no camping place
till 9:30—cabin by creek.*

SATURDAY, AUGUST 17. *Half mile to Blewett . . . lunch
in beautiful pine woods above road . . . Rode late—camped
under wheat stack near Teanaway River, with horses tethered at
roadside—buggies and carryalls going to dance.*

SUNDAY, AUGUST 18. *Skipped early—very chilly—revellers
returning much the worse for wear and beer. Uneventful ride to
Cle Elum . . . Easton at 6 o'clock—supper at hotel—60¢ for oats
. . . Went on and on until 11 p.m. when foreman of C. M. & St.
P. construction camp overtook us . . . invited us to spend night
at camp.*

No camping place till 9:30 . . . Rode late . . . Went on and
on until 11 p.m.—they were pushing both themselves and the
horses now. In the clear moonlit evenings they added three or
four hours to the usual daily stint, picking their way along the
road that climbed a timbered spur of the Cascades at Blewett
and dropped down beside Swauk Creek. Keyed up with expectations of the homecoming just ahead of her, Ella disregarded
fatigue on these night marches, and refused to think of the bears
and cougars that might be prowling the forest on either side. It
had been scary enough, winding up Peshashtin canyon, to hear
the stream roaring in its black chasm several hundred feet be-

low the trail and know that from here to there was straight down.

Sunday's ride took Ella and Quincy over the foothills that rolled southward in gentle swells from the Teanaway ridge. Beyond Cle Elum they turned upstream along the Yakima River. It was the first day of hunting season and the woods were full of barking dogs and banging rifles. Ella didn't pay much attention to either the noise or the hunters, most of them Italian coal miners from Cle Elum and Roslyn. Her eyes were on the mountains and her thoughts on what lay beyond them. Following up the Yakima, the road entered a deep corridor leading northwest to Snoqualmie Pass. Dark forested walls flanked each side and framed a view ahead of higher peaks, knife-edged and marked with hieroglyphic streaks of snow. The Cascades were her mountains. These eastern fronts were unfamiliar, but from the time she was eight years old until she was twenty, she had lived with their western faces. Though often veiled in fog or haze or clouds, the Cascades were there, and they had given her a special feeling about Seattle. It had always been a fresh and happy surprise to waken, after a spell of dark wet days, and find the veil magically withdrawn, revealing the skyline from Rainier northward cloaked in dazzling new snow. These were her mountains, and by tomorrow (if fortune favored) she would be on their western slopes with a downhill stretch home.

If it was fortune that met her and Quincy the next day in the person of the railroad company doctor, fortune was decidedly not in her favor.

The Milwaukie Road was pushing its line along the southwest side of the canyon, clearing trees and blasting a roadbed to the summit tunnel. The canyon reverberated with the roar of explosives, the crash of falling rock and the staccato chuffing of donkey-engines. Hike and Hobo plainly didn't like it. But having received their baptism of fire from the Italian huntsmen, they kept going. At the foot of Lake Keechelus Ella and Quincy found the company doctor debating with his plump assistant what to do.

"The ferry's out of order," the doctor told them. "It's no use for any of us to wait. We'll have to ride around the lake." He was a tall, well-muscled young man whose eyeglasses and natty attire added to his air of authority. Having settled the matter for all concerned, he raised his hat politely to Ella and started off, followed by the assistant, who looked anything but cheerful at the prospect ahead of him. The road had been submerged when the lake had filled in behind the dam, and the only way around was to scramble on a steep hillside between the water and the railroad construction, partly through deep woods, partly across open areas angled with downed timber and exposed to showers of rock and shreds of stumps from the blasting above.

The doctor and his helper were riding fresh horses and soon disappeared into the forest ahead. Ella and Quincy had to travel more slowly, picking the levels that would put least strain on the horses and detouring around fallen trees. But detours weren't always possible. Just as Ella was trying to coax Hike to straddle over a log half his height, Quincy called, "Look! On the lake!"

Several hundred feet below, and a quarter of a mile out on the glistening waters of Keechelus, the barge ferry steamed smoothly along past them.

Quincy clenched his fist. "That confounded doctor! No use to wait, he says. If I ever catch up with him, I'll—I'll—well, there won't even be enough left of him for the autopsy!"

Ella jerked off her bandanna and waved wildly, but the woods were too dense here for the signal to be seen from the lake, and it would have done no good in any case for there was no way for the barge to land on that stretch of shore. She wanted to sit down and cry. They had covered only about a third of the way, and already she was out of breath and shaky in the knees with the constant effort. Most of the two hours had been spent on foot, leading the horses and cajoling them into unusual feats of twisting, balancing, clambering and skidding, all the while holding them steady against the sudden assaults of the blasting.

At the next pause for rest, Quincy leaned wearily against Hobo's sweat-darkened shoulder.

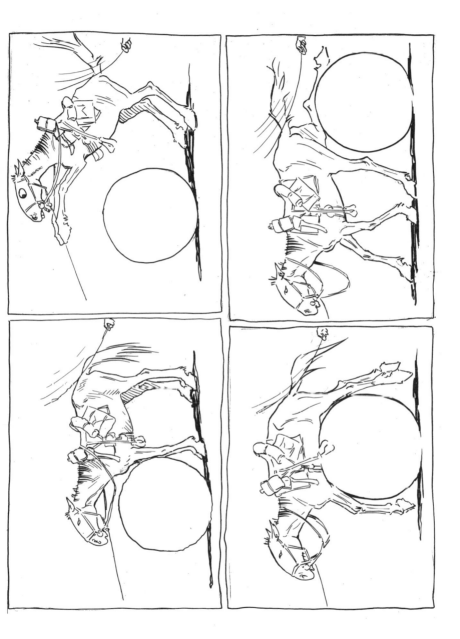

"Scrabbling over this ground must be pretty hard on your lame foot," said Ella anxiously. "Is it troubling you much?"

"I get an occasional twinge, but if Hobo, the old roan idiot, will kindly not plant his hoof on my instep more than three or four times today, I think I'll hold out. And I'm certainly not complaining about either him or Hike. They've learned a lot this summer. We never could have managed a traverse like this with them in the early part of the trip. This morning they're scared by the explosions, they're knocking the skin off their shins on these logs, they don't know where they're going or why, but neither one of them has balked."

It wasn't balking that brought Hobo to grief in the late afternoon, but simple exhaustion. As Quincy was leading him across the top of a steep rock slide, the roan's legs abruptly gave way, crumpling under his belly. He started slipping sideward. Quincy was jerked off balance and barely regained his footing. Turning, he gripped Hobo's headstall with both hands, leaning back to check the horse's downward slide. For ten seconds man and horse poised, a tableau of arrested motion. Then, with a heaving sigh that expanded and collapsed his ribs like an accordion, Hobo began to take control of his muscles. Front legs strengthened and straightened, hind quarters came up. Finally he stood, trembling and wheezing, but upright. Quincy let him rest until the trembling stopped, then guided him gently across to where Ella and Hike waited at the far end of the rock.

Quincy gave her a weak grin and looked down at his hands. "Hobo's nine hundred and thirty pounds, counting saddle and gear. I'm not exactly ashamed of singlehandedly keeping all that weight from dropping to destruction."

"You had *two* hands on the headstall," she said, proud of him but teasing.

"Then I'm not ashamed of doublehandedly et cetera. But it took about my last ounce of zip. Let's locate a place to camp."

At the head of Keechelus they reached the road again. They spread their blankets at one end of a semi-circle of damp ground beside the road, the only place they could find with grass for the horses.

Quincy said, "Darned lucky we didn't take the advice of that railroad advertising man in New York who told us to follow the construction route all the way West. The trail's torn up with the blasting and chopping and hauling. Mud and dust everywhere. The grazing's ruined, and if the construction camp prices along this stretch are any gauge, we'd have been bankrupt long ago buying grub for ourselves and hay for the horses."

Just before dark, while Ella was wringing out a towel between two sticks to make a hot compress for Quincy's foot, they had a visitor. He came shuffling out of the woods, swinging a lantern made of a candle stub stuck in a tin can. Like so many of the other old men they had met across the West, Amos Vedder had outlived his times, bewildered and irritated by the changes he couldn't understand or put a stop to. He took a few minutes first to curse the railroad ("I got to run outa my cabin and get behind a tree when one of them explosions goes off 'cause the cabin bucks and shakes like a ornery cayuse—coffee pot upset this mornin'.") but his focus was on the past, and as he squatted by the campfire it was the talk of long ago that made his deep-set eyes glisten and his lips quirk in satisfaction between their fringes of tobacco-stained whiskers.

"I rode five times atween Californy and the City of Mexico, I did. One of them trips I been without water so long that finally to get a drink I bled my horse. Not to death, mind you. But I figured he had some juice to spare."

And he went into great detail about the winter when he had been snowed up for eleven days with a band of Pawnee Indians, huddled in a hollow on the prairie, the drifts over their heads and no food but horsemeat.

"Fifty-two Pawnees and me. But praise be, the blizzard stopped before the horsemeat run out. I *knew* Pawnees wasn't man eaters, but I was getting a mite nervous just the same."

Vedder invited Ella and Quincy to bring their blankets to his cabin for the night, and sputtered angrily when they declined. "Hell, if I'd a known you wasn't goin' to accept my hospitality, I wouldn't a wasted my time comin' all the way down here to ask yuh."

He lit his candle lantern with the end of a stick from the fire and grumbled away in the dark. After about fifty feet, he yelled back over his shoulder, "Remember, fifty-two Pawnees and me, eleven days."

Tired as they were, Ella and Quincy sat on by the dying fire for a few minutes after Vedder had gone. One last spurt of flame threw its glow on the horses, a dark mass and a pale mass in motion near the edge of the clearing. The slow thud of hoofs and the crunch of jaws were noises so familiar by now that Ella noticed only if they were interrupted. The blasting had ceased before sundown. Except for the muted sounds of the horses and the *tu-whu* of an owl, nothing broke the healing silence. She rested her cheek against Quincy's shoulder, tilting back her head to watch the stars winking in the little circle ringed by the converging treetops. Anyone who had lived all his life in a forest like this would find it hard to believe the prairie night sky, that enormous black bell jar sequined with stars right to the flat horizon. And a plainsman, she supposed, would be incredulous before mountains like these, furred in their pelt of evergreens. But she was at home now with both prairies and mountains, and presently she helped Quincy douse the fire and then was off to sleep beside him the moment she closed her eyes, a veteran camper oblivious to the scratchiness of the horse blankets over her and the lumpiness of the ground underneath.

They rolled out at dawn to start what turned out to be the most wearying day of the whole trip. The road was so steep that in many places they had to dismount to get the horses up. Here were no dry, piney, open woods. The gigantic cedars and firs shut out all but small coins of sunlight that sank through the cool deep green air like gold doubloons falling to the bottom of the sea. Salmonberry bushes, rhododendrons, and huge ferns grew head high or higher, and under these thickets damp mosses carpeted the ground, still soggy from the last rain. Progress was a matter of slip and slither, up the last few miles to Snoqualmie Pass, then down, down, down on the western side.

Quincy was limping when he left camp, and before long he

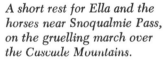
A short rest for Ella and the horses near Snoqualmie Pass, on the gruelling march over the Cascade Mountains.

cut a staff to support some of his weight. On the steeper slopes he crawled. They reached the three-thousand-foot pass before noon. Resting at the summit, he shook his head. "Somehow, after the craggy skyline west of Wenatchee, I expected something more spectacular at Snoqualmie than this—just a high spot in the road and nothing to see but trees. Let's hope that going downhill will be easier than climbing up."

It wasn't. Sections of the road had been corduroyed with lengths of small tree trunks embedded side by side in the earth. It made treacherous footing. Repeatedly Ella tried to persuade him to give up for the day. "Maybe the road will be drier tomorrow, and you not so lame."

His answer to each urging was, "No, there isn't time to wait over." If there was an undertone of anger in his refusals, she knew it was not for her, but for the pain, and the delays at Wenatchee and Keechelus that had set back their schedule. This was August 20, the day he had promised her they would reach Seattle. Obviously that wasn't going to be possible. But tomorrow? Yes, if he could keep going, if there were no more hindrances. She would let him set the pace, but remain watchful for any sign that he was pressing too close to the edge of his endurance.

She was near her own limit when they dragged into North Bend that evening. They had done twenty-six miles. The horses were shambling with fatigue, and Quincy hobbled like a gimpy old man.

They put the horses in a livery stable and stopped a woman outside to ask about a place to get a room.

"Better go to the Home Hotel. The other one's more expensible."

Before they cast themselves on the mercies of the less "expensible" hotel and its fat chummy cook, Quincy sent off in the night mail a postcard to Ella's mother: "Expect us on the last Kirkland-Seattle ferry tomorrow (Wednesday)."

August 22 in Seattle was a "smiley day." That had been Ella's childhood term for weather when the sun's heat and glare were gently tempered by a salt air haze from the Sound, and she repeated the phrase to herself as she stood on the deck of the ferry that was nosing its way across Lake Washington. This morning the colors of the lake and the tree-covered hills fringing its shores glowed in soft pastels. Rainier mounded up in the southeastern sky, a giant scoop of ice cream served on a dish of lesser mountains. Most of the city was hidden behind a row of hills, but Ella was straining to glimpse a few familiar landmarks.

Somewhere back in the dusty miles of Montana she had vowed, "Whatever it takes to make it through to the end, I'll give." Close as she was to the end now, she wouldn't count it made until she and Quincy tied up the horses in front of her mother's house.

She had been so sure that *yesterday* would be the last day, only to have it wind up in a crushing disappointment. At intervals on the route down out of the Cascades from North Bend, Quincy had asked people the hour of the last horse ferry leaving Kirkland. The answers varied considerably, and to add to the uncertainty, misdirections in Redmond wasted precious minutes. But Ella had continued to believe that they would catch that last boat and ride home through Seattle under the shelter of a friendly dusk that would conceal their patches and tatters and grime. So she had loosed the reins and urged Hike to run with Hobo the remaining few miles to Kirkland.

"Sorry, folks. The last horse ferry pulled out at five-forty-five, twenty minutes ago." The lanky dock tender had been sympathetic but positive. It was too far to ride around the lake. There was nothing for Ella and Quincy to do but resign themselves to spending the night on the east side, frustrated by the few miles of water that lay between them and Seattle.

But Ella's disappointment vanished in the elation of an unexpected reunion. Her mother, having waited in vain at the pier on the city side of the lake, crossed on the late passenger boat. She got a welcome that left her breathless. And she brought the assurance that Jessie would not be leaving Seattle for five days. "She didn't come to the ferry because she thought someone should be at home in case you changed your minds and arrived by a different route." Ella's mother paused to straighten her small rose-trimmed straw hat, pushed awry by the hugging and kissing of her welcome. She was shorter than Ella and comfortably built, with crisp dark curly hair frosted with gray, and brown eyes that glanced keenly through steel-rimmed spectacles. Her voice still kept its Kentucky softness. "Riley is down at the *Post-Intelligencer* office. He'll be out with a photographer to get your pictures for the paper directly you reach home over yonder. There'll be a reporter and photographer from the *Times*, too."

Quincy insisted on engaging a room for Ella and her mother at the lodging house near the ferry landing. He would take the horses a mile back along the road, he said, and put up in a farmer's barnyard. Ella felt she ought to go with him, yet she had so much to tell her mother that she gave Quincy a grateful and slightly guilty goodnight embrace and went off to the lodging house bubbling with talk, until the day's excitement and weariness took their due. Soon after slipping into bed she fell asleep with a happy sigh. "Tomorrow, Mother . . . tell you tomorrow."

And now it was tomorrow, the smiley day. The ferry had reached the slip at Madison Park, and Ella was helping Quincy lead the horses off the boat. Her mother, who had crossed with them, started toward a waiting trolley, to go home and put a roasting chicken in the oven and await their arrival. Quincy saw her safely aboard, then came back to Ella and the horses.

"Well, Bunny?"

She grinned back at him. They swung into the saddles and set out on the final ride of the journey.

It was a short but merry one, along city thoroughfares. Over the hill, across the Lake Union bridge, up the mild slope of Fifteenth Avenue, past the forested campus of the University. Word traveled ahead of them that something unusual was coming up the street, and from the ferry slip onward, people appeared in scattered clusters along the sidewalks to stare, to cheer, to click their cameras, and to yell questions.

"Is it part of a circus?"

"How far have you come?"

"Are you advertising a Wild West show?"

"Hey, cowboys, ain't one of you a girl?"

In the jubilance of achievement, Ella responded happily to all the faces along the streets. Grownup faces, curious or sceptical, envious or admiring. Children's faces wide-eyed with awe and delight. She ceased worrying about the state of her outfit, realizing that the patches, tatters and grime authenticated the answers she and Quincy were tossing back to the onlookers. If they had been embarrassed by the newness of their clothes in St. Paul, rolling on the hotel room floor to accumulate some dust and wrinkles, why should they be ashamed now? Riders who had pushed for a hundred and eleven days through snow, rain, mud, wind, sun, hail, high water, dust, and sand *ought* to look ragged and tough!

When they were well along Fifteenth Avenue, Quincy reined Hobo close to Hike.

"It's almost ended, Bunny darling. Are you glad?"

"In a way, yes." She pushed back a wisp of dark hair that had escaped the bow tied at the nape of her neck. "But I'm more glad that we planned this honeymoon on horseback, and that we've done what we set out to do. Aren't you?"

"You bet! And let's wind up with a real western flourish. Vag should be here to lend us some style with that circular swish of his tail. Are you ready?"

"Ready."

"Then let's go. Yippee!"

And they took the last quarter mile at a gallop.

XIV

There weren't enough chairs in May Herrick's flat for all the friends she had invited to welcome Quincy and Ella back to New York. Some of the artists and students and newspapermen leaning against the wall joined those already sitting on the floor.

"Go on, Quincy," called out one of the girls. "What did the old Irishman tell you?"

"We asked him about crossing the Little Missouri, and he said, 'Now, I niver see ye afore, and ye niver see me afore, but —un'stan', I'm tellin' ye as a fren'—I'd niver go in the river!'"

At the other side of the small room Ella was half listening to Quincy while answering questions from an attentive group of her own. Yes, she and Quincy had returned east by train. No, it hadn't been easy to part with the horses. Stubborn, lazy and whimsical as they could sometimes be, Hike and Hobo had come through stoutly, both in the crises and the long pull.

"But what was it like for *you*, Ella?" demanded May.

That was exactly what Ella had been trying to tell these interested friends tonight, hoping they would feel with her the flow of the prairie wind and the comic miseries of pitching camp in the rain. She wanted to make them tremble before the awesomeness of a Rocky Mountain thunderstorm, to sweep them with her through a dozen more experiences that came crowding into memory. But suddenly she understood that it was impossible. Only one other could fully know—the man with the blue eyes and the sun-faded auburn hair, the tall young man who was reeling off Old Mac's brogue with such skill and gusto. Quincy knew. He had been with her out there, harried by the same anxieties, drooping with the same weariness, laughing at the same nonsense. They had made love with fifty miles of sage-brush for a bedroom, and divided one small corncake to make supper. They had responded to the same beauties of sky and earth, and had shared the rebuffs and welcomes, the hilarities and pathos of the people met on the way. In testing themselves against the country, they had tested each other, and though there had been few great moments, the days were strings of little moments woven by the summer into a sturdy bond of self-confidence and mutual trust.

She wondered if it was a sense of this bond that had caused Quincy's father to say, the night after their return to New York, "I've been watching you two, and I see that the horseback trip was a sound idea after all. It's made your marriage."

It was a neat phrase, so neat that she was almost content to believe it. But not quite. For what she and Quincy had brought home was less—and more. Not a marriage made, but the makings of a marriage, to be worked at persistently and tenderly for all the rest of their days together.

She glanced over at Quincy as his voice rose above the chuckles rippling about him. "And Old Mac said, 'Ye're man an' wife, ain't ye? Shure? I took ye so—it's all right.'"

Man and wife. Ella's eyes caught Quincy's in a flash of deep affection. Man and wife, woman and husband. Let Old Mac and the whole world take them so, for it was indeed all right.

The End

Postscript

Quincy and Ella Scott moved west four years after their honeymoon journey, to bring up their children where they could see the mountains from the main street. For Quincy there followed twenty years of work for civic and advertising organizations in Washington and Montana. In 1931 he returned to his first joy, becoming editorial cartoonist for the Portland *Oregonian*, a post he held until his retirement in 1949.

Ella, called Nell in later life, resumed her professional work during the 1920's in Seattle. When she and Quincy retired to a seaside home at Neahkahnie, Oregon, she began painting in oils and exhibited her western landscapes and ocean scenes in several one-man shows.

Meanwhile the three children grew up, married, and launched into careers of their own.

Hugh, a retired Army Reserve colonel, is advertising and public relations officer for the United States National Bank of Oregon. Allen is professor of physical chemistry at Oregon State University, known in this country and abroad for his work in solid-state chemistry. Dorothy carries on her free-lance writing in California.

Quincy lived to age eighty-three, Ella five years longer. During her last year someone asked her about the horseback trip. "Didn't you, at least once during those weary months, feel completely discouraged, too miserable or scared to go on?" She thought a moment. "No, I never got that discouraged. I knew Quincy would get us through." We think her own endurance and venturesome spirit also had a lot to do with the outcome.

The Editors

INDEX

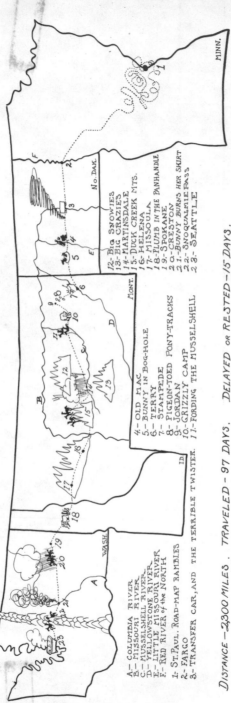

A.— COLUMBIA RIVER.
B.— MISSOURI RIVER.
C.— MUSSELSHELL RIVER.
D.— YELLOWSTONE RIVER.
E.— LITTLE MISSOURI RIVER.
F.— RED RIVER OF THE NORTH.

1- ST.PAUL ROAD-MAP RAMBLES
2- FARGO
3- TRANSFER CAR, AND THE TERRIBLE TWISTER.

4.— OLD MAC.
5.— BUNNY IN BOG-HOLE
6.— TERRY
7.— STAMPEDE
8.— PIGEON-TOED PONY-TRACKS
9.— JORDAN
10.— GRIZZLY CAMP
11.- FORDING THE MUSSELSHELL

12- BIG SNOWIES
13- BIG CRAZIES
14- MARTINSDALE
15- DUCK CREEK MTS.
16- HELENA
17- MISSOULA
18- PLUMB IN THE PANHANDLE
19- SPOKANE
20- CRESTON
21- BUNNY BURNS HER SHIRT
22- SNOQUALMIE PASS
23- SEATTLE

DISTANCE — 2300 MILES .   TRAVELED — 97 DAYS .   DELAYED OR RESTED — 15 DAYS .